RESISTING REPRESENTATION

RESISTING REPRESENTATION

—

ELAINE SCARRY

—

New York   Oxford
OXFORD UNIVERSITY PRESS
1994

Oxford University Press

Oxford   New York   Toronto
Delhi   Bombay   Calcutta   Madras   Karachi
Kuala Lumpur   Singapore   Hong Kong   Tokyo
Nairobi   Dar es Salaam   Cape Town
Melbourne   Auckland   Madrid

and associated companies in
Berlin   Ibadan

Published by Oxford University Press, Inc.,
200 Madison Avenue, New York, New York 10016

"Willow Bark and Red Poppies: Advertising the Remedies for Pain," originally appeared in *Word and Image*
4 (Summer 1985), 112–40.

"Work and the Body in Hardy and Other Nineteenth-Century Novelists," originally appeared in *Representa-*
tions 3 (Summer 1983), 90–123.

"Six Ways to Kill a Blackbird (or Any Other Intentional Object) in Samuel Beckett," originally appeared
in *James Joyce Quarterly* 8 (Summer 1971), 278–89.

"Untransmissible History in Thackeray's *Henry Esmond*," originally appeared in *Literary Monographs*, ed.
Joseph Wittreich, vol. 7 (Madison: University of Wisconsin Press, 1975).

"The Well-Rounded Sphere: Cognition and Metaphysical Structure in Boethius's *Consolation of Philosophy*,"
originally appeared in *Essays in Numerical Criticism of Medieval Literature*, ed. Caroline D. Eckhardt
(Lewisburg: Bucknell University Press, 1980), 90–141.

Library of Congress Cataloging-in-Publication Data
Scarry, Elaine.
Resisting representation / Elaine Scarry.
p.   cm.
ISBN 0-19-504270-0   ISBN 0-19-508964-2 (pbk)
1. Literature, Modern — History and criticism.   2. Representation
(Philosophy)   I. Title.
PN710.S327   1991
809´.91 — dc20   90-22508

3 5 7 9 8 6 4

Printed in the United States of America
on acid-free paper

for Eva Scarry

Contents

RESISTING REPRESENTATION

Introduction

The problematically abstract and the problematically concrete are the two starting places of the essays in this book. One group of essays looks at the ability of language to accommodate conceptions of truth and cognition, subjects whose immateriality or alacrity might place them beyond the reach of speech and writing. The other group examines phenomena such as physical pain and physical labor whose materiality might leave them outside the reflexes of language. By the side of the problematically abstract, language sometimes seems full of the weight of the world. By the side of the problematically concrete, language can seem inappropriately quick and cavalier. In both instances, what is overtly at issue is the knowability of the world, and that knowability depends on its susceptibility to representation. This is the case, whether the particular world whose knowability is in question is (as in Hardy) the deep interior of another person at labor or (as in Boethius) the metaphysically expansive ground that lets one "learn how to die." In this sense, all the essays are about the labors of cognition.

A second feature shared by these writers is the continuity they display between grammatical structures and narrative structures. A given subject resists representation. In order to overcome that resistance, the artist bends the sentence into a particular shape. But precisely that same grammatical or syntactical shape may then, in magnified form, reappear in larger patches of language such as a scene or finally even the narrative as a whole.

Why should this be the case? Perhaps there is no need to answer this question. It may be enough simply to notice how persistently it is the case—not only in writings by Beckett, Hardy, Thackeray, Boethius, but in many other artists as well as in philosophers like Plato, Rousseau. The continuity between small and large patches of language seems—in the precision of the match and in the pressure toward totalizing linguistic structures it implies—neither casual nor incidental but (at least for these writers) artistically needed, necessary. But why should it be necessary?

One way of answering the question is to point to the "extendibility" of language, the coherent way it can be steadily elaborated and unfolded. Once opened and elaborated, it can be contracted again. The unceasing practice (every day, all day long, not only in intellectual conversation but in the stories accompanying all daily tasks) of elaborating what was a moment ago brief and, conversely, of redacting what we have just finished making long, reflects our desire to affirm the consistency between folded and unfolded versions, like making certain that a sheet has two hundred threads a square inch in both its folded and unfolded states. The shift to concrete objects is useful. Large narrative structures can be expected to have grammatical attributes in the same way that bridges, buildings, and human skeletons are presumed by engineers to have structures only partially distinguishable from the materials out of which they are made. "Structures are made from materials," writes J. E. Gordon in *Structures: Or Why Things Don't Fall Down*, "but in fact there is no clear-cut dividing line between a material and a structure."[1] Since narratives are made out of sentences, it would be strange if the vocabulary for describing the attributes of sentences (nouns, verbs, appositives, definite articles, connecting particles) were wholly distinct from the vocabulary for describing the attributes of large narrative structures (acts, chapters, denouement, character, plot), or if there were no accepted way of aligning those separate vocabularies.

When grammatical or syntactical features remain constant across small and large stretches of language, they do so in two distinguishable ways. The first way might be called *iterative* constancy and the second, *imitative* or mimetic constancy. (The writers in this book practice the second.) Iterative constancy can be illustrated by Harold Weinrich's ingenious account of words like "a," "an," "the," "one." He argues that "the definite article has the function of directing attention to pre-information while indefinite articles direct it to post-information."[2] When a fairy tale mentions *"a* girl," we have just been told that we do not yet know anything about the girl; we have been put on watch. When the fairy tale mentions "the girl," we have just been told that this person is someone we have already met; we suspend the work of identification. The disposition of articles in the sentence, "There once was *a* girl who lived in *a* sunny house, and one day *the* girl decided to leave *the* house," cannot easily be inverted. Further, the distribution of the articles in this sentence recurs in long and varied stretches of language such as Camus's "La Pierre qui pousse," Perrault's "Little Red Riding Hood," and (as Weinrich notes) Weinrich's own article about articles. In both short and long patches of language, indefinite articles appear earlier, as well as at "decisive points" in the narrative where a "new or unexpected direction" occurs, and the definite articles greatly outnumber the indefinite.[3] The text, argues Weinrich, has a "macrosyntax"[4] carrying forward the requirements of the sentence beyond its own boundaries. This can be called iterative or literal constancy because the words in question—"a" and "the"—remain the same. The movement from syntax to macrosyntax entails a magnification only in the sense that the number of iterations increases: the thing being counted stays the same. But presumably one might additionally notice some narrative unit larger than, or different from, the solitary word that performs the same function and this would be mimetic constancy. Music in a film, for example, acts like a steady stream of indefinite and definite articles, situating the auditors in relation to pre- and post-information, now instigating, now relaxing, our readiness to perform the work of identification. This second form of constancy can be illustrated by turning away from Weinrich's indefinite articles to J. L. Austin's connecting particles.

Connecting particles such as "still," "therefore," "moreover," and "although" can all, as Austin has shown, be unfolded into speech acts.

> We may use the particle "still" with the force of "I insist that"; we use "therefore" with the force of "I conclude that"; we use "although" with the force of "I concede that." Note also the uses of "whereas" and "hereby" and "moreover."[5]

The connecting particle ("still") contains within it a speech act ("I insist that"). Conversely, the speech act ("I insist that") — although composed of a pronoun, verb, and conjunction — may be understood as a species of connecting particle. It imitates the labor of that part of speech without repeating the word "still." So, in turn, the specific grammatical attributes of this longer phrase might themselves be carried mimetically forward into progressively more expansive verbal terrain. The set of performative utterances that particularly preoccupied Austin are centered in sentences such as "I take this man as my husband," "I pronounce him guilty," "I bid three aces," "I contract." They have been summarized by Jürgen Habermas as a set of "institutionally bound" illocutionary acts[6] to distinguish them from the much wider class of performative utterances explored by other philosophers. It can be argued that the attributes of these sentences reappear in the language-drenched institutions (marriage, the courts, the social contract) to which they are attached and by which they are enforced. As one moves from the sentence to the institution, the prominent grammatical requirement of a first-person pronoun is sustained not by vastly multiplied iterations of sentences that begin with the word "I" (though that might also be the case) but by large structural features that preserve and distribute the exercise of the performative. Constitutional protections of free speech guarantee the first-person action of speaking; the provision for trial by jury distributes to the full population, rather than to a small number of judges, the capacity to announce the words, "I find him guilty";[7] voting rights distribute to the adult population the capacity to perform the sentence, "I vote for" or "I consent." These constitutional guarantees sustain the first-person requirement of performative speech even though the First, Sixth, Fifteenth, Nineteenth, and Twenty-Sixth Amendments of the U.S. Constitution are not themselves framed in sentences with first-person pronouns. A society that distributes the right of self-description has a different grammar from a society that gives an executive (king, president, or party), attended by a cadre of security officers, the right to describe all other citizens in the third person.

It would take time to show the mimetic constancy of grammar as one moves from a sentence to an institution because the institution is only partially verbal. Showing mimetic constancy in a literary or philosophic text is less difficult because the text is exclusively verbal. The essays in this book on Hardy, Beckett, Thackeray, and Boethius all begin with the attributes of some small patches of language; they then show the same structures at work in isolated scenes, and then, finally, in the narrative as a whole. Although the essays provide an extended portrait of mimetic constancy, it can here be quickly glimpsed by thinking about a sample scene.

In any given scene, the character is made up wholly of sentences. The house in which the character dwells is made up wholly of sentences. The character's movement as she crosses the room to the door at the side porch is made entirely of sentences. While it does not follow that the scene itself must therefore acquire syntactical features, it would on the other hand not be surprising if it did. Each writer might summarize this scene in a sentence whose syntax would reappear in the larger structure of the scene. Hardy would say:

> Eve turned from the worktable and, dressmaking still, walked toward the man at the door.

Thackeray would say:

> He would remember to the end of his life the look of the setting sun shining on her face as she moved to the door to meet me on the eastern porch.

Beckett would say:

> Once at the door, she was on her way, to what no matter, she was on her way.

Boethius would say:

> Then gliding toward the door, she spoke freely to me of the impediments restraining my capacity for straightforward argument.

The felt weight of the woman as she moves across the floor would be different in each scene, as would scores of other attributes. Precisely because each writer needs to solve a different problem of representation, each requires a sentence bearing a different grammatical shape. That shape, the "acoustical signature" of the resistance the sentence must overcome, holds visible within a small compass the larger shape of the scene as a whole.

For Hardy, the problem is how to represent the unceasing activity of physical labor when the linguistic structures that accommodate actions — sentence verbs and story plots — more easily accommodate discrete actions that start and stop. He solves this problem by transporting the action out of the realm of the verb, across the hybrid terrain of the gerund, and into the realm of the noun, where he places it in apposition to the person whom it now permanently accompanies, even in the midst of many other actions that themselves have nothing to do with labor. The sentence

> Eve turned from the worktable and, *dressmaking still*, walked toward the man at the door

can be written in the more familiar apposition form

> Eve turned from the worktable and, *dressmaker still*, walked toward the man at the door.

On the level of the scene, the gerund and appositive are mimed and magnified by grafting the materials of labor to her body:

> Eve turned from her worktable and, *enveloped still in a haze of silver thread and tiny filaments of wool and silk*, walked toward the man at the door . . .

As she crosses the room, the light might scatter, glint, across the small fragments of silk, flash suddenly on the silver scissors at her belt, exposing in the continual shimmer the tremor of her own desire for the man at the door. Hardy thickens the world, and lets us see the pulse that runs through it. His appositives affirm the continuity of the worker and the materials of her labor by compounding the subject, joining substantive to substantive. In his relation with his characters, Hardy is profoundly enabling. By embedding verbs within substantives, he gives action a permanent residence within the interior of persons who are made ample, able, even in the moment of passivity. In the disarray of desire, still his men and women work. Although subject to fatality, they down to the final second reproduce their lives.

For Thackeray, the opposite is the case. The passage of the woman from the interior to the door cannot occur, except as an intellectual claim that passes fleetingly through the mind it will soon disappoint. If the scene were rendered in bodily terms, the woman would slip and slide across the floor. But it is in the cognitive categories she illustrates, rather than the room she occupies, that she is made to take her fall:

> He would remember to the end of his life the look of the setting sun shining on her face as she moved to the door to meet me on the eastern porch.

Thackeray creates a syntax of disablement. The features of "orientation" required to permit the coherent passage of the woman to the doorway are simple: all that is needed is that she not move in two directions at once, or that she not turn to the right and see objects we know to be on the left. Those simple requirements of orientation are exaggeratedly fulfilled by a literal invocation of the compass points, and eroded by the disabling overlay of east and west: the sun setting in the west shines on the face looking east. The shift between the third- and first-person pronouns — between the "he" who remembers and the "me" who is met — similarly disables the sentence and situates both auditors and characters in a defective space. Doubling a pronoun for a single person, always mildly disorienting, is here licensed by the fact that the person is at once the teller of and the participant in the story. But normal pronominal habits — which reserve the more intimate first person for the spatially and temporally proximate act of story telling and third person for the earlier (hence now distant) and externally observed story action — are here inverted so that the woman is about to cross over the doorway out of the story into the space of the storytelling, while the man standing with his back to us on the eastern porch confides to us the day's memorability.

Thackeray wants to make an argument about the nontransmissibility of both objective and subjective history. The problem of representation he must solve is how to argue that assertions do not have enough stability to secure their own content, while himself enlisting the deep coherence of language to enable him to transmit that speculative argument. On the level of the individual sentence, both external referent (east, west) and internal referent (he, me) must be implicated. Across the larger scene, the same syntax of disablement must be at work: names must change; names, nouns, pronouns, and titles must have multiple referents; words must scatter and phrases contradict; discredited idioms must disappear yet return in moments of personal urgency. The overall narrative architecture, like the solitary sentence, must question both external and internal assumptions about reference. It encourages us to imagine that *both* public history *and* private history are knowable, then invites us to imagine that *not* public history *but only* private history is knowable, and then requires us to imagine that *neither* public *nor* private history is knowable. The three stages of syntactical scaffolding — *both* . . . *and*; *not* . . . *still*; *neither* . . . *nor* — dismantle our basis for cognitive optimism.

The passage of Beckett's woman through the door first posits, then erases, the object toward which she moves.

> Once at the door, she was on her way, to what no matter, she was on her way.

Elementary ways of being — here, being on one's way — are concretely rendered by reducing the clutter of irrelevant nouns. The structure of solitary sentences, the structure of scenes, the structure of full works are persistently preoccupied with the task of regulating the disappearance of objects from the world, either through overexposure or, as is more often the case, through underexposure. In the instance of underexposure, the woman during the scene refers repeatedly to the object without ever specifying what it is. In the instance of overrepresentation, she joins Joe Breem on the porch, then returns, then leaves and moves about through the city. She returns, then walks out with a telescope to a nearby hill. Returns, then walks out again to the flower market. Returns, then goes to a repair shop.

Given the steady erasure of the object world, one might argue that Beckett shares Thackeray's merciless incredulity about our epistemological aspirations. The syntactical disability that had no physical correlative in Thackeray (whose young woman does not slide on the floor) even has one in Beckett whose woman sallies forth with an inflected gait or limp. The fact that all states of consciousness are nearly objectless also means that his women and men inhabit the neighborhood of physical pain.[8] But the scepticism that for Thackeray is an exhausting final conclusion (denied, delayed, half-conceded, and at last acknowledged) is for Beckett a good-natured first premise. Because so little labor has been spent here, it can be invested instead in catching in language the fragile reflexes of the phenomenological state, the lilt and cadence of being on one's way. Beckett has a nearly *idiot savant*-like openness, an openness so remarkable it appears a preternatural talent. This openness also marks his incorporation of grammar into large narrative structures. Because his magnifications of grammar are so overt, his readers often remark on the linguistic features not just of sentences but of long passages (Richard Ohmann's description of speech acts in *Watt*[9] is a sample) as well as in the shape of the work as a whole ("*Not I*," writes Keir Elam, "must be the first drama in history whose central agon has to do with a grammatical category"[10]). But Beckett, though not ordinary, is also not alone in this. For Boethius, too, words, sentences, the features of poetry and prose, logical and analogical tropes are things to be seized, prayed over, and unfolded not only, or even primarily, in "the sentence" but in the larger work.

Boethius's woman in the room attends to language—her own and that of the man near the door—with an exquisite and sustained level of acuity. Solitary sentences duplicate their subject matter in their very action of enunciation.

> Then gliding toward the door, she spoke freely to me of the impediments restraining my capacity for straightforward argument.

The display of volition in the motion of speech is what she speaks about and what her manner of speaking itself demonstrates. Over the expanse of the scene, the woman alternates between poetry and prose so that her nouns will sometimes carry immaterial particulars into the room and sometimes universals, and so that her intellectual and verbal motion will be regulated now by meter and now instead by logical connectives. The linguistic attributes of poetry, prose, prayer, complaint, argument, analogy are crucial to her because those collective attributes (in their many arrangements and recombinations) are the materials out of which she will recreate the universe. In back of all her other assertions lies an extreme claim about linguistic representation — that it can reproduce its own content. Rigorous speech does not merely describe godlike cognition; it induces its practice and so brings it into being.

Boethius bring *Resisting Representation* to a close. His writing takes place on a ground very distant from that on which the book opens — advertising the remedies for physical pain. The two belong at opposite ends because they are, among the essays, the two most widely separated in time, tone, and metaphysical aspiration. Yet they are, in several respects, strangely similar. Because each seeks to instigate a certain mental practice, each is openly utilitarian.[11] Each makes itself available to us as a set of instructions for prescribed action. Equally noticeable, the perceptual practice is in both instances closely bound up with (though not identical to) the very concrete project of diminishing pain. A "consolation" is for Boethius not a loose set of genre requirements but a direct work of help extended to those in an immediate state of distress, the severe isolation that comes with imprisonment or approaching death. That his project differs greatly from that of the advertisements is clear. But in fact, even those advertisements, taken alone, in themselves contain two strikingly disparate genres — on the one hand, the oddly restrained portraits of aspirin and nonaspirin substitutes addressed to a wide public; on the other hand, the decadently lavish portraits of pharmaceuticals addressed exclusively to physicians and surgeons. In making human thought a remedy for hurt, Boethius widens the spectrum of ethical possibility that, in much narrower form, is already set in place by the two advertising genres in their divergent narratives of promised transformation, their representations of the human body, and their strategies for product identification. If Boethius's "well-rounded sphere" were for a moment imagined as a species of opiate (one that works by linguistic rigor rather than narcotic relaxation), it would vastly extend a line already drawn by the divergent points of willow bark and red poppies.

What distinguishes the opening and closing essay from the essays they frame is their overt urge to intervene in the world. But the writers contemplated in all the essays, precisely because they solve hard problems of representation, may seem drawn to the same act of world-meddling. At the same time, their linguistic virtuosity may distract us from the world. Because they enable us to witness a problem in the exact moment they are uncovering a solution, it may be only the "fullness" or the "perfection" or even (quite mistakenly) the "ease" of representation that we see, rather than the ordinary state of difficulty. Of the two general subjects considered here — the problematically abstract (the varying accounts of "truth" in Boethius, Thackeray, and Beckett) and the problematically concrete (the picture of pain in advertising, the picture of labor in Hardy and other nineteenth-century writers) — the second is by far the more difficult terrain, especially since the question of "truth" is often understood as a question about language, rather than a question about something taking place outside language that needs to be brought in. But even on the inaccessible ground of extreme materiality, where events do take place outside language and do need to be brought in, it may — once we are inside the writer's sentences — again be the extraordinary resourcefulness, the expansive ingenuity of the human voice that we hear.

Notes

1. J. E. Gordon, *Structures: Or Why Things Don't Fall Down* (Harmondsworth, 1978), p. 29.

2. Harold Weinrich, "The Textual Function of the French Article," in Seymour Chatman, ed., *Literary Style: A Symposium* (London, 1971), p. 233.

3. Weinrich, "The Textual Function of the French Article," p. 227.

4. Weinrich, "The Textual Function of the French Article," p. 221.

5. J. L. Austin, *How To Do Things With Words*, 2nd ed. J. O. Urmson and Marina Sbisà (Cambridge, 1962), p. 55.

6. Jürgen Habermas, *The Theory of Communicative Action*, vol. 1, *Reason and the Rationalization of Society*, trans. Thomas McCarthy (Boston, 1981), pp. 294, 295.

7. We ordinarily think of the jury trial as an individual right protecting the person on trial; but Akhil Amar, drawing on the writings of Tocqueville, calls attention to its equally important role as a collective right, enabling citizens to participate in the legal process ("The Bill of Rights as a Constitution," 100 *Yale Law Review*, 1186–89).

8. For an extended account of physical pain as an intentional state without an intentional object, see E. Scarry, *The Body in Pain* (New York, 1985), Chapter 3 "Pain and Imagining," pp. 161–80.

9. Richard Ohmann, "Speech, Action, and Style," in Seymour Chatman, ed., *Literary Style: A Symposium*, pp. 245f.

10. Keir Elam, *"Not I*: Beckett's Mouth and the Ars(e) Rhetorica," in Enoch Brater, ed., *Beckett at 80/Beckett in Context* (New York, 1986), p. 136.

11. The kinship between the instrumental goals of classical writing and the "applied practical art" of modern advertising was argued by Leo Spitzer in his juxtaposition of Cicero and *Sunkist* oranges, and probably requires no elaboration here ("American Advertising Explained as Popular Art," originally published in 1949 and republished in *Essays on English and American Literature*, ed. Anna Hatcher [Princeton, 1962], p. 250).

1

OBDURATE SENSATION: PAIN

Willow Bark and Red Poppies: Advertising the Remedies for Physical Pain

Advertisements for aspirin and nonaspirin substitutes are remarkably tedious. They are so uniform in their imagery, so narrow in their claims and so unmemorable in their dramatic methods that it might indeed be difficult to remember them were it not for the sheer frequency of their appearance in the coveted spaces of prime-time television and large-circulation magazines. Anything endlessly reiterated is likely to be tedious; anything barely noticeable is likely (once noticed) to be tedious; the two together do not produce what would ordinarily be understood as a winning combination. But the opening designation of this tediousness as "remarkable" is not meant only as word-play; for when the advertising industry — not notorious for its restraint — suddenly becomes restrained, something at least moderately remarkable has in fact happened; and this restraint in turn must be recognized as only the visible sign of the anomalous and mystifying conditions that have brought it about.

Aspirin and aspirin substitutes work to diminish pain, and commercials assert that they do so. But in the very modesty of their assertions, they violate four categories of claim ordinarily present in advertisements. Category one is intensification. Most advertisements identify what the product actually does and then exaggerate that actual function into a fictional extreme. Tires certainly do enable a car to move along the surface of a road; and some brands of tire no doubt enable the car to maneuver in rain and snow more effectively than others; but an advertisement for Michelin tires pictures a car moving confidently forward into a nuclear mushroom cloud (Figure 1). The jaunty sentence printed across the bottom of the photograph—"The Michelin XA₄ all-season tire can handle just about anything the weather can throw at you"—cannot retroactively change the fact that what compelled the *Newsweek* reader to stop turning pages was the unmistakable image of a nuclear cloud, even if that reader now (after reading the sentence) dutifully revises the image downward into a mere hurricane or tornado. Aspirin commercials do not claim to make us immune to nuclear war, conventional war, hurricanes, or tornadoes. They say nothing about eliminating the external agents of pain, whether international or domestic, but speak only about diminishing the sensation of pain itself; and they never claim total relief from extreme pain but only *some* relief from *minor* aches and pains *relatively* quickly. No wonder America is yawning.

Category two is the negative counterpart of category one, the threat of what will happen to us without the product. The ominous "Don't leave home without it" of American Express is only the most familiar negative in a steady cascade of negatives: "The right suit might not make you

FIGURE 1.

The right suit might not
make you president of the bank.
But the wrong suit
could keep you out of the running.

Reaching a senior executive
level is the reward you receive
for perseverance, a flair for
your work and sound business
judgment. Choosing the suit
that will take you there is an
important decision, because it
says a lot about you. That's
why Hart Schaffner & Marx
is the brand successful
executives choose above all
others. When their suit speaks
for them, they want it to say
the right things.

Hart
Schaffner
& Marx.
The Right Suit.

The Right Suit
in Heritage® Cloth, a fine blend of 55%
Dacron® polyester/45% wool worsted,
woven by Burlington Menswear.

For the name of the retailer in your
area, call toll-free: 1-800-FASHION
In Nebraska, call: 1-800-562-6500

FIGURE 2.

president of the bank. But the wrong suit could keep you out of the running," announces Hart Schaffner and Marx in the *Sunday New York Times* (Figure 2). The photograph shows a several-foot thick bank vault door, so studded with intricate mechanisms and dials that it might have resisted Linus Yale Jr. himself, but which seems to have swung effortlessly open in response to the sheer matter-moving charisma of the man in the right suit. The door (the only door that matters, the *ur*-door, the door to the bank vault) will never open for the man in the wrong suit. While not every advertisement announces its penalty so explicitly, perhaps no advertisement, however free of *overt* warnings, is ever wholly free of negation, as Hannah Arendt long ago suggested in her analysis of the coercive psychology embedded in the lilting commercial for facial soap: behind the advertiser's crooning assurance that the right soap will bring a woman the right husband is that advertiser's fantasy of omnipotence, his belief that the woman who fails to use his product deserves never to find a husband.[1]

The logic of negation Arendt exposes is almost equally applicable to all products. Though empty of overt threats, advertisements for aspirin and nonaspirin substitutes certainly contain the implicit threat that, without the Excedrin, Bayer, Tylenol, Advil, or Bufferin, one's headache will continue. But the scale and intensity of any negative threat will be directly determined by the scale and intensity of the positive claim made: those who fail to buy Excedrin deserve to have an ongoing headache, but those who fail to buy Michelin tires deserve to be annihilated.

Thus by this second criterion, as by the first, advertisements for pain remedies must be given a low rating. This is perhaps especially surprising because a moment's reflection reveals how easily these products might lend themselves to negative advertising: "Don't wait until you are already in the middle of that crucial business meeting to take the aspirin; be smart, take it before the meeting, and your headache, even begin." People who do not take aspirin before business meetings deserve to fail at business. The recent medical finding suggesting that aspirin may reduce chances of heart attack or stroke, though widely reported in the news, was for several years never even subliminally alluded to in advertisements, and has so far not been coercively alluded to even after the medical speculation has become actual "evidence." The hypothetical examples introduced here are, at the very least, unpleasant. But that unpleasantness alone cannot explain why the advertising industry abstains from this genre of advertising, since the examples given are tonally consonant with the strategies for selling endless other products we every day encounter.

The third category is the wide frame of extraneous claims. Advertisements ordinarily push the object's actual function into a fictional extreme (category one); but they also include claims about originally fictional outcomes — that is, outcomes or functions that the product does not produce at any level. Thus, before our very eyes, the most fragile of objects becomes the most robust, and the most robust asserts and magnifies its reputation for sturdiness while simultaneously acquiring a logo of rose petal fragility; the pre-scientific transforms itself into the apotheosis of space age invention, and the ultrascientific becomes the vehicle of our return to agrarian values; the domestic becomes the professional; the homely acquires the scale of the cataclysmic; the non-erotic explodes into the orgiastic; ice skaters become preachers; the male becomes female; the high-tech becomes the high-dec, and Frank Perdue can host a dinner party as elegant and street-wise as Calvin Klein's because this is the commodity culture of change and exchange, Bertolt Brecht's alchemy of theatrical transformation, where anything can become a new thing, and all things vanish and reappear, merged in an ever-widening democracy of glamour.

Television is our national theatre; and the periodic commercial interruptions are like rhythmic recitations of the pledge of allegiance, affirming (in their succinct, thirty-second dramas of transformation) a political ideology whose central provision *is* the *power* of *alteration:* Give me your tired and your poor; Nothing need stay as it is; None of us need be what we are. Thus a large red bottle of Tide emerges before us on the television screen; it tips over into a downward spin, rotates through the air; and when it comes to a stop, its shape has changed into a map of the United States; it spins once more and reacquires its bottle shape. Having, in its very name, assimilated one of the large facts of nature, Tide now becomes, with equal ease, an emblem of the polis itself. Because it can change dirty clothes into clean clothes, it is a legitimate vehicle for the ideology of transformation; it is a palpable, purchasable fragment of citizenship.

In the midst of this, aspirin remains stubbornly itself; and people who take aspirin remain stubbornly themselves. Although the brow of the person who has just taken Anacin is less furrowed than it was a few moments ago, that person has not turned into Sophia Loren, nor is there any implications that she has suddenly become the hip employee of a high-tech computer company. Despite her arthritis, the woman who takes Bufferin can play the piano (Figure 3), but she has not suddenly become a concert pianist, and it will cross no one's mind that she is playing *The Goldberg Variations*. Although her freedom from pain now allows her to enjoy the camaraderie of her friends, we are not invited to suppose that it is her skill itself that has earned her their friendship, nor that they loved her less when she was in pain. Nor, finally, can we even think she is now *wholly* free of pain and stiffness; the position of her neck does not allow us to. Like most advertisements for aspirin and nonaspirin, the form of pleasure claimed here is that of modest enablement, not a level of "enablement" that entails extraordinary litheness or agility. Swallowing an aspirin is not like inserting a tampax, which (according to its advertisers) enables one to hurl and spin through the air as though one had just been transformed into Kathy Rigby and the inserted product had just been transformed into a supercharged battery (or a miniature bottle of spinning red Tide).

In a widely televised commercial for APF, the woman who an hour ago could not zip up her dress can now do so. But she is the same woman. Her husband is the same man. Remarkably, her dress is the same dress. (All that has changed is that she herself can now fasten it.) The advertisers do not suggest that while troubled with arthritis, she was confined to the loose, slip-it-over-your-head genre of housedress, and that having regained the full use of her hands, she now enters into the transformational grammar of high fashion, with its intricate fastenings, hooks, eyes, and zippers. Advertisers of aspirin are perhaps in more danger of underrepresenting rather than overrepresenting their product: from the inside, the striking sense of enhancement that comes with the recovery from pain and the extended use of one's hands is not wholly unlike the feeling of being glamourous or the warm pleasure of receiving adulation for one's musical skills. But commercials for aspirin and nonaspirin analgesics tend never to represent either the intensity of the original pain or the intensity

"I don't let my arthritis get me down. I do something smarter."

She takes Bufferin. Taking Bufferin® for arthritis is smarter for two reasons: It's smarter than taking Tylenol because Bufferin can effectively relieve the swelling and inflammation that may occur with arthritis. Tylenol can't. That's because Bufferin contains aspirin, the pain reliever doctors recommend most for the temporary relief of minor arthritis pain and inflammation.

And Bufferin is smarter than taking plain aspirin because Bufferin contains special buffers that help protect against the stomach upset plain aspirin can cause.

That's why...Bufferin is smarter for arthritis.

Because arthritis can be serious, if pain persists more than 10 days or redness is present, consult your doctor immediately.

USE ONLY AS DIRECTED

FIGURE 3.

of the pleasure that comes with the cessation of pain as they would be experienced from the inside, but only as an onlooker might see the change from the outside where it appears quite modest.

In a culture that celebrates transformation, one might expect aspirin to be presented as the quintessential transformational object, for it entails the pronounced temporal categories of an emphatic *before* (the disabling absorption in the physical fact of the body) and an emphatic *after* (the regaining of an external world that comes only when one's attention is no longer coercively appropriated by the headache, earache, toothache, whether minor or severe). But, as even the random objects encountered along the way here have suggested, it is not aspirin alone but all of material culture — car tires, suits, soap, Calvin jeans, and Perdue chickens — that presumably work to diminish discomfort or extend the world of pleasure. The full spectrum of pleasure includes not just physical and mental enablement but romantic love, erotic allure, professional achievement, good food, the thirst quenching-and-creating dance of reggae and rock, camaraderie and good cheer (or, as we call it in the United States, Cheer), the acquisition of knowledge (True), or all of these together (Total). Aspirin must somehow wedge its way into that full spectrum and defend its own discrete, however narrow, band of territory. But precisely because its position occurs at the cross-over point, the self-conscious boundary between physical pain and the absence of pain, its narrow territory is also pivotal. If, in other words, material culture as a whole is our pleasurable workbench of alchemical transformation, then aspirin is the small white philosopher's stone, the elemental pebble of access to all subsequent realms of transformation.

Category four is itself a composite of categories one, two, and three; and having failed to meet the standard of those three, advertisements for aspirin and nonaspirin substitutes must again fail here. Commercials have been repeatedly credited as one of the technological precedents for the visually sophisticated rock videos because those advertisements have a complexity and density of texture that results from the pressure to accomplish so much so quickly. Within the spatial confines of a single page or the temporal confines of a thirty-second sequence, they must identify the object's function, magnify it fivefold into a fictional extreme, then moderate it downward twofold so that, though it still remains magnified by a factor of three, what we seem to have just experienced is disarming honesty (as in the owning and disowning of the good-natured Michelin advertisement with its visual urgency and its verbal wink). Further, because they persuade by means of both promises and penalties, they must somehow woo without putting at ease, and threaten without ceasing to be winning. Finally, they must spin the object through endless formal alterations while simultaneously ensuring that the product's identity remains stable enough to be indeed identifiable. As a result, they contain themes and counterthemes, overlays of imagistic connotations, subterranean narratives, and excavatable surprises. Aspirin commercials, in contrast, claim little and thus have little to disown; they are unwooing, unwinning, unthreatening, and seem at work to deprive their object of its inherent spin. Though not wholly one-dimensional, aspirin commercials aspire to the unexcavatable.

It may be that the sheer factualness of physical pain inhibits and subverts the inherent fictionalizing process of advertising. Perhaps the industry abstains from its usual procedures out of a kind of quiet respect for the aversive reality of (even minor) aches and pains. Or, if that explanation strains our credulity, perhaps it abstains not because of its own respect but because it senses in its audience a widespread cultural reverence for those in distress, and concludes that it would be better to err on the side of tedium rather than tactlessness, underrepresentation rather than overrepresentation. While we cannot know whether or not this is so, there are five explanations that we *can* know cannot be so.

First, it is not the case that this restraint arises out of any indifference to selling. The sheer frequency of commercials suggests what the financial figures confirm: like tribesmen preferring shells or beads to money, Americans in one recent year (according to a Smithsonian report) traded 1385 million dollars for 64,800 million aspirin and nonaspirin tablets. Second, it is not the case that the restraint arises from any inherent lack of drama in the product itself or the problem it works to remedy. Third, it is not the case that the object's attributes are incompatible with the attributes ordinarily sanctioned and celebrated by the culture, since willed alteration is held to be of central value, and aspirin is an agent of willed alteration.

A fourth, tempting but ultimately erroneous, hypothesis is that the inherent resistance of physical pain to verbal or visual representation accounts for the quality of the advertisement that we have so far been identifying as restraint. The accurate part of this hypothesis is the first half of the sentence: people in pain, as well as philosophers and artists who work with problems of representation, have repeatedly acknowledged that physical pain *does* resist objectification, does so perhaps more than any other human experience. But the conclusion that advertisers do not represent pain because (like patients, philosophers, or artists) they *cannot* do so is erroneous; for there exists graphic evidence that the ever-resourceful advertising industry has gone fairly far in inventing visual analogues for pain, though most of us do not encounter those visual analogues on a day-to-day basis. In one relatively hidden corner of the advertising industry, there exist strategies of representation wholly unlike those with which we are familiar. Because these strategies are available to the national advertisers of aspirin and nonaspirin analgesics, one must conclude that when they refrain from them, they do so out of conscious choice. The differences between the two genres of advertising will be examined below, after first contemplating for a moment a fifth, closely related hypothesis.

Pain is a medical problem; even small pains are a medically related problem; aspirin is a medically related product; and, not surprisingly, aspirin advertisements constantly remind us of the object's connection to the world of professional medicine. If there is a single piece of information that the makers of Nuprin want us to know, it is that their over-the-counter product is related to a chemical formula that is (as the white-coated man tells us each night toward the end of the evening news) "over 100 million prescriptions strong." The makers of Teldrin devote a full page in *Family Circle* to an image of their product resting on a rather large prescription pad, framed by the headline, "For allergy relief this effective, you used to need a prescription" (Figure 4). Tylenol, too, stakes its name on a single claim, to the exclusion of all other claims, in the pages of *Good Housekeeping* (Figure 5). In the large headline at the top, the woman tells us, "Ever since the hospital gave me Tylenol, it's become our family pain

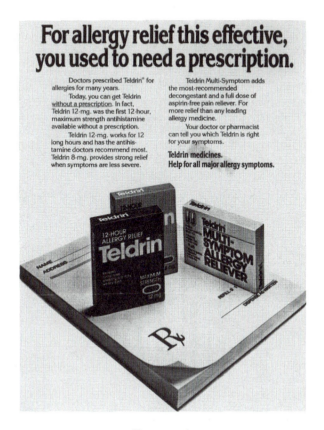

For allergy relief this effective, you used to need a prescription.

Doctors prescribed Teldrin® for allergies for many years.

Today, you can get Teldrin without a prescription. In fact, Teldrin 12-mg. was the first 12-hour, maximum strength antihistamine available without a prescription.

Teldrin 12-mg. works for 12 long hours and has the antihistamine doctors recommend most. Teldrin 8-mg. provides strong relief when symptoms are less severe.

Teldrin Multi-Symptom adds the most-recommended decongestant and a full dose of aspirin-free pain reliever. For more relief than any leading allergy medicine.

Your doctor or pharmacist can tell you which Teldrin is right for your symptoms.

Teldrin medicines.
Help for all major allergy symptoms.

FIGURE 4.

reliever." The small print elaborates the original hospital circumstances. The product itself is backgrounded against a stethoscope. The woman herself is backgrounded against a family photo showing the three sons whose passage into the world was made easier for their mother by the existence of Tylenol. The advertisement ends at the bottom of the page by a fifth reiteration of the idea first introduced at the top, "Trust TYLENOL. Hospitals do." The full page presents a steadily elaborated but reassuring homogeneous tone: although the steady declarative voice slips to the imperative in the penultimate, "Trust TYLENOL," it quickly returns to the plane of the declarative in the final, "Hospitals do."

Given the fact that pain remedies are connected to the professional medical world, and given the fact that the advertisers so clearly wish us to remember that connection, one might conclude that the overall restraint of aspirin and nonaspirin advertising arises because it must remain tonally consonant with the professional "dignity" and ethical "sobriety" of the hospital and doctor's office (even when a given image is not directly calling

FIGURE 5.

attention to that professional realm). It is therefore somewhat disarming to discover that when the advertising industry addresses the men and women who actually inhabit these offices and hospitals, they do so by means of advertisements that are not primarily characterized by dignity, sobriety, restraint, or understatement. The visual and verbal imagery that reaches the wide public through CBS, ABC, NBC, *McCalls, Good Housekeeping, Saturday Evening Post, Family Circle, Reader's Digest* is not the verbal and visual imagery that reaches the medical professionals through the pages of such magazines as *Contemporary Surgery, The Journal of Surgical Practice, Primary Cardiology Clinics, Clinical Pediatrics, Hospital Tribune, Hospital Practice, Hospital Medicine, Human Sexuality, Hospital Therapy, Resident and Staff Physician*, and *The New Physician*. The two genres of advertising differ dramatically in their narratives of transformation, in their representations of the human body, and in their strategies of product identification. Each of the three will be looked at below.

I.   Narratives of Transformation

Spread lavishly across the full two-page expanse of an open magazine is a visually stunning photograph (Figure 6). It arrests attention both because of the scale of space devoted to it (the side and bottom margins have been completely eliminated) and because of its own mesmerizing content. It depicts the near-uniformity of sky and sea at sunset, interrupted only by the motionless boats whose upward masts are reiterated downward into their watery reflections. The masts form a sequence of vertical lines joining air and water, and thus work to reaffirm the continuity of sea and sky they for a moment seemed to interrupt.

It is perhaps always the case that at the horizon of the sea, the world is poised between abstraction and representational content. But this particular photograph unfolds and elaborates the mental shift back and forth between the two. What on the right-hand side is only a near-abstraction (forever recapturing its own sensuous bounty) dissolves on the left into the serene geometry of unequivocal abstraction. The substance of the horizon (right) disappears into a contentless horizontal line (left). The masts-and-reflected-masts (right) vanish into their contentless vertical counterparts (left). Thus, as the eyes move back and forth over the full surface of the photograph, one enters the dreamlike suspension of a world acquiring content, dissolving, abandoning that content, reacquiring it. The visual action elicited is the action of "gazing," the steady focusing and unfocusing of the eyes, the continual finding and losing of the visual object. The mental action elicited is one of drift, as when on the edge of sleep, the mental image slips away and is then refound. The photograph thus initiates the viewer analogically into the pleasurable analgesic state that the drug being advertised reportedly creates: Vistaril-i.m. produces a state of "Calm" (the word looms large in the print above the photograph); and when we eventually read the small print given on the following page, we will learn that one of its side-effects is "transitory drowsiness."

But regardless of whether the reflexes of consciousness are described in the idiom of "gazing" or "drifting" or something else, they are of course only the prelude to the real visual action demanded by the photograph; for suddenly the mind (off guard, adrift) slams up against the fact that the horizontal line on the left is not an abstract rendering of the horizon but a graphic rendering of a surgical incision; the vertical lines are not the two-dimensional counterparts of masts-and-reflected-masts but the sutures closing the incision.

Precisely how the overall action (which perhaps lasts several seconds; perhaps only a fraction of a second) comes about probably varies from person to person. It may be that the eyes stray in and out of the photograph to the large words printed above — "Following surgery . . . the perception of pain diminished by CALM" — and thus come to recognize in the

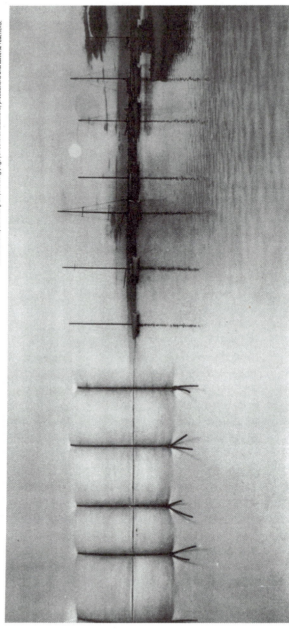

FIGURE 6.

picture the pain and the surgery as well as the calm. Or perhaps our eyes only roam around within the confines of the photograph itself, but keep getting caught on the illuminated tucks at the top of each vertical line, and the splayed triangles at the bottom, neither of which can be accounted for as a counterpart of anything over on the right.

In either event, the final jolt of recognition is a breathtaking one, for the block of space that had initially been perceived as the source of abstraction suddenly acquires the most concrete of all content, the human body, and not just the body, but the body hurt, the body cut (however artfully), the body opened and not yet healed. The sense of vertigo is amplified by the fact that the object realm on the right exists deep in space, a distant half-mile from the viewer's face, while the object on the left is now only one inch away. One can feel the spatial break against the surface of one's eyes: we have projected ourselves forward into the open expanse of ocean and air, but only the right-hand line of vision passes through; the left-hand side is blocked. We are stranded on the magnified surface of the body; we can see but no longer reach and enter the alluring realm beyond. It is, of course, Vistaril-i.m. that can carry us from the worldless pain and surgery of the left to the world-restoring serenity of the right.

This is, within the pages of the glossy medical magazines, the equivalent of the "before and after" narratives known to most of us only in the many commercials that begin "I had a headache; now it's gone," "She couldn't zip up her dress; now she can." But aside from their shared emphasis on temporal categories, the two are in nothing equivalent. As noted earlier, the advertisements that make their way into the wide public realm represent both the pain and the cessation of pain only as they can be perceived from the outside; the woman used to be able to open her hand this much, but now she can open it this much; a tape measure appears on the screen beside the hand to register the scale of the increase that the advertiser rightly worries may not be discernible to the unassisted eye. From the inside, this widening arc of action may bring with it the rush of pleasure of a trapeze swing; but the iconography of the advertisement does not provide an external analogue for events occurring at the interior of consciousness. The Vistaril-i.m. photograph, in contrast, recreates in the viewers themselves both the rhythms of pleasure (the beauty of the seascape, the aesthetic play between the sensuous and the abstract, the folding and unfolding of space, the luxury of gazing and drifting) and the jolt that, though not "painful," has the abrupt, non-negotiable character of pain. The difference between pain and pleasure is made graphically available to us, even if we have been made to experience the serene equilibrium first and the disequilibrium second, reversing the normal "before and after" sequence. The practitioners of advertising are at liberty to rearrange the world, including the world of temporal categories. In fact, although the photograph has often appeared in hospital magazines as reproduced here, it has turned up equally often with its left and right panels reversed, reminding the physician that Vistaril-i.m. can be used not only post-operatively but pre-operatively.

Once we turn back the cover of *Hospital Practice* or *Hospital Tribune* or *Contemporary Surgery*, we have consented to imagine entering a sphere that includes extremely severe pain. But the discrepancy between the visually stunning Vistaril-i.m. advertisement and the muted advertisements for Bayer and Tylenol cannot be explained in terms of the discrepancy in the intensity of the pain each product works to diminish. It does not follow that, as pain intensifies, so the iconography of advertising should intensify. If anything, one might anticipate the opposite outcome: the more severe the pain, the more restricted and professionally subdued the presentation of the remedy.

Nor, for that matter, is there any absolute break between the two kinds of product. The continuity between over-the-counter and prescription drugs is acknowledged by the manufacturers and advertisers of both. Just as Nuprin, Teldrin and Tylenol remind us that they are connected to the hospital and doctor's office, so, conversely, the advertisements for prescription drugs often announce their own connection to aspirin: advertisements for Clinoril explicitly present their product as a competitor to aspirin; an advertisement for Indocin begins by saying it should only be used if "an adequate trial of aspirin and rest" have not brought the desired relief. Further, it is not only advertisements but some drugs themselves (Percodan, Empirin Compound c̄ Codeine) that combine prescription and nonprescription elements. And, finally, some very serious forms of pain require treatment by nonprescription drugs: aspirin is prescribed for very severe, as well as minor, forms of arthritis; Mylanta-II is prescribed for very severe ulcer pain.

The difference between the two genres of advertising does not, then, follow from the varying level of the pain or from the varying nature of the product. It seems to follow, instead, from the discrepancy in the two audiences addressed. Commercials for aspirin and nonaspirin substitutes are addressed to the people who themselves have the aches and pains: the advertisers are probably correct in believing that almost everyone has occasional small aches and pains, and a large number of people have some aches and pains fairly regularly. They need not present their product through the coercive strategies used for many other commercial products in part because physical pain, even when minor, provides its own coercion, its own compelling message that it must be gotten rid of. Without the informative assistance of advertisers, one might live many decades without knowing that dandruff or perspiration or limp hair or old suits should be "gotten rid of." But one does not spend many minutes with an ache without desiring its cessation. It contains its own pressure toward alteration. The advertisement need only ensure that the existence of its pain-altering product is known, that the name is familiar, that the bottle or box is easily recognizable. This helps to explain the inordinate amount

of time that aspirin and nonaspirin commercials devote to product identification (a subject that I will return to), rather than to narrative elaborations
of the product's function. It also helps to explain why the "before" and
"after" categories need never be presented mimetically. The viewers need
not be told what the one-inch gain on the tape measure might feel like
from the inside because a certain percentage of the viewers come to the
television or magazine with an interior account already in hand; they can,
without assistance, see in the markings of the tape the swing of the trapeze.

But the advertisements in the medical magazines are addressed to people who must work to diminish pain even when they are themselves wholly
free of pain — that is, people who cannot begin to work for pain's diminu-
tion only at the moment when the coercive interior signal happens to arise
within the circle of their own bodies. The advertisements thus present
the temporal categories mimetically, reminding physicians, for a brief
moment, what pain, and hence relief from pain, feels like from the inside,
why it must be gotten rid of. The fact that the motive is financial does not
eliminate the possibility that one of its outcomes is humanitarian. If it
seems either unnecessary or presumptuous for advertisers to instruct physicians on the felt-experience of pain, one need only remember how widespread in the United States is the complaint that doctors do not listen to,
or hear, or understand the patient's reports of pain. It is not overprescrip-
tion, but underprescription, that people who have stayed in hospitals most
dread. The attempt to provide external analogues for interior physical
events again becomes visible in the way medical advertisers depict the
human body. The dangers of this reservoir of compelling images will also
become visible.

II.　The Representation of the Body

The peculiar quality of television and magazine advertisements for aspirin
and nonaspirin substitutes in part arises from their attempt to speak about
the problematic contingencies of the body (aches, pains, stiffness, physical
discomfort) without representing the human body itself. Often there is
no person, hence no locus of embodiment, included anywhere in the
advertisement: the visual image for Teldrin (see Figure 4) has its counterpart in the images used for many other pain-relief products, as will be
elaborated later. But even when persons do appear, the photograph typically works to eclipse and disguise the fact that they have bodies, and does
so by one of several paths.

As the earlier Tylenol and Bufferin advertisements suggest (see Figures
3 and 5), the person is usually wearing the maximum amount of clothing
compatible with an indoor photograph. Even the neck is considered too
resonant to be exposed: high-collared blouses with large bows appear
often, and the blouse itself is usually covered by some second layer, wheth-

er sweater or jacket, having a pronounced texture of its own that thus substitutes for an deflects attention from the actual texture of the body's surface. Clothing, of course, contains its own iconography: a double-layer of clothing mimes the double reality of the body's outside and inside surfaces, especially if the underlayer is pink (as in the Bufferin photograph) or red (as in the Tylenol photograph). But blouses and sweaters are not identical with the thing that they cover; and these advertisements, decorous in isolation, are even more decorous when seen in the wide field of commercial images that ordinarily take every occasion to undress the human figure (while simultaneously failing to convey anything about the nature of embodiment).

When advertisements for aspirin and nonaspirin analgesics explicitly call attention to the sensation of hurt in any discrete part of the body, it is almost always the head or hands, not only because each is a major locus of enablement (and thus, when aching, a major locus of disablement), but also because each exists at the periphery of the body. Though emphatically part of the body, head and hands extend into the world, are the parts most intensely engaged with the world, and thus come to be perceived as the locations most intimately bound up with personhood rather than sheer physical existence. Pains in the head are usually referred to diffusely as "headaches," rather than, for example, earaches or toothaches which in their specificity too quickly carry us into the messy matter inside the head, where the pain actually happens. The interior of the torso (whether abdomen or back), like the interior of thighs, shins, knees or feet, is usually bypassed altogether. Some bodily territory other than head or hands may be *verbally* alluded to, either as the locus of pain (the childbirth of Figure 5) or the locus of enablement (the full bodily participation of tennis in Figure 7); yet, as both Tylenol images show, what will be *visually* depicted are the face and a small tip of the hand. Thus one of the most common forms of aspirin advertisement is the talking head, or sequence of talking heads (Figure 8).

When very occasionally the secret interior of the body is visually represented, it tends to be represented by means of a chalk drawing, silhouette, or stylized outline. In its two-page advertisement for *McCalls* (Figure 9), Encaprin devotes one full page to the product, the other full page to what it introduces as "AN INSIDE LOOK AT HOW IT WORKS." But the dangerous invitation to enter the depths of the body is safely subverted by the visual insistence that there are no depths, but only two dimensions, and only the edges of the two-dimensional. The sources of pain, indicated by bright red spots on the shoulder and hand of the navy blue figure, reside securely on the outside edge. The interior, empty of complications, has no organs, only an isolated line-drawing of a stomach. Even the Encaprin grains themselves float mysteriously to the periphery of the body.

While not every aspirin advertisement conforms to the hierarchy of possibilities outlined here, in general four rules are at work: one, eliminate

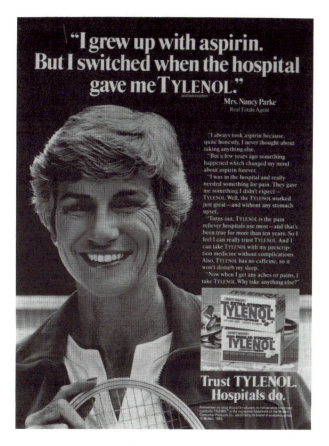

FIGURE 7.

the problematic issue of bodily representation altogether by excluding human beings from the visual image; two, fully clothe and reclothe any person still present in the image; three, if a specific location within the body must be visually alluded to, let it be the head or hands; and four, if any more intimate part of the body must be represented use a silhouette or line drawing. Not surprisingly, medical advertisements follow a different set of rules.

In medical advertising, the surface of the body is directly seen and often oddly seen, in order to permit it to be reseen, or seen for the first time. Although the Vistaril-i.m. photograph (Figure 6) is often printed in black and white, it more frequently appears in color. A startling, airy expanse of light pink (broken only by the fragile intervention of a red horizontal line and blue-grey vertical sutures) covers the entire left panel and extends over into the right, where it now begins to alternate with an

FIGURE 8.

equally airy, light blue. The photograph is thus dominated by a single shade of pink that is at once delicate and totalizing: it must simultaneously represent both the radiant flush of the world at sunset and the vulnerable flesh-toned surface of Caucasian skin. In its use of ethereal pastel colors, this image is exceptional among medical advertisements. It is typical, however, both in its pressure toward totalization, and in its passage from the body's outside surface to its interior (the window into the body provided by the open incision).

The woman in the advertisement for Darvocet-N 100 (Figure 10) is, like the women appearing for Bufferin and Tylenol, fully clothed, even clothed in multiple layers. Like Encaprin's silhouette man, she is two-dimensional. But what the page as a whole lifts directly into view is the looming shape, depth, and scale of a physical interior that has become uncontainable within the fragile external dimensions of the human form. Like the photograph for Vistaril-i.m., the image provides an external representation of pain not as the person in pain is seen from the outside,

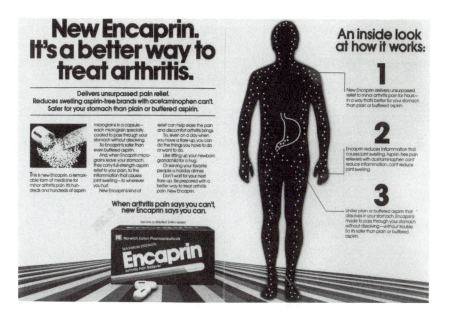

FIGURE 9.

but as the pain itself is felt from the inside where, by appropriating all attention, it has become total. Pain is not a detail in the woman's existence. Instead, the woman, draped across her pain, has become a detail on its surface. Pain sabotages and subverts personhood. When it becomes three-dimensional, the person becomes two-dimensional: it drains her of all content from below in order to widen its own graphics of extension.

Because it is upright, it reduces her (even in the midst of her action of walking) to the helplessness of the horizontal. Larger, longer, wider than she, it contains her, folding her into its shape, and gradually becomes connected to everything beyond itself, as the colors of the page insist. The top triangle of color is dark brown. Behind the monolithic block letters — letters only in the sense that the rocks of Stonehenge and Easter Island might be called letters — the ground becomes orange-red, then changes in the foreground to a crudely bright blend of violet and magenta. The letters of pain are themselves purple: their front surfaces are inflected with bright violet from below; they become black at their deep interior, as though absorbing the blank spaces of consciousness from their haunted source above. The woman, clothed in bright white and very light blue, is isolated from everything on the page except the white printed letters of Darvocet-N 100 and the logo *Lilly*, which thus act as her fragile source of connection with the world outside. Darvocet-N and Lilly are allied with persons against the monolithic destroyer of persons, physical pain.

While the images of the human body within medical advertising are

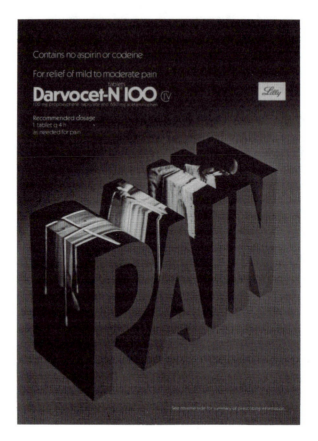

FIGURE 10.

too diverse to be summarized in a set of rules, the Darvocet-N 100 advertisement is itself a compilation and distillation of the multiple strategies of
representation visible in Figures 11–19. Because pain subverts a person's
consciousness of any external world, inside and outside surfaces seem to
change places. Thus the external agents of pain appropriate the surface of
the body, as in the blanket of sharply articulated nails that displace the
skin of the man drawn in a rigid posture of attention for the Vicodin
advertisement (Figure 11). Conversely, the interior matter of the body is
lifted out into the world, stranded from its home in the body, and subjected to raw actions and harsh textures, as in the prostate and rope of the
coercive Geocillin advertisement (Figure 12). We are no longer in the
realm of line drawings. The background of this photograph is dark, magenta brown; the moist organ is orange-red. But even when it is not the
inner content of the body that an advertisement literally depicts, it is
often the colors of the body's interior — red, orange, muddy purples, dark

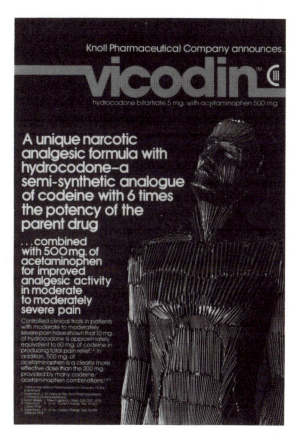

FIGURE 11.

brown—that dominate, rather than the daylight world of pastels and primary colors found in the aspirin advertisements. Figures 11, 12, 13, 14, 15, and 16 all position red or orange against an alternative field of black, brown, or green.

The habitual, stylistic interchange of internal and external surfaces—the drawing of what is outside inside (nails) and what is inside outside (prostate)—leads medical advertisers to an extensive use of geographical images. Thus in representations of ulcer pain, the stomach lining becomes a dislocated landscape of eruption, as in the volcanic imagery of Mylanta-II (Figure 13). Again in Tolectin's depiction of arthritis (Figure 14), the knotted fingers, lurid with color, become the jagged plates of vertical terrain holding in the hot substance they cannot contain and that flows down the backs of the hands in discrete, precisely etched lines of bright pain. The geological metaphor is pushed further in the Darvocet-N 100

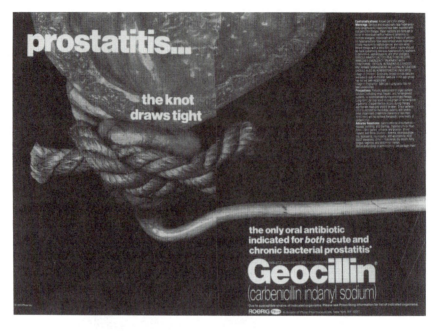

FIGURE 12.

image: as the body becomes the only world, so pain becomes the only body.

Nowhere in the images for Vicodin, Geocillin, Mylanta-II, or Tolectin is there a human face or an ordinary human form that would link these depictions of pain to the familiar faces and forms that the medical professionals see everyday in the hospital rooms or corridors. While the Darvocet-N 100 page is a distillation and extension of the representational strategies present in these advertisements, it also contains a realistic (however derealized by pain) human figure that is drawn from the subgenre of representation visible in Figures 15–19. The two groups of the images (11–14 and 15–19) are not mutually exclusive. As both Paul Schilder and Eugene Minkowski have written, physical pain often distorts a patient's conception of his or her own bodily shape; in particular, the location of the pain is often experienced as an opening into the body.[2] The representation of pain as an opening, already present in the images encountered earlier, again appears in the illuminated interior sphere of the elbow in Figure 15, the visible wound that mimes the invisible sensation in Figure 16, and the exposed haze of breast and heart in Figure 17.

Although this second constellation of images more closely approximates the images familiar from aspirin and nonaspirin advertisements, the space separating them remains great. In commercials for aspirin, the person who aches is not always, but often, a woman between forty and sixty

FIGURE 13.

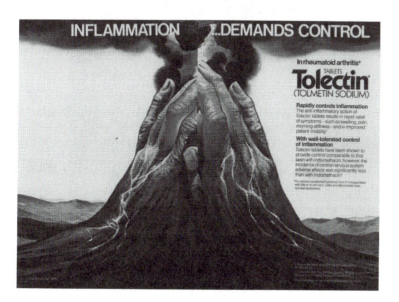

FIGURE 14.

FIGURE 15.

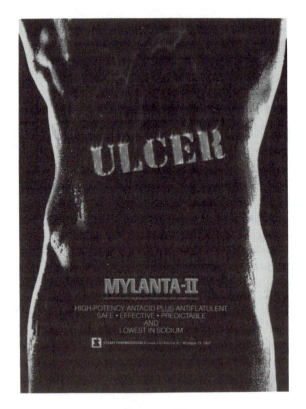

FIGURE 16.

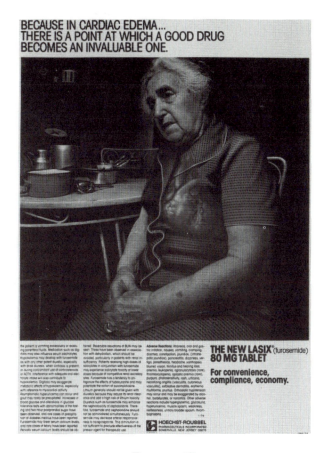

FIGURE 17.

(even if a male voice names the remedy and narrates the solution); in medical advertisements, both men and women have pain, and the age range begins at infancy and continues to the end. The judgments about what portions of the body engage the world are often mutually exclusive, as the representations of tennis by Tylenol and Dolobid 500 suggest (Figures 7 and 15). The woman in Figure 17 could never appear on behalf of aspirin because even if one could cajole her into long sleeves (which seems unlikely), no amount of clothing could disguise the profound embodiment of her arms.

The idea of a child in pain is perhaps to the medical advertisers what the idea of any person in pain is to commercial advertisers: it appears to inhibit the otherwise habitual reflexes of graphic invention. Thus the advertisement for Auralgan (Figure 19) most closely approximates the visual strategies found in aspirin advertisements: a talking head; an un-elaborated narrative assertion that the pain is over; an exclusive absorp-

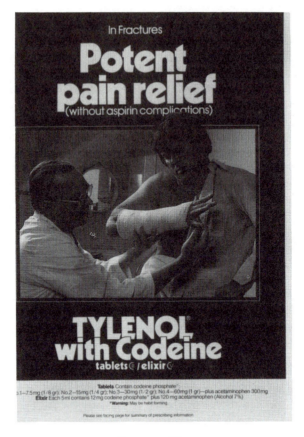

FIGURE 18.

tion in the face and hands. But precisely because it so resembles these familiar images, it can be taken as a final test case of the distance between the two realms of advertising.

What separates the Auralgan image from its aspirin and nonaspirin counterparts is, quite simply, that it is compelling. That this person should have had pain seems intolerable; that she did have pain is something the viewer does not even wonder about; that she is free of it now is self-evident. How could we disbelieve her? She looks out at us as someone for whom the jack-in-the-box of bodily well-being has just popped into view, someone who cannot quite contain her amazed disbelief at what the world has brought her, yet simultaneously wishes to assure us that, surprising as it is, it is so: the pain's gone. Using only the most conventional forms of portrait and verbal testimonial, the medical advertisers have managed once more to bring about mimetic reenactment, an emotional symmetry between the state of feeling the picture depicts and the state of feeling the

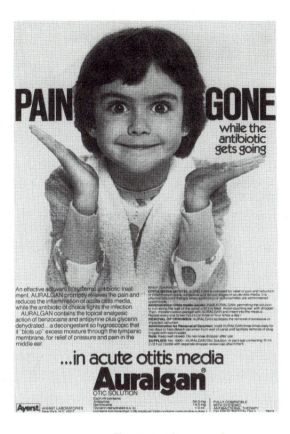

FIGURE 19.

viewer feels when encountering the photograph. They have found a face that is pleasure-bearing: the page turns; she comes into view; one feels, at that split second, glad to be in her presence. And "gladness" is the feeling they wish to elicit, because gladness *is* the feeling of "pain gone." The believability of the advertisement does not depend on her being a fragile child. Commercial advertisements using children are often among the least believable. More importantly, the medical advertisers are able to bring about such emotional symmetry using people of any age. One advertisement·for sleeping pills is so full of saffron colours and radiant pleasure that, for a time, one believes that there could be no pleasure on earth so great as being sixty-five and waking up in a sunny room on a summer morning. Even at a distance, the thought lingers, "Perhaps it is so."

This, then, is the quality that unifies the medical advertisements about pain. Those for aspirin eliminate the human body because the locus of embodiment (and hence, the locus of belief) is in the viewers themselves: their attention to pain remedies only requires that they believe in the reality of their own bodily aches and pains, over which the admakers need exercise no persuasion. But what is at stake in medicine is not the doctors' awareness of their own bodies but their capacity to see the bodies of others, on whose behalf they must act and prescribe. The pain of others must be believed in (as though it were, at least mimetically, their own), but has tended traditionally to be disbelieved or underbelieved. The medical admakers therefore design pages that compel belief. Sometimes they do this through visually stunning images—that is, images that literally stun the mind into inaction, suspend critical thought, hence elicit belief. At other times, they use combinations of innovative and conventional techniques to produce photographs which generate mimetic continuity between the image seen and the one who sees.

Medical advertisements thus become small exercises in re-enactment and coercion. The dangers of this high-powered cauldron of images are especially apparent if one envisions these images beginning to slip out of the private theatre of professionals into the national theatre of television and large circulation magazines. The increasing pressure for advertising medical services within the public realm will, as has often been noted, bring with it not only a wide distribution of medical information but also a wide distribution of resonant terms such as "emergency care," "instant care" and "plastic surgery."[3] Whose strategies of bodily representation, whose narratives of transformation, will be used, those of aspirin and nonaspirin advertising, or those done on behalf of Vistaril-i.m., Darvocet-N 100, Vicodin, Auralgan and Geocillin?

The presentation of medicine through public advertising is especially problematic because medicine's subject is the most inherently political of all subjects, the human body. Further, what will be advertised will not be a discrete, material product but a diffuse service, and the possibilities for compelling belief become much more emphatic when the product disappears. What is widely considered most offensive about advertising is that "all this" is being done on behalf of a product, in order to sell it. At the same time, the saving grace of commercials has always been the product, for the product betrays the motive for the drama, and thus provides the single check on the believability of the ideologies embedded there. It is the only invitation to critical thought; it is the locus of scepticism and disbelief in what without it would merely entrance. When advertisements become severed from any concrete, purchasable products, all checks are lifted. The political advertisements in any American presidential campaign provide a glimpse of what is possible; but the theatre of belief has what is so far its most perfect model in certain public service commercials that have been present for a much longer time. The contemplation of advertising that is unanchored to any identifiable product carries us back to the contrast between the realms of Bayer and Vistaril-i.m.; for, in the first form of advertising, the product is stubbornly present; in the second, the product disappears. In their elaborations of the human body and evaporation of the product, medical advertisements become a dangerous rehearsal ground.

III. Product Identification

Magazine and television advertisements for aspirin and nonaspirin substitutes actually devote only a modest amount of their space to imagistic and narrative explorations of the product's function. These narratives are not only narrow, modest and two-dimensional, but quickly evacuated from the field of vision altogether so that attention is directly focused on the box or tablet or both. The blue and white Encaprin box with its miniature rocket-like capsule (see Figure 9), the green, gold, and yellow packages of Teldrin (see Figure 4), have their counterparts in the competing magazine images for the blue and yellow packages of Anacin-3 (Figure 20) and the red and yellow package of APF (Figure 21).

Often, twenty-five seconds of a thirty-second television sequence will include in the visual field either the object or its package; and sometimes the full thirty seconds is devoted to the act of identification alone. One Advil commercial begins with an image of an aspirin tablet (with a voice-over triumphantly announcing the year in which it was first made available to the public); then an equally large Tylenol tablet appears on the screen (with a voice-over triumphantly announcing the year in which it was first made available to the public); then a large Advil tablet appears (with a voice-over triumphantly announcing the year in which it was first made available to the public). The commercial pictures the competition it seeks to displace, while simultaneously acknowledging that Advil's very eligibility for competition is based on the fact that it is worthy of being introduced into the company of the other two. But the self-subverting logic here is unimportant because the Aspirin! Tylenol! Advil! sequence is only a narrative excuse for holding the object in front of the viewers' eyes for as long as possible so that we will be able to recognize it quickly when the occasion arises to go out and purchase a pain remedy. The strained quality of many other aspirin commercials is similarly determined by the need to excuse the holding steady of the object on a medium ordinarily devoted to split-second shifts in the visual field.

What is striking about the Advil commercial is that the admakers have clearly decided that the amount of attention deflected away from their product by picturing the competitors is much less than the amount of attention that would be deflected away from the product by including a human being in the picture. With the scandalous exception of Robert Young, neither recognized stars nor strikingly attractive unknown persons are ever used in aspirin commercials because such people demand attention and recognition, and all the viewer's mental energy of "recognition" must be directed onto the product. When men and women do enter the

FIGURE 20.

visual field, they tend to be, though certainly very pleasant-looking, some-what unnoticeable and unmemorable. The problem is that the face of even an "unmemorable" person is brimming with sensuous detail, espe-cially when compared to the ghostly lack of sensuous detail in a chalky white tablet. Thus the best strategy is to keep them away altogether.

In the Encaprin advertisement (see Figure 9), it is the product on the left-hand panel rather than the human being on the right-hand panel that is permitted to have sensuous substance and a material form. APF (Figure 21) pictures Robert Young but his face is smaller than the APF box and much smaller than the giant tablet. The advertisement for Anacin-3 (Fig-ure 20) contains human figures smaller than the name of the brand, and the one for Teldrin (see Figure 4) contains no human being at all. The issue of outside-and-inside bodily surfaces inherent in the subject of physi-cal pain is carried only by the insistent visual emphasis on the outside surface (box), and inside surface (tab) of the product itself. Many of the

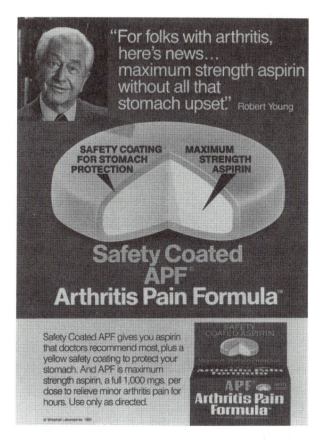

FIGURE 21.

tablets are themselves designed to have an outside skin and inside content: the m&m-like form of APF; the buffered surface and unbuffered undersurface of Bufferin; the plastic capsule containing powder of Tylenol. The use of the photographic insert in Tylenol advertisements (see Figures 5 and 7) reveals the same emphasis: while the cut-away window in the medical magazines leads us into the interior of the human body, here it leads us into the product.

The task of designing an advertisement for aspirin begins to look, from the outside, like a professional nightmare: they are asked to design an advertisement (*a*) for a medium, whether magazine or television, whose very strength is its ability to carry sensory information; (*b*) about a product connected to the resonantly sensory and inherently dramatic subject of relief from pain; while (*c*) confining their attention and the viewer's attention exclusively to the sensuously vacant surfaces of the object itself. Because the chemical substance in the product remains relatively constant across competing brands, while the amount of that substance in any one table varies from brand to brand, the virtue of any one brand is often asserted to be the small number of tablets one needs to take (only three rather than four, only one rather than two, once a day rather than every three hours). Thus the admakers are in the anomalous position of having both to celebrate the material content and form of the object while simultaneously celebrating how few of the objects one ever has to handle.

The necessity of absorbing our attention in the physical properties of the product and package does not, however, wholly explain away the subdued quality of these advertisements. Other commercial presentations of bottles and boxes, such as Tide's bottle-map of the United States, show that the act of product identification does not, by definition, result in visual modesty. Labels from nineteenth-century pain remedies, such as the one for Samaritan Nervine recently included in the Smithsonian exhibit on pain and its relief (Figure 22),[4] again show how morally and geographically totalizing a package alone can be. Both Tide and Samaritan Nervine, like the medical advertisements for Tolectin and Mylanta-II (see Figures 14 and 13), map the world.

If, in other words, aspirin and nonaspirin advertisers need to concentrate exclusively on the physical properties of the product itself, they are not constrained by the given attributes of the object because those attributes are not "fixed" givens. In concert with the manufacturers, they of course have the option of increasing the sensuous character of the tablet or package, aestheticizing it, dramatizing it, covering it with pastel flowers (like the boxes for hand-carved hand soap), or including on its surface a line drawing as beloved as the one on Morton Salt. Aspirin's own remarkable history—its physical origin in the bark of the willow tree—itself provides endless possibilities for packaging and advertising, possibilities that seem to be rejected precisely because the heightening of the object's sensuous qualities would ultimately entail a disappearance of the object into aesthetic mystification. The conscious restraint (rather than externally imposed constraint) of aspirin advertisers is in nothing so apparent as the fact that there is no brand of aspirin called "Willow Bark," there is no package entwined with willow wands, whether spring green or Chinese blue, there is no magazine or television advertisement that carries us under the comforting branches of this tree, and reminds us why it was that it came to be seen as the tree of empathetic commiseration and comfort.

The willow tree that is absent from the realm of aspirin advertising has as its counterpart and antithesis the poppy that is present in the realm of medical advertising (Figure 23). Looming up out of a ground saturated with ink and blackness is a huge scarlet poppy, so lucidly red, so luminously red, so multiply red in its tissue of petals that one sees and understands for the first time the epithet "blood-red poppy." It returns at its center to the black mystery of the ground, just as the ground, at its own

FIGURE 22.

horizon, grows into a soft red haze of light. The slender green stem, halfway down, becomes a silver nail; its metallic point directs attention to the words below; "Endo laboratories tames the poppy." These astonishing words do not astonish, for, although the image luxuriates in all that is untamed, one's mind is so dazed by staring into the open face of the flower that the startling contradiction barely registers and has no power to disturb.

This is how the act of "product identification" takes place in the hospital magazines when it takes place at all. As the earlier figures accurately suggest, it is not a task undertaken very often. In those earlier images, the whole surface of the page is overwhelmed by the representation of the human body itself; no product — no pill, no liquid, no bottle or package — is pictured. Although the product ("Vistaril-i.m.," "Geocillin") is named, and although those names have been frequently cited here in order to specify the particular figure under discussion, the initial viewing experience is one in which the visual content eclipses the name, making it difficult to read and impossible to recall a moment later. On the back of each of those pages, complete verbal information is given about the product, its administration, limitations and adverse reactions (this information is itself carefully monitored by the FDA, and full-page apologies sometimes occur, retracting misinformation originally occupying only a single line of small print). While, then, a verbally precise product description does appear, it is important to remember that it appears "on the *back* of each of those pages."

But even, finally, here in Figure 23, where at last what is pictured is not the pain or the body but the pain remedy or product, where is the pain remedy, where is the product, what does Nubain look like, where did it go? It has subsided beneath the surface of its own aestheticized history: it has not simply reverted back (from whatever Endo laboratories has made) into the opium substrate, but reverted back one step more into

FIGURE 23.

the original flower itself. The image is as atavistic as it is opulent. So completely has the sensuous fullness of the human body been transferred to the product, that the product has disappeared and, of course, the body has reappeared: it is there, as before, overwhelming in its layered openness; the image even strays into the realm of the sexual, a trespass that normally is (to the credit of advertisers) mercifully absent in both medical and commercial depictions of pain and the products which relieve it.

The panel pictured here is actually only the first of a six-page long advertisement. The next four pages have the same proportions of deep black ground and narrow sky. Now, however, the haze above the horizon is neon violet edged with light blue. Each page contains a strangely beautiful bottle: its grey-blue tinted glass is moist with condensed vapor. Here and there, small charts float on the black ground like lost fragments of technical elegance. The bars of the color-filled graphs are stylized hypodermic needles, comparing the effects and side-effects of Nubain and morphine. Nubain "OFFERS LOW POTENTIAL FOR ABUSE," but the imagery entices one into the very narcotic haze that the absent product itself is asserted to be relatively free of. We have lost our bearings and cannot remember how we strayed from the hospital into this synthetic half-light: geometric shapes and chemical structures emerge out of the ground, and Billy Holliday's voice is almost audible at the horizon.

It is, then, mimetic enactment that occurs even at the moment of product identification. The advertisement is narcotic not because it identifies a narcotic-product but because the narcotic-product has been dispersed, and with it, the invitation to sceptical disbelief and distance. Nubain has something to do with poppies, moist vapors, stylized hypodermic needles and empty spaces; but we cannot, out of these fragments, reconstitute a single, concrete, visually graspable image of the product. Like the narratives of transformation and modes of bodily representation looked at earlier, the aesthetic mystification of the object can be benignly interpreted in terms of the specific professional audience that is being addressed. The relation between the medication and the physician is, after all, itself half-way gone toward dissolution. It is mediated across the abstraction of the prescription pad. The person who licenses the purchase is not the person who makes the purchase (pays the money, holds the product in hand, or uses the product). Even if the medication is administered in a hospital, it is often handled by a nurse or resident rather than the prescribing physician.

Whether these advertisements are helpful or hurtful to the physicians who see them (as well as to the patients of the physicians who see them), is something that can, from the outside, be wondered about rather than answered. What seems less ambiguous is the effect these techniques of mimetic enactment would have if transferred to the public realm. Prescription drugs themselves will not be the subject of public medical advertising, since the public cannot on its own purchase such drugs. But these representational strategies can be easily divorced from their original subject, especially since that original subject is, through these strategies, already gone.

Notes

1. Hannah, Arendt, *Totalitarianism* (New York, 1951), p. 43.
2. See Paul Schilder, *The Image and Appearance of the Human Body: Studies in the Constructive Energies of the Psyche* (New York, 1950), p. 98ff; and Eugene Minkowski, "Findings in a Case of Schizophrenic Depression," trans. Barbara Bliss, in *Existence: A New Dimension in Psychiatry and Psychology*, eds. Rollo May, Ernst Angel, Henri F. Ellenberger (New York, 1958), p. 134.

3. For an extended discussion of the problems of advertising health care to the public, as those problems are understood by the advertising industry itself, see "Special Report: Healthcare Marketing," *Advertising Age*, 8 November 1984, 11–32.

4. This label as well as other nineteenth-century labels are presented in Nancy Knight's beautifully designed catalogue, *Pain and Its Relief: An Exhibition at the National Museum of American History* (Washington, D.C., 1983).

Note

The advertisements reproduced in this chapter originally appeared in 1984–85 issues of the following publications:

Figure 1: *Newsweek*
Figure 2: *New York Times Magazine*
Figure 3: *Reader's Digest*
Figure 4: *Family Circle*
Figures 5, 20: *Good Housekeeping*
Figures 6, 11, 18: *Contemporary Surgery*
Figures 7, 21: *Modern Maturity*
Figure 8: *Saturday Evening Post*
Figure 9: *Ladies' Home Journal*
Figures 10, 13, 16, 23: *Hospital Practice*
Figure 12: *Medical Aspects of Human Sexuality*
Figure 14: *Hospital Medicine*
Figure 15: *Resident & Staff Physician*
Figure 17: *Cardiology Clinics*
Figure 19: *Clinical Pediatrics*

2

PARTICIPIAL ACTS:
WORKING

Work and the Body
in Hardy and Other
Nineteenth-Century Novelists

I

Early in *The Woodlanders*, an idle surgeon spends a long afternoon watching the wet white paint on a swinging gate detach itself from the gate's surface and latch onto first the body of one, then a second, then a third young woman crossing into his neighborhood. Much later that same surgeon, not now idle but engaged in the exhausting work of self-rescue, crawls toward the home of a wealthy woman, lifts himself over the stile, and leaves behind on its altered surface his own red blood.[1]

These two moments, clear counterparts of one another, belong to a long succession of moments in which a gate or threshold or stile or doorway or fence is crossed to permit the passage of one person into a space belonging to a person of another gender or of another class—gates, fences, and doorways that thus open into scenes resonant with economic and political and sexual disturbance. Hardy's concern here with the crossing of three young laboring class women into a space watched over by a middle class man and again with the crossing of that middle class man into a space whose very air is radiant with monied femininity, at the same time requires him (requires him because he is Thomas Hardy) to be attentive to another sort of crossing: the crossing of the white paint from the non-sentient surface of the wooden gate to the sentient surface of the human body, and in turn the crossing of the red blood from the sentient surface of the human body to the non-sentient surface of the wooden stile. This

49

FIGURE 24. Jean-François Millet. *Winter, Women Gathering Wood* (*L'hiver, les bûch-eronnes*). 1868–74. Unfinished oil on canvas. National Museum of Wales, Cardiff.

second kind of crossing is at least as essential to Hardy as the first. His subject is not the passage of persons through the world but the passage of embodied persons through the world, and he is, on this subject, without peer in the three centuries of the English novel.[2] The human creature is for him not now and then but habitually embodied: it has at every moment a physical circumference and boundary. Thus it is, in its work and its play, in the midst of great yearning and in the moment of great fatigue, forever rubbing up against and leaving traces of itself (its blood) on the world, as the world is forever rubbing up against and leaving traces of itself (its paint) on the human creature.

So it is that a girl passes through a swinging gate. Soon she is through the gate. A minute later she is beyond the gate which, if she were to look back over her shoulder, would be invisible, eclipsed by an intervening lilac bush. The act is over, yet it is still with her: one might say to her not "You have paint on your shoulder," but instead, "You have gate surface on your shoulder," or instead, "You have passing-through-the-gate on your shoulder." An action has become a substance, a film or skin grafting itself onto her, just as "the passing of the man over the stile" solidifies into "a coat of blood on the stile." Fleeting gestures become materials with shape, weight, and color. Verbs generate their own nouns as objectifications and memorializations of their own disappearance from the world. A patch of paint or blood is a patch of history. The paint can be removed from the girl and the blood from the stile; but such an act of removal, like any tampering with history, is itself laden with cultural and political significance.[3]

The two incidents are very brief, each occupying only a few seconds of narration, yet even in their brevity they echo the central stories of Hardy's men and women: they have, in miniature, the same structure as those large stories; they are abbreviations, or architectural models, of those larger structures. The story, for example, of Tess Durbeyfield, whose childish body collides one night not with a painted gate but with a painted man, is for all its haunting magnificence, for Hardy a magnificent commonplace, an extreme and extended amplification of what he elsewhere takes to be habitually the case. He so persistently calls attention to the visible record of the exchange between the human creature and the world immediately beyond the boundary of the human body that at times it seems an unselfconscious reflex of his style, a form of notation entering into the verbal texture of his descriptions as routinely and inevitably as notations on color or direction might enter there.[4] Man and world each act on the surface of the other; each alters the other's surface either by adding new layers to it or subtracting layers from it: an addition takes the form of a film or skin like the smoke film on the walls of Grace Melbury's room (77), the thumbprints on a deck of playing cards (106), a thin spun film of orchard matter coating Giles Winterborne's head (205); a subtraction appears as an imprint, an inscription, or a polishing, like the footprint left behind in the dirt (49), or the gleaming silver nail in the boot sole (125).

Any one of these details enfolds within it a story. The aspiration of Grace Melbury toward another class and another way of life gets translated into the act of reading and studying, an act repeated over a sequence of midnights; and in turn that action gets translated, as it moves across a burning lamp, into a film of smoke on the wall. What is at first an interior and invisible aspect of consciousness, "aspiration," is lifted out into the world of visible action, "reading"; and now that visible but continually disappearing action acquires an enduring sign of itself in the materialized persistence of a smoky film that need not be renewed each night, because it will not only be there in the room each night but be there still in the daylight when the girl and her aspiration and her reading are many weeks gone. Human consciousness is always, for Hardy, embodied human consciousness: all states of being—not just overt, physical activity but even what appear to be forms of physical inactivity like reading or perceiving or feeling—inevitably entail reciprocal jostling with the world.[5] Had she pounded the walls with her fists, she might have left behind the print of her hands; but so, too, the film of smoke registers the fact of her actual conflict with the walls of her world, the walls of her room, the wooden walls that she has "pushed" out of her way, or "smoked" out of her way with a magic reading lamp that makes such walls begin to lift.

The material record of the interaction between man and world often survives the interaction itself: it may, as here, outlive it by several months; it may instead outlive it by less than a day as the chalk marks on a mahogany table memorialize the scoring of those who sat there gaming a few hours earlier (108); or it may, finally, outlive it by generations, as the large ellipse on the back of each playing card bodies forth the image of a sea of "damp and exulting thumbs" belonging to hands now "fleshless in the grave" (106). There need not, of course, be any discrepancy between the longevity of a given human activity and the longevity of the material- ized residue of that activity. The sign will accompany rather than outlive the activity whenever the activity itself is habitual and ongoing. The trans- lucent tissue of sap and seed coating Winterborne's head registers the fact that some interaction between the man and the orchard has just taken place, but it will also accompany him as he reenters the interaction the next day. So, too, the silver gleam of the nail in the bottom of his boot attests to his foot's persistent contact with the earth: though the nail be- comes visible only at the moment when his contact with the earth is broken (Winterborne works suspended in the branches of a tree), it is contact that will soon be reestablished. In both instances, the sign—like a loyal friend—bodies forth the image of the activity during the brief inter- val when the activity itself is suspended. Hardy would himself very much prefer that signs always be, as here, the companions rather than the survivors of occurrences—which is perhaps only a way of saying that Hardy would very much prefer all activity to be sustained, habitual activ- ity: his deepest sympathies belong to the realm of work rather than to the realm of play.

Viewed through the peculiarities of our own intellectual framework, his greater sympathy for work may for a moment seem inconsistent with what is often called the "sensuousness" of his writing: we tend in the late twentieth century to surround "play" and "desire" with connotations of inventiveness, innovation, spontaneity, sensuousness and to surround work with connotations of numbing routine, diminished consciousness (perhaps even false consciousness or unconsciousness). For Hardy, the connotations distribute themselves very differently. Though acutely aware of the sensuousness of play (for in play, the senses become self-experi- encing), work is, for him, more sensuous or, at least, entails a far deeper embodiment: the human creature is immersed in his interaction with the world, far too immersed to extricate himself from it (he may die if he stops) and thus almost without cessation he enacts a constant set of move- ments across the passing days and years. In contrast, it is required by the very nature of play that the person be only half submerged in the world of his activity, that he be able to enter and exit from it freely: the activity, even if never engaged in before, can be started in seconds, or ended just as quickly. The difference between Suke Damson who works the meadow each day and Fitzpiers who enters the meadow one night, or between Marty who supports without cessation both the beauty and the weight of the hair on her head and Felice who can put on its beauty one hour and take away its weight the next, is a difference Hardy never tired of elaborating, as in the difference between Tess who walks through the world and Angel who "goes on" a walking tour, between Tess who works in the dairy and Angel who (until he goes to Brazil) plays at being a farmer, between Henchard who is inseparable from the fields and streets of Casterbridge and Farfrae who sings of a country for which he has no ache of longing. The person at play, protected by the separability of himself from his own activity, does not put himself at risk and, though he acts on the world outside his body with less intensity than the person at work, he may put that world at greater risk precisely because his own immunity from risk makes him inattentive to the forms of alteration he is bringing about. In the details cited from *The Woodlanders*, it is not accidental that the material record brought about by work includes translucent tissue and the silver flash of nails, while that brought about by play includes chalk marks, smoke smudges, and thumbprints, not quite damaging the world (as will happen in more major events in the novels) but causing the moderate damage of "dirtying."

Dirt is, however, as Hardy reminds us in "The Dorsetshire Labourer," only "matter in the wrong place"[6] and thus the fact that the residues of play (or more precisely, the category of signs that outlive the activity that produced them) happen here to take the form of dirt should not be credited with a greater import than it has. Though it is for Hardy inferior to some outcomes, it is preferable to others. His hierarchy of signs would have four tiers. First and most preferred are material signs that accompany the ongoing activity. Second (less positive than the first but infinitely preferable to the third and fourth) are signs that outlive the activity that produced them. Third is the absent sign, the lack of any material objectification of an interaction having taken place: so averse to this possibility is Hardy that characters he is fond of will, even when it is to their disadvantage, "make" a sign if none arises naturally (Tess's letter, Michael's oath). Fourth and most startling is the erased or falsified or substituted sign, which not only misrepresents the antecedent action but in doing so actively asserts the realm of human action to be "dismissible." Within the frame provided by these four possibilities, it is possible to restate with more clarity the relation between the first two.

Hardy prefers that signs be companions rather than survivors not because he dislikes the longevity of the sign (on the contrary) but because he dislikes the brevity of the activity; the ease of extricating oneself bewilders him. If, however, a given activity must end, it is consoling that in its absence there is at least a materialized record of its having occurred. That is, while it seems most appropriate to Hardy that man and world should get permanently woven to one another, given that they do not (the card game starts and then is gone), a record at least means that a small piece of one (a film of sweat on the thumb) has broken off onto the other, that they have not disengaged from one another as though that engagement had never occurred. Hardy's world is made up of women and men in intense interaction with the realm of animate and inanimate objects, any two fragments of which are like friends who can not part without turning around repeatedly, as though to show that the frame of contact has not yet been successfully broken. This is a familiar characteristic of deep embodiment whether occurring in the context of immorality, as in the story of Lot's wife's inability to not turn around, or in a morally neutral context, as in the similar story of Orpheus's inability to not turn around, or in the context of deep moral compassion, as in the work of John Keats who, like Hardy, could not bear the cessation of interactions between man and world, and who in his farewell letter to Charles Brown shortly before his death writes what may be not only the most searing but the most accurate single sentence of self-description in English, "I always made an awkward bow." Like the painted imprints of hands at the Sanctuary of Hands at Kap Abba Cave or again at Gargas (the sea of slender fingers extended, reaching out in a delicately frozen gesture of greeting or farewell across time and space) so the residues and fragments in Hardy reach out, the thumbprints of one generation touching the surface of the still embodied thumbs of another generation who now pick up the cards in the resumption of the game, affirming in the meeting of thumbs the continuity of an activity that appeared to be over but was instead only in a prolonged state of interruption. Thus, strictly speaking, play (which includes festivals and agricultural holidays) and work are differentiated not by the fact that one ends and the other continues but by the difference in the length of the interval during which their activity can be suspended.

It is, though, work and the first tier of signs that are Hardy's central subject, and the subject of the discussion that follows.

II

Although for Hardy the human creature reveals itself through many forms of action and activity — Michael Henchard striding through a meadow, Tess stretching out her arms in a yawn, Winterborne standing still watching the soft collisions of snowflakes on a woman's back — human character has for him its deepest registration in the activity of work. It does so because his essential subject is the reciprocal alterations between man and world, and though these reciprocal alterations occur inevitably in almost any activity (walking, watching, reading, playing cards), they occur there (however inevitably) accidentally and incidentally, almost as a by-product:

in work, in contrast, they do not simply happen to occur but are consciously sought; they are not simply the outcome of the activity but seem instead to constitute the very activity itself.

When, for example, the weight of a girl leaving home moves down across her shoe and presses the outline of her foot into the ground, or when her aversion to her home moves across the burning light of a reading lamp and imprints itself on the wall, an alteration in the world has occurred but one very different from that which occurs when with the full power and precision of conscious intention a girl presses her weight out across an ash haft and inscribes herself into the hazel wood by cutting it into thatching spars. If there is a structural similarity — the projection of the self out into the world across a mediating object like a shoe, lamp or bill-hook — the first two are at most shadowy, labile approximations of the third: shoe and lamp are only analogous to tools; footprint and smoke film are only analogous to artifacts; the sequence of mediations so unpremeditated that they are just barely recognizable as mediations. Marty South's cottage, with its luminous tones of amber, brown, and red and its textures of willow wood, ash wood, hazel wood, leather, and human hair, is unified through the concentrating agency of the laboring act, human intelligence inscribing itself into the surfaces of the vegetable, animal and human materials accumulated there.

The account of the interaction between man and world given earlier — each acts on the surface of the other, either adding layers to it or subtracting layers from it — is a structurally accurate but, in the case of work, a tonally narrow and neutral description, innocent of both the concussiveness and the largesse of that interaction. While, for example, a "subtraction" or inscription may well, as suggested earlier, take the form of an indentation (in the dirt) or polishing (of a nail), it will if occurring in live tissue take the form of a wound. The surfaces both of trees and of the human body are throughout *The Woodlanders* ("Let me look at your hands — your poor hands!" [52]) scratched, blistered, cut, flayed, and lightly lashed as again in *Tess* animal tissue, human tissue, vegetable tissue repeatedly collides with something outside its own boundaries and is punctured (Prince, Alec) or hacked (turnips). Again, while the "addition" or the substance transferred in the interaction was earlier alluded to as a "film" (of dirt, of apple matter), it may be not a thin surface layer but a large integral chunk that is severed from its source and transferred to a new location as when the gigantic branches of a tree are separated from the trunk (125), or when Marty South's impossibly abundant tresses are separated from her head (41), or when Grammer Oliver's startlingly large brain is, at least in conversation and imagined futures, spatially separated from the rest of her physical body (55, 153).

It is not simply the surface of the body but the deep entirety of its interior that is in work put at risk. Tess's encounter with Alec brings about a profound change in her body as it first swells to a large size and then breaks into two: while this particular alteration may belong to the realm of desire rather than work, the encounter is between an employee and her employer (for the world outside the body contains, among many other things, human bodies) and what happens to her is (as is routinely recognized in the twentieth century and as Hardy deeply understood) a hazard of the workplace, an industrial accident. John Melbury's body is a tracery of aches and pains that map and record the history of his working life: a cramp in the left shoulder memoralizes the "carrying of a pollard, unassisted, from Tutcombe Bottom home; that in one leg was caused by the crash of an elm against it when they were felling; that in the other was from lifting a bole" (61). Felling, lifting, carrying—the rhythm of his work, etched into his body and made a sentient presence there, survives by many years the actual physical activity and accompanies him throughout the mercantile activities of his later years. Such outcomes are not, of course, limited to the agricultural world, nor are they limited to Hardy's representation of work; they belong as well to mining, to cottage industry, or to factory life. Zola's eleven-year-old Jeanlin announces in the contortions of his bone structure, posture, and gait his childhood years in the mines; of Grimm's three spinners, one has a startlingly enlarged thumb from twisting the thread (twisting the thread, twisting the thread), a second has a colossal lower lip from licking (licking, licking), and a third has a huge foot from treading (treading, treading). And Dickens's Phil Squod has a physical countenance which in every millimeter of its damaged surface maps the complexities and vagaries of the industrial revolution.[7] The literature of the nineteenth century represents in its pages what is a literal fact about work, one which is perhaps even more available in historical accounts than in fiction, whether it is a specific person described (the fingers of William Cobbett's right hand bent from years of digging and hoeing before the age of fifteen)[8] or instead the bodies of unnamed persons (as those described in the parliamentary bluebooks on which Marx, among others, depended so heavily). Such details in Hardy are sometimes there to protest or lament injuries that should not have occurred, but other times they are unlamented as though (especially in the acquisition of new habits of labor as with Marty) they are part of the resculpting or remaking of the body that is seen by Hardy as inevitably entailed in work. Important in themselves, they are also a particularly resonant version of Hardy's overriding concern with the relation between actions and the signs or residues they leave behind. If there is a general "significance" to wounds-as-signs it is that the human being in work puts himself, by his very depth of engagement, continually at risk—that he alters the world only by consenting to be himself deeply altered.

The concussiveness of the interaction between the material creature and his material world is, though important in Hardy's novels, far less central to them than is the largesse of that interaction. There is an enhancement—almost a physical enlargement—of the individual that results from his immersion in the materials of his work; for the two do not, as described earlier, simply leave a residue on one another or transfer parts of themselves back and forth across an intervening space, but are instead grafted together so that there ceases to be a clear boundary separating them; the surfaces of the two are continuous with one another. Their inseparability is in Hardy's fiction expressed through an elaborately extended sequence of images, but if one had to begin with a single image, it might be that of Giles Winterborne and a small companion blossoming apple tree moving together down a road to town, then standing still together in the town's center, the man grasping the tree in his outstretched arm and the tree, in turn, holding the man within its own form of reach, containing him and all his actions (his meeting with Marty South, his

FIGURE 25. Jean-François Millet. *The Spinner* (*La fileuse*). 1850–55. Oil on Canvas. Museum of Fine Arts, Boston, gift of Quincy Adams Shaw through Quincy A. Shaw, Jr., and Mrs. Marian Shaw Haughton.

FIGURE 26. Jean-François Millet. *The Winnower* (*Le vanneur*). 1847–48. Oil on Canvas. National Gallery, London.

reunion with Grace Melbury) within the nodding arc of its branches (63, 67). Each acquires the other's attributes, the once rooted apple tree for a time inheriting the man's mobility and the man (awkwardly restricted to a single spot in the town's center) inheriting the other's rootedness.[9]

In isolation, this image (extraordinarily beautiful in its combination of filigree, fragility, and clumsiness) can only begin to convey the interlacing of man and his materials. The two of them, the six-foot man and the slender ten-foot tree, are at this moment brought before us as comrades nearly equal in stature; but their immersion in one another means that each may be absorbed into the other, so that the man may be suddenly dwarfed beside the one-hundred-foot vertical reach of a giant elm tree and ingested into it (124f) as first Giles's head, then his trunk, then his legs and feet disappear from view, just as alternatively (as in the scene of the planting of the delicate infant pines) the tree may seem to shrink beside the man until it is almost small enough to disappear within his own closed hand (93).

Throughout the entire course of the novel the two move unceasingly together or somersault in slow motion through one another. The images described are only three of thirty or perhaps three hundred, and this multiplicity is crucial to Hardy's working method. Any one of these passages in isolation might have for its visual equivalent Millet's *Spinner* (Figure 25) in which woman, wheel, and wool are inseparably contained within the triangular boundary of the large tool whose circular motion is required and completed by the disposition of the woman's hands,[10] or again its equivalent in the *Winnower* (Figure 26) where the dark mergence of man and world creates a uniform blue and brown surface on which there float luminous white pools of grain, hands, ankles, back—the shared radiance of the materials of work and those parts of the human body most acutely engaged in the activity. But Hardy's narrative as a whole, with its steady sequence of images, works not like Millet's *Spinner* or his *Winnower* but like his *Women Gathering Wood* (Figure 24) and *Faggot Gatherers Returning from the Forest* (Figure 27) where there is, within one canvas, a rhythm established by the three figures, each merging with the other and with the wood they carry: the foremost carrier is still distinguishable from the wood she carries; the second is less so; the third is even less distinguishable, and behind her looms up the forest itself which merges with her load and becomes the snowfilled thing she (and by extension, her comrade) carries on her back—just as any one image of Winterborne merges with an entire sequence of Winterbornes (and Souths) and in turn with a sequence of

FIGURE 27. Jean-François Millet. *Faggot Gatherers Returning from the Forest* (*Fagotteuses revenant de la forêt*). About 1854. Black conté crayon on wove paper. Museum of Fine Arts, Boston, gift of Martin Brimmer.

apple trees, elm trees, infant firs, and a stand of pines which finally become "the woods and orchards" in some integral unity collectively acting as an extension or "prolongation of the human body."[11] Tess's body, too, is continuous with the surface of the earth,[12] as is implicitly acknowledged in the many comments on, for example, the "correspondence" between the changing landscape of close hills and open expanses and Tess's own changing body. This "correspondence" is misrepresented, however, when the image of the hills or of the valleys or of the cows or of the turnips is identified as (or described as though it were) a literary device or "symbol" used by Hardy to express Tess: rather Hardy, in representing a woman and worker, of necessity includes the material in which she expresses and objectifies herself. The "she" in that sentence does not stop at the boundaries of her own body (despite the problematic noticeability of those boundaries) but instead extends out into the earth over which she walks and in which she works. Michael Henchard's character, too, as will be elaborated below, is even in the most extreme moments of intimacy inseparable from his work as hay trusser-merchant-mayor.

What it is Hardy is doing here, ethically as well as aesthetically, will be easier to recognize after stepping away from the immediate subject for a moment and summoning up the larger representational context, a context that can be at least crudely summarized in two assertions: first, work is a subject extensively represented in the eighteenth- and nineteenth-century British novel, and a subject that has in fact a natural affinity with the novel; second, though it is a natural subject for the novel and though it occurs there far more than has been acknowledged in twentieth-century readings, it is a subject that in some fundamental ways is very difficult to represent. To unfold and substantiate either of these two assertions would require a richness of elaboration far beyond the scope of the present discussion; each will be reasserted below only long enough to make the claims they contain intelligible (and provisionally believable) so that their counterparts in Hardy will be clear: it is not the mere fact of his inclusion of the subject of work that so distinguishes Hardy but, rather, his particular response to certain deep problems in its representation — problems which he solves by making the structure of all narrative action entail (and often even depend on) the physical continuity of man and his materials.

While the name of Emile Zola can be invoked to silence the suggestion that any British novelist ever even for a moment thought of the subject of work, it is in fact the case that what is carefully researched and stunningly imagined in the novels of Zola has a substantial presence in the works of his English counterparts where it is, if less striking in its occurrence, nevertheless acutely observed and richly imagined. It is central not only to writers such as Gaskell and Disraeli but to at least some of those who have always been regarded as central: it is certainly true of Charles Dickens (Orwell notwithstanding),[13] as it is both of George Eliot and of Thomas Hardy that to "read out" the subject from one of their works is not just to perform a peculiar act of editing on the content but to truncate and damage the formal structure of the work and, perhaps most important, to disguise some of the revelations contained there about the nature and source of the human imagination.

If twentieth-century descriptions and discussions of the novel have partially erased the subject from the text,[14] that "act" of erasure has probably occurred passively: our habit of inattention to work is the natural counterpart to our intense (and in itself benign) preoccupation with courtship and desire. What is somewhat startling about this, however, is that the very basis of our critical absorption with courtship is much more self-evidently and elaborately true of work. Our attention to courtship has never been primarily moral and didactic. Everyone, as Bruno Bettelheim once lamented, already knows how to court: flirtation, desire, the initiation of love, the proposal of marriage, all obsessively represented in the novel, are all subjects about which people are in little need of instruction, while the perpetuation of love, the sustaining of vows, the keeping of the promise, the daily rerepair of marriage, are subjects about which many people would gladly accept inventive instruction, and subjects about which literature is nearly silent.[15] But we continue to be intrigued by literary depictions of courtship for reasons that are formal and imaginative: we see the marriage contract (the assertion of a human bond as binding and enduring and inalterable as a biological bond) as a product of man's fiction-making powers and consequently as an analogue to other products of man's fiction-making powers such as literature in general or the novel in particular. Ian Watt's *The Rise of the Novel*, for many (both in literature and in other fields of inquiry such as the philosophy of fiction) one of the most compelling descriptions of the coming-into-being of a new object in the world, has at its very center the demonstration of the way in which the formal properties of the new genre required that both romantic love and marriage exist and that the two entail each other. The recognition that marriage is a made thing, that the novel is a made thing, *and that the second made thing only gets made by incorporating into its interior an image of the making of the first made thing*, is perhaps at least latent in our endless critical attention to endless love triangles in endless novels and periodically surfaces into brilliant explicitness as in Tony Tanner's *Adultery in the Novel: Contract and Transgression*.

Yet if in tracing the intricacies in the interior of courtship it is really the interior of created objects (or even, the interior of the imagination) whose secret shape we seek, the subject of human work, human labor, provides at least as rich an occasion for exploration; for while there is an initial analogical leap required in seeing the kinship between "making a marriage" and "making a book," almost none is required (as Robinson Crusoe and Daniel Defoe long ago made clear) in "making a house" and "making a book," or "making a table or a journal or a whole new world on an island" and "making a book." Throughout the nineteenth century, in

Britain as in America and on the continent, the equation is simply assumed as the space of labor—factory, field, forge, or mine—comes again and again to represent both the external space of diurnal making and the internal space at the hidden center of the artist's own dark act of making. Mining the hidden ore, weaving a web or a tale, forging the image, harvesting the seed, are all elaborated into visual explanation of the human powers responsible for putting a new industrial world into place or a new art work where once there was none.

Any one of these forms of labor entails a rich array of representations. Predictably, for example, the making of textiles (the largest nineteenth-century industry) is in all of its phases one of the most elaborated of analogues. The spinning of thread and the weaving of cloth is objectified as it occurs in the factory (Dickens's *Hard Times*), as it occurs in cottage industry (Eliot's *Silas Marner*, Grimm's "Three Spinners," "Rumpelstilt-skin," "The Lazy Spinner," "The Spindle, the Shuttle, and the Needle": the tales themselves are believed to have arisen as accompaniment to home spinning),[16] or as they occur in some hybrid intermediary between home and factory (Hauptmann's *The Weavers*, Kollwitz's *Weavers*). When the making of the cloth gives way to the remaking of the cloth into clothes, the analogue to imaginative making continues: the tailor metaphor which makes only a slight appearance in *Great Expectations* is monumentally at play in *Sartor Resartus* and again, like a thread emerging from one side of cloth and disappearing through the other side, it darts in and out of the pages in Grimm, some of whose many tailors[17] are explicitly designated "talers." And finally the cloth-made-clothes become raw material in another industry, paper-making, where as throughout all earlier alterations, it is part of the depiction of the terror and beauty of the creative process as in Melville's "Paradise of Bachelors, Tartarus of Maids."

At times, the analogy between one form of physical work and imaginative activity will simply elide with an analogy between a second form of work and imaginative activity as in *Sartor Resartus* where, in the midst of an ongoing exploration of human inventiveness carried through the tailoring metaphor, the text suddenly simply shifts to an image of mining.[18] Different forms of physical labor come over time to be relied on to convey different dimensions of imaginative labor as here, for example, in the difference between weaving and mining where the one comes to objectivity something of the felt rhythm and reflex of the mind in the moment of invention and the second conveys the sheer discomfort, the felt impossibility, the anticipated exertion of locating the existing image in the recesses of the mind and transferring it from the interior of the mind to the realm outside the boundary of the body. The imagination is here being conceived in two very different ways: the first comes close to crediting invention with the materialization of something out of nothing (or the almost nothing of "thread," for what is crucial in this metaphor is the minimalness of the raw material) while the second conceives of invention essentially as a radical act of relocation, the redistribution of something already given (an emphatic given, for the weight and unwieldiness of coal underscore the incontestable facticity of its prior existence in the mind). Whether these are two separate conceptions of the imagination or, instead, two different temporal moments in the same conception is the kind of question that needs to begin to be answered. At times, the different forms of work will be explicitly presented as competing models of the imagination. The first third of Dickens's *Great Expectations*, for example, depicts two different arenas of labor, two different images of the interior of creation, a forge and a brewery. The antagonism between the Havisham world and the Gargery world is often misdescribed as an antagonism between the imaginary (beautiful, haunting, cruel, perverse, and insubstantial) and the real (modest, lovely, banal but sturdy). But Dickens's crucial contrast here is not between art and reality or the imaginary and the real but between two forms of imagining, two models of making, that of passive intoxication and that of active smithing. If life had required Pip to learn the distinction between the artificial and the real, he might not have had such a difficult time; but he is instead required to make the much more difficult and interesting distinctions between failed artifice and successful artifice, between failed work and successful work, between irresponsible imaginings and responsible imaginings. These distinctions, in their full philosophic complexity and ethical import, are also among the most difficult questions of our own times.

It is important to stress that here — as elsewhere — distinctions are made between different forms of physical work, or between different ideas of the imagination, but not between work on the one hand and imagining on the other. Pip's crudest error, in fact, is his perception of a separation between physical and imaginative labor, an error which begins to dissolve when Herbert renames him "Handel," alerting him with a tact bordering on genius to the composer's musical assertion of the continuity between the hammering in the forge and the hammering in the harpsichord or pianoforte.[19] This continuity, repeatedly affirmed throughout the century in representations of weaving, tailoring, paper-making, brewing, forging is in Hardy again confirmed in field, dairy, woodland, and market where rituals, stories, superstition, lore, and family chronicle rise up out of the immediate act of labor and become, as he describes it in *The Woodlanders* (56), a palpable layer surrounding working hands and accompanying them in all their movements. Throughout his writings, physical and imaginative labor both accompany and occasion one another as the unturned vat of milk at Talbothay's brings forth a series of stories, and those stories in turn eventually bring forth the alteration in the milk.

The easy eruption of symbolic-making out of the realm of physical-making, simply assumed in works like *The Woodlanders* and *Tess of the D'Urbervilles*, is an overt and extensive subject in *The Mayor of Casterbridge* where the very market town itself emerges up in the midst of an agricul-

tural expanse with no intervening or moderating structures (21), reminding us that the physical labor of the merchant, the activity of exchange,
rises up out of agricultural labor and is itself already halfway gone toward
disembodied imaginative activity.[20] If one were ever tempted to identify
as unique Bertolt Brecht's wonderful insistence on making the store front
his persistent subject and setting — whether it is Widow Begbick's traveling
canteen, Mother Courage's wagon, Wong's waterpole (a very fragile store,
small enough to carry), Shen Te's tobacco shop, Shui Ta's tobacco factory[21] — one should at least recognize in Hardy a kindred and anticipatory
impulse, for he includes in *The Mayor of Casterbridge* every possible version
of "the store," portable and immobile, fixed structures, carts and vans,
and empty or filled wagons (45, 136, 147). All major action of necessity
happens here, for on each page the setting we inhabit is the store: a
furmity tent, later a furmity bucket without tent (the old woman's "store"
now has the size and fragility of Wong's waterpole), the Three Mariners
Inn, the King's Arms, the elaborate open market street of Casterbridge
with its array of stalls and vans, Henchard's own factory-storehouse, later
his seed and grain shop ("not much larger than a cupboard" [231]), later
still his tool basket out of which he sells only his own labor, the town itself
(which not only in its market street but throughout its entirety is a structure built for exchange). And just as Brecht's canteen, wagon, waterpole,
shop, and factory each undergoes many transformations but remains at
all times that particular form of space which itself celebrates the principle
of transformation, namely the theatre, so each of Hardy's stores is explicitly presented as a theatre. The furmity tent is the space where a private
act becomes a public spectacle as a domestic sentiment is absorbed into
the expressive structures of an auction; a band plays (as though in the
orchestra pit of a small theatre) in front of the bay window of the King's
Arms through which the townspeople stare at the mayor's party; the Three
Mariners Inn is not only the space in which food and money are ex-
changed but that in which Farfrae sings, just as it later becomes the arena
for psalm singing; in the Three Mariners, the forging of a partnership
between two men is converted into a small moment of theatre when it is
publicly witnessed by a woman in the next room; Elizabeth-Jane changes
her room at the back of Henchard's house for a room at the front of the
house when, with the departure of Farfrae, the public space she wants to
watch changes from her father's storehouse to the street; Lucetta's house,
with its theatrical masks engraved in the door (108), is explicitly presented
(106–125) as a front row seat in a market-street theatre that has many
acts including circus vans, actors, and clowns (46, 47);[22] the Roman am-
phitheatre is not the "only" but simply the "largest" theatrical space, one
large enough to accommodate and absorb Henchard's oversized gestures
(54); the acute competition between the town's two leading businessmen
becomes visible as a contest to determine which man can better provide
the community with good entertainment (79); the theatre-of-cruelty

Skimmity Ride makes it clear that the town as a whole is a theatre whose invisible Mixen Lane is its own never-seen backstage where a spectacle is conceived, the costumes found, the props gathered, the production machinery put in place for a performance to be executed in a more forward space before eyes innocent of all preparations. The sometimes troubling continuity of economic and imaginative exchange is, then, asserted even in the major structural outlines of the novel, the unfaltering progression through a series of stores that is also a series of theatres. To move through additional forms of labor and additional literary works would only be to re-encounter the same essential point: that just as work becomes a major subject in philosophy in the nineteenth century, so it is a major subject in literature where it is richly represented both for its own sake and for the sake of what is perceived to be its special kinship with the artist's own inventive activity.[23]

Although, then, work is extensively represented in the novel, although it has in fact a natural affinity with the novel, it is at the same time (we now arrive at our second point) a deeply difficult subject to represent. The major source[24] of this difficulty is that work is action rather than a discrete action: it has no identifiable beginning or end; if it were an exceptional action, or even "an action," it could—like the acts in epic, heroic, or military literature—be easily accommodated in narrative. It is the essential nature of work to be perpetual, repetitive, habitual.[25] There is no formal convention in any genre of literature that would make it either possible or desirable to portray it in all its constancy and repetitiveness; yet, on the other hand, to take one arbitrary segment of it, a "typical" eight-hour stretch, for example, is to falsify it precisely because it is in its repetitions that it is what it is—it can no more be represented by one segment of itself than the rhythm or rhyme of poetry can be indicated by the recitation of a single word, no matter how indicative the accent and lilt of that word; and it is precisely in the way the motion of work departs from and rhymes with the reenactment of its own activity that out of something quite modest something immodest (the creature's own survival, his self-recreation, his continual recreation of his own activity, his creation of new parts of the world) is set in place.

Two particular solutions arise in response to this problem. One is to subdivide the activity of work not into temporal units but into task-units.[26] Zola is of course the master of this technique; for he is able to take a massive and immensely complex form of work like coal mining and make the intricate interior of the process accessible by dividing it into a huge array of separate tasks, each of which emerges into the narrative at a separate moment surrounded by its own drama. Another classic portrayal of work, George Sturt's *The Wheelwright's Shop*, follows this same technique, which is in literature relatively uncommon. Hardy is doing something very similar—certainly responding to the same problem in the representation of work—in his choice of seasonal labor (Giles's movement over the

year through the varying demands of apple, elm, and pine), migratory
labor (Tess and chickens, Tess and cows, Tess and turnips), or a series of
jobs each emerging out of its predecessor like a new fringe of petals on an
always opening flower (Henchard as trusser of hay; Henchard as merchant of the trussed hay; Henchard as mayor of the merchant town that
arose in the midst of fields to exchange the trussed hay).

A second and more common approach is to take the massive fact of
work precisely at the moment when there is a tear or lapse in the activity
that must be repaired, replaced, or rescued. While an eight-hour segment
of ordinary activity usually fails to convey the overall fact of work, an
eight-hour act of repair *can* convey that overall fact precisely because it is
the whole of the process (not just that day's segment) that is put at risk
and must be rescued, and hence the whole of the process that gets rein-
vented: in the quiet act of the boy with his finger in the dike is the massive
action of the building of the dike, the taming of the ocean, the resculpting
of a terrain. There are lacing Hardy's narrative many small moments of
repair. A line of four or five pairs of eyes and a second line of four or five
bent backs move forward across the ground in search of infinitesimal
sprigs of garlic. In doing so, they make available to us not only the
extraordinary patrolling of nature's boundaries perpetually occurring in
the banalities of everyday labor but also the overwhelming fact of the
making of the milk itself; that an almost "invisible" fragment from the
vegetable world (and thus one almost outside the realm of the human
senses) should enter the cavernous interior of the animal body and re-
emerge on the London breakfast table where, far from being beyond the
human senses, it should now be unavoidably present as an "unmistakable
taste," dramatizes the larger alteration of grass into milk, the benign
conspiracy and startling intimacy of the vegetable, human, and animal
bodies. So, too, with the restoration of Henchard's bad bread (33): not
only is a bond between two men made and the bread itself remade but
Farfrae's nearly magical reclamation also makes visible the essential ex-
tremity of self-alteration risked in the everyday work of exchange, its
dangers (moving into one's own personal sphere many pounds of damaged
goods), its equally frightening freedoms (moving those goods on to someone else), and the anticipatory precision required of the successful merchant who neutralizes those dangers and freedoms by ensuring (both by
technological and legal means) the stability, uniformity, and "unaltered-
ness" of the goods he buys and sells. The same logic of representation is
enfolded within many other moments of accident and repair, whether the
collision of a cart carrying beehives or the covering of the hay ricks in a
storm.

Hardy, George Eliot, and Zola[27] are unusual for how particularized
are their acts of rescue. In other writers, rescue is less specific to a particular form of labor; instead, a generalized act of repair[28] or universal idea of
rescue is invoked to dramatize by proximity "labor in general" or "the

essential structure of work." Robinson Crusoe's daily work and world recreation take place, of course, within the overall frame of self-rescue. His American counterpart, Benjamin Franklin, throughout the obsessive and stunning acts of invention and self-reinvention recorded in his autobiography, thinks of creation as reclamation: he repairs the vagaries of the eyes with bifocals, the limited reach of the grocer's arm with a mechanical stick. When as happens on almost every page a problem or defect is noted — a dirty street, a failing streetlight, an absent treaty — one can almost sense his nostrils begin to flare and the nerves beneath the skin of his cheeks begin to flicker like a wild animal whose quarry is invention and who has just caught the scent.[29] In his attempts at recreating himself, he takes his specific vocabulary of repair — "errata" — from his early work as a printer. Again, the overall structure of action in *Great Expectations* is best summarized as an extended sequence of afternoon visits framed on either side by two elaborate acts of rescue. The book opens with the unselfconscious rescue of Magwitch and returns at the end to the now vastly elaborated and deeply self-conscious repetition of that act; but in between there is the Christmas dinner scene and the visit of Pumblechook and Wopsle; Pip's initial visit to Satis House followed by an eight- or ten-month period where he returns every other day; a visit to Pumblechook's house; Pip back at the forge arranging for an afternoon off in order to visit Satis House and inspiring Orlick to demand time off as well; the sequence of visits continues in London with a visit to Jaggar's house and multiple visits to Wemmick's house in Walworth; any one visit often ends by opening out into another as when Joe visits Pip in London, reports on his own visit to Satis and communicates an invitation or instruction to Pip to visit Satis; Pip visits Estella at Richmond; he dines with the Finches of the Grove; he "visits" Newgate; he visits Clara at Hammondsworth, and so forth. The at first startling perception that this is the same visit structure used by Jane Austen is quickly displaced by the recognition that Dickens's use of this form of action is expansive (we are carried into many quarters and classes), while Austen's is restrictive. The analogy with Austen is not idle, however. Both Dickens and Austen know that it is the "work" of a gentleman to visit and be visited, a pastime in which not-working is acted out and one strikingly different from the work of rescue with which the book opens and closes and in which Pip experiences the immediate power and value of the now burned and bandaged hands he had earlier disowned as "vulgar appendages." Rescue and repair become effective models of work precisely because "survival," which is always at stake in ordinary work, becomes for the first time *visibly* at stake. At the same time, however, it somewhat misrepresents (or inadequately represents) work because, unless the given repair is very modest (as is usually true in Hardy), it turns the habitual inside-out into the exceptional and makes of activity that is perpetual a discrete action.

In both solutions there is a deconstruction of work: in the first, work is broken down into its parts; in the second, work itself breaks down. In both it is the reconstruction of work itself that we then witness. Both enable nineteenth-century writers in general and Hardy in particular to include within the action of the narrative a representation of work-as-an-action. But they are for Hardy only minimal solutions precisely because though they do not falsify the habitual, repetitive, perpetual nature of work (as some other "solutions" would), neither do they convey it; and it is, as noted earlier, this very repetitiveness — the human being's deep immersion in and inseparability from his own activity, his daily reacceptance of his own responsibility for his survival, his deep camaraderie with the material realm in which the everyday drama of survival takes place — that earns him Hardy's (at moments painfully acute) respect and affection.

Forms of art that have no temporal element (painting) or a very repetitive relation to time (music) convey the "activity" of work with more ease than does literary narrative. Millet's paintings, for example, habitually depict the worker in the midst of a gesture or action, whether it is the broad sweep of the arm of *The Sower* or the delicate dance of fingers in the *Seated Goat Girl in Auvergne Spinning* (Figures 28 and 29). The motion of her fingers seems to radiate through her entire body and lift her from the ground. What in each instance we seem to watch is not arrested motion but perpetual activity. So it is too in work songs (or in the incorporation of the work song into another genre as in "The Harmonious Blacksmith"), for here the rhythm of the song is the very rhythm of the bodily action the song accompanies, and thus its "action" (its movement and direction) is a blueprint of the body, conveying the nature of that embodied activity that is its subject, both in its interior repetitions and its pressing requirement to be repeated in its entirety.

In order to convey the full repetitiveness and constancy of the "activity," Hardy lifts it out of the realm of narrative "action" altogether and situates it in the formal realm of inaction, character. In doing so he transforms what within the realm of plot remains a problem into what within the realm of character becomes much more than a solution. Narrative action cannot convey the full coincidence of work identity with human identity because when the representable action stops (the milking hour ends; the search for garlic is completed), the ongoing activity of work would, if not being carried through any other formal element, seem to dissolve. By showing the materials of earth (trees, woods, plants, animals, oats, soil) as extensions of the human body, Hardy enables work-as-perpetual-activity to continue even when work-as-an-action has stopped. Thus the characters in the novels perform many different kinds of action, some of which are work (cutting branches of a tree, digging turnips, purchasing barley) and many of which are not (talking to a friend, courting a woman, writing a letter, walking down a road); but work is carried forward into the second category of action because the materials of labor are grafted to the body of the person who is performing the action.

FIGURE 28. Jean-François Millet. *The Sower (Le semeur)*. 1850. Oil on canvas. Museum of Fine Arts, Boston, gift of Quincy A. Shaw through Quincy A. Shaw, Jr. and Mrs. Marion Shaw Haughton.

Hardy's approach can be illustrated with its equivalent in the realm of sentence structure where the totality of the relation between the acting subject and his act can be conveyed either by devoting the verb to the work (John steams and shapes and bends the wood for the barrels) or instead through the apposition construction (John, cooper, walked with his child along the riverbank). The sentence, "Winterborne cut branches in the tree," is translated into narrative by a passage made up of many similar sentences describing that action in extended form; in contrast, the sentence, "Winterborne, woodsman, met his beloved when she returned from school," becomes in narrative Giles and his apple tree traveling side by side to meet Grace. His inseparability from his materials is the equivalent within the novel of the apposition structure within the single sentence. So, too, the peat and pollen (and treacle) of agricultural labor will sur-

FIGURE 29. Jean-François Millet. *Seated Goat Girl in Auvergne Spinning* (*La fileuse, chevrière auvergnate*). 1868–69. Oil on canvas. Musée du Louvre, Paris.

round a woman's body and move forward with her into the half-recorded action of her seduction; as the grass and grains in which a hay trusser works will enter and rise up in his body as furmity or rum and thus accompany him in his act of selling his wife. Each continues to work the land in these other scenes of desire and distress. Though the labor of each is suspended, the motion of the body at work seems to surround them like a ghost image of perpetual action.

The continuity of man and his materials takes many different forms and becomes visible (as was described earlier) as many different degrees of reciprocal absorption: the world may seem to have allowed itself to be swallowed by the human being and to have left behind only a small fringe of apple leaves on his hat, or the man may seem to have allowed himself to be swallowed by the world leaving behind only an extended foot or hand. Hardy establishes such a deep and varied texture of images that he can even risk scenes portraying this interaction in its most extreme form, with the human body wholly absent and the human being existing only as a voice emanating out of the materials as when Tess "sees" Angel Clare's voice answering out of the body of a cow, or Grace Melbury seems to hold conversation with a huge elm tree that speaks to her in tones of longing, or Lucetta watches a bright red and yellow machine complete its own portrait of self-delight by breaking not simply into speech but into lilting Scotch accents. As man may lend his voice to the less articulate materials of work, so conversely those materials may become for him a surrogate voice at moments when he is speechless: a sudden flush of powdered grain from a winnowing machine announces Elizabeth-Jane's presence to Farfrae when she is stupefied with shyness and silence (89, 90); just as Giles's longing to give himself generously to Grace, lacking any direct form of objectification, inscribes itself into the wood of his work in the outrageously high bid he makes on some timber (85).

That these most radical portraits of the man-materials relation so consistently occur in the context of scenes of human desire and courtship perhaps expresses Hardy's sense that one does, in desiring a person, desire the whole world bodied forth in that person, or to phrase it in another way, one loves not just the person but the world out into which the person projects and inscribes himself or herself. At the same time, however, the context of courtship seems intended to invite the recognition that there is not only between two human beings but between man and his materials an extraordinary intimacy and comradship, even a wholly asexual love, that each regularly enters the interior of the other, that they sometimes wound each other, but that they also habitually speak on one another's behalf, each routinely expressing the other's hidden attributes and unarticulated vulnerabilities. No matter how imaginatively engaging Hardy's depiction, it is of course a literal truth about work that he expresses: the things we build or grow or invent or "work" do speak for us, express us; and in turn we speak on behalf of the materials of our work. The literalness of this interaction is perhaps most visible in the work with which one is most familiar: those who study literature, for example, assume that the words in novels and poems speak for us, objectifying not only forms of love or discomfort that seem beyond speech but perhaps above all the nature and significance of our own powers of invention; and in turn literary critics perform the reciprocal act of ventriloquism, lending their voices to the materials of their work when it is felt that the attributes and powers of those materials are insufficiently self-announcing.[30] So the voice in this chapter emerges not out of the speaker's own body but (like a voice out of a cow or an elm or a red and yellow machine) out of *Tess, The Mayor,* and *The Woodlanders,* materials from which it for a time becomes inseparable.

In Hardy's depiction of the interaction of man and materials, each so often acts as an externalization of the interior of the other that inside and outside regularly change places as in a dance. Elaborately true of major characters and their work, it can be briefly illustrated with a very minor character, Suke Damson, and the hay that is the material of her labor. The act in this scene is not an act of work but an act of flirtation: the equivalent sentence would be not "Suke Damson worked the hay in the field" but "Suke Damson, hay trusser, ran through the field one night."

Almost before we can realize what is happening, Fitzpiers one midsummer's eve jumps over a stile into a moonlit meadow "belonging" to Suke, belonging because in the daylight world it is the realm of her work. It is not daylight now and so their dance of hide and seek takes place not in the color world of daytime but in the black and white world of night light — or rather (because it is an open meadow and there is a moon) silver gray with here and there the sudden radiant yellow of the meadow ground and the "half-made hay" under which she hides and the unkempt yellow hair that has been repeatedly identified with the hay of her work (179). Hardy knows that dreams most often take place in black and white, and though the event is meant within the narrative actually to occur, the scene has all the formal properties of a dream — all, that is, the formal properties of the activity of disembodied imagining. As in a dream, where with unconscionable ease one person takes the place of another, the scene has at its very heart the principle of substitution, for Suke and Fitzpiers begin the chase seconds after each swearing themselves the eternal partners of another man and another woman. The scene slips into view, then is just as suddenly gone, as though the action enters from the periphery of vision on the left, glides quickly across the front of the eyes and slides off the edge of vision on the right, all without breaking or pausing for a moment: this too is a formal property of dreams.

Like an erotic dream and hence far removed from the habitual daylight realm of work, the scene is nonetheless inseparable from the realm of work not only because of its political resonance (the disparity in their classes and the related disparity in their willingness to carry forward the principle of "substitution" into the waking world where it will take the less winning forms of "lying" and "infidelity")[31] but because even the present-tense action — the act of flirtation itself — is expressed through the materials of labor. Irenäus Eibl-Eibesfeldt describes the antithetical gestures of rejection and encouragement that flit across the face of a flirting girl:

> A flirting girl can make eye contact but hide the rest of her face behind her fan, or she can turn away so as to show her shoulder, and also she can alternate between looking and looking away. . . . She can, for instance, drop her eyes to indicate breaking of contact while raising her brows as a ritualized expression of encouragement. A smile of friendliness can be checked so that it becomes a smile of embarrassment.[32]

Suke is acting out in full body the contradictory gestures and rhythm of flirtation: in her midsummer dance of concealing and enticing she plays across the surface of the meadow the way the muscles of Eibl-Eibesfeldt's flirting girl play across her face; but because the half-made hay is also her own (now magnified and magnificent) half-combed hair, it is her own face across which she dances. It is an extraordinary scene: the materials of her labor, her own element and own extension, involve her in a play of scale, a continual slipping of the boundary between body and world, and between inside and outside. As she hides herself under the hay and reappears and hides once more, it is a girl letting her hair fall over her face, lifting it back, then letting it fall once more. Under the moonlight there appear Suke in her own person and Suke's face in huge outline drawn out by Suke's own running.[33]

Each individual scene in Hardy is crafted with such unthinkable care that it is tempting to move scene by scene, tracing the peculiar logic and power of each. The relation in *The Woodlanders* between Marty and Giles — intimate, asexual, comradship — is a human relation that is close to that which Hardy perceives as existing between man and his materials, or man and his tools. It is a relation that exists at a great distance from that of Suke and Fitzpiers; for Marty and Giles are the presiding intelligence of the vegetable world; between them as between the north-south axis formed by their names, the seasons come and go; though they do not enter each other's interior, it is in part because they already share the absolute intimacy of a common interior; for Hardy stresses that the content of their perceptions is identical (358). Hardy expresses the nature of the relation in an indirect love scene. In her run through the meadow, it is the very different Suke who invites us into the reading of this second scene and thus who once again initiates us into the intricacies of labor; for Marty's heavy tresses, too, are elaborately bound up with her work through the multiple connections Hardy draws between them and the branches of trees; so, too, her cutting of her own hair is inextricably bound up with the cutting of those branches. Hence, in a scene rich with many meanings, Giles at once lost in the branches of the gigantic elm and moving there with complete knowingness and absolute tact, seems by narrative transposition Giles lost in and found amidst Marty's massive tresses in a complicated act of shearing and caress that has the beauty of Yeats's beloved wound and bound in cosmic hair while expressing the complicated moral character of the interaction between man and world in work.

III

Throughout the novels, the characters' labor moves with them into many other forms of action, unfolding in startling directions in countless individual scenes. But despite the multiplicity of scenes, it is also true that the materials of earth acquire a singular and stable gravity of meaning over the course of any given novel. Hardy is able to discover in a specific material a specific expression of the human being which he makes steadily available to us on every page and which, if it eludes us, does so only because it does not belong to a wholly familiar psychological category (or, alternatively, because it is an aspect of consciousness too familiar and habitual to have ever occasioned categorization). Thus out of the affinity between trees and the woodsman in *The Woodlanders*, between a changing terrain and its human attendants in *Tess*, between materials that can be passed from person to person and the persons who do the passing in *The Mayor*, Hardy develops his major themes. Out of the three single attributes belonging to each of the three novels there emerges the composite portrait of Hardy's embodied imaginer.

It would not be entirely inaccurate to identify the "rootedness" of trees as what brings Hardy to the realm of forests and orchards in *The Woodlanders*, for when in his essay "The Dorsetshire Labourer" he contrasts the nomadic worker and the one who stays still, he describes the latter as experiencing the "condition of a serf who lived and died on a particular plot, like a tree."[34] Given his interest in depicting the passing feudal world presided over by a feudal lady, and given his emphasis on the difference between those who stay still and those (like Felice, Grace, and Fitzpiers) who move easily in and out of a spot, the woodsman's work is a natural choice for a subject. But the description would be almost inaccurate, for while trees are rooted, wood and bark and fruit and sap are not, and in the novel we more often see wood in a state of mobility (passing into the timbers for houses and spars for furniture; carried away on a van; hauled in a twelve-ton load down a road; travelling in full blossom in a cart to market). If one were to articulate Hardy's interest in trees in terms of the tree's own anatomy, one would have to locate it not in the roots but in the branches.

There are two major ways in which living things extend out into the world: the first, shared by the human and most of the animal world, is the capacity to move, to be detachable from the immediate ground on which one stands; the second, shared by most of the vegetable world, is to be fixed in one spot but to branch and reach, then again in each branch, branch and reach again, until the space in the world available to the live thing is vastly amplified. The two forms of access are not mutually exclusive; and though the human being is able to move, his basic form is like that of the vegetable world, so much so that even technical descriptions of his anatomy often make unavoidable the recognition of his kinship with a tree: "The [human] trunk," as James Gibson writes in his classic text on perception, "branches into four limbs and each limb branches into five digits" to which he implicitly adds the head as a fifth limb which branches into forms of reach (seeing, hearing, etc.) that extend the human being hundreds of feet further than the twenty small branches on his other four limbs; and again "The terminals are of many sorts, not easy to distinguish. First, there are free nerve endings, the bare branches of the afferent fibers that can spread out, spray, or cluster in basket-like or flower-like arrangements."[35] As we move through the intricate relations of men and women and trees in *The Woodlanders*, we continually encounter in the given outline of body structure, in the deep facts of perception, in the psychological habits of aspiration, ambition, and desire, and in the daily activity of creation and survival, the singular and (as it gets elaborated in the intricacies of human consciousness) immensely complicated human attribute of reach.

Even when Hardy is describing a tree's roots, it is not their "rootedness" but their branching reach that he discovers in the delicate spread of fibers (94) displayed across Winterborne's own extended fingers; just as Marty shorn of her hair continues to be in the brute fact of sentience a branching creature who has three headaches, one in her poll, one over her eyes, one on top of her head (95). As in the literature of desire the genitals become the spoken or unspoken locus of orientation, so throughout the literature of creation the hands become the most resonant and meaning-laden part of the human anatomy. In their human and vegetable form they reappear here again and again, often like the fingers of deaf children containing in their movement breath and voice (47, 83). The kinship between the branches of trees in their own activity of survival and the limbs of man in his is made inescapable in many ways, not the least of which is the fact that tree limbs are used as substitutes for or extensions of human limbs as in the detail of the gnarled walking stick (84) that like the leg it aids, has wounded spots; or as in the forked stick that substitutes for Marty's hand in the planting of young pines (95) or that Grace Melbury uses to open a painted gate (143); just as those who exempt themselves from this world come to be represented by the image of the absent foot, hand, or head, the negative imprint of a footprint in the dirt (49), a glove turned inside-out (248), or an empty hat (301) belonging to Grace, Felice, Fitzpiers.

Though important, the act of the hand is only one kind of act; for touch is (even speaking of the sensory realm alone) only one of many forms of reach,[36] though it is at once the most intimate and, because the most exclusive, the most political. The text makes continual distinctions between those spaces which can be entered in one's own body and those spaces which can be entered only with a substitute object such as a tool (only the barber's scissors and cane trespass across Marty South's door-way) or some other materialized surrogate (Giles hands Grace food across a doorsill he can not himself step over), as it also makes continual distinctions between boundaries that can be crossed with the sense of touch and those which can only be passed over with some other form of perceptual reach. Grace can enter the interior of the elm in which Giles works only with her ears and not with sight or touch (125); Giles is able to reach out over an expanse of space and "touch" with his eyes the snowflakes that themselves actually touch the woman he cannot himself touch (85). In contrast, to be politically powerful is to be unconscious of the existence of any realm beyond one's own power of touch, to refuse to acknowledge and revere the existence of such a realm: both Felice and Fitzpiers (in his own cruel inversion of the doctor's access to the human body) are able to touch both the exterior and the interior of many persons. So, too, Hardy is attentive to the difference between moments in which human consciousness is characterized by perceptual unity, as in Marty's making of spars or Giles's and Marty's quiet movement together through the woods, and moments in which it is characterized by perceptual irrelevancies as when Felice, half immersed in miserable consciousness of Fitzpiers (and a minute later, Giles) sees Timothy Tang trespass on her land, pinch snuff, and roll down a hill (227), or as when Fitzpiers (simultaneously, like a moral octopus) reaches the windowsill with his hands, reaches Grammer Oliver with his voice, reaches Suke Damson's smoke with his eyes, and reaches the sawyer's conversation about Felice Charmond with his ears (357). What differentiates the woodsman from others is not the possession of the attribute of reach but the power to objectify that (once objectified, universal) attribute in the materials of his or her labor; to reach and project the attribute of reach is also Hardy's work in his representation of woodsmen in *The Woodlanders*.

Dorothy Van Ghent long ago called attention to the changing terrain in *Tess of the D'Urbervilles*, a ground that becomes so radically different within what is asserted to be a countable number of miles that we might not believe any given spot could be connected to any earlier spot were it not for the fact that we have Tess's own footsteps to certify both the proximity of her various work residences and the step by step contiguity and continuity of earth between one and the next.[37] Vegetation, soil, terrain all quickly change as the deep interior facts of earth sometimes emerge effortlessly out onto its own surface — its largesse suddenly breaking through the ground and standing there in the quiet mass of a beautiful cow whose own hidden interior in turn rises to and emerges out onto its surface in the form of milk — and at other times, as at Flintcomb Ash, are held back by a reluctant, refusing surface, withholding itself, except under the worker's forced insistence. This is not background but foreground. Hardy's subject is this attribute both of the earth and of the men and women who here work the earth: self-alteration both as it occurs mutely and unconsciously, and self-alteration as it enters consciousness and becomes something that is knowingly risked, knowingly willed.

The capacity for self-alteration, always a central part of work (as is acknowledged in the widely accepted definition of work as that activity in which man creates the world and recreates himself) becomes even more pronounced in a nomadic population moving over the land. One can, like Angel, simply decide to be a farmer in Brazil, or one can, having been like Alec a nouveau riche dandy in one terrain, choose to become a working class minister in another, or can, like all of them, have a love relation in one geography that is not necessarily known by the people in the next. So much is self-transformation the abiding characteristic of the worked earth and working humanity that it is the inability to undergo transformation, as when the milk will not turn, that comes to be perceived (with astonishment and fear) as a failure. Tess, now a young girl, now a young woman, herself undergoes a fundamental alteration when (as was commented upon earlier) her body becomes big and then becomes two bodies. It is the alterability, the impregnability, the capacity of the body to become pregnant that astonishes Hardy here—the child-conceiving and bearing power of the maternal body, not the fact of the child who is born; for Sorrow quickly disappears from the narrative, and the milk cows are shown in their state of perpetual pregnancy rather than in calving season. The pregnant body and the baby are enduring material signs that a fleeting act has earlier taken place: as sentient memorializations, they are the most extreme form of sign because they are potentially autonomous, and thus themselves sign-generating. In this case, however, those signs soon themselves disappear, leaving Tess at liberty to determine whether there will be a verbal objectification and memorialization of the act that took place, then disappeared, leaving a body that grew large then disappeared, leaving a hungry infant who then disappeared, leaving only Tess and the language of self-substantiation.

Tess's troubled refusal to disown her earlier self, her younger body, is one of the crucial issues of the book. If, as readers have sometimes asserted, Hardy is in love with Tess, surely the attribute that most compels his love is her capacity for self-substantiation in the midst of transformation. Once more the kinship between Hardy and Brecht surfaces, for Brecht's dramas are built on rituals of substantiation and failed substantiation: in *A Man's A Man*, Galy Gay disowns himself in the presence of a day-old acquaintance, Widow Begbick, and then goes on to disown himself in the presence of Mrs. Gay; so, too, Jesse, Polly, and Uriah disown their connection with Jip in front of the temple priest; again Mother Courage (like any good business woman able to compute the cost of substantiation with the speed of light) denies knowing her son, Swiss Cheese, when enemy soldiers ask for an identification; once more, the family in *Good Woman of Setzuan* disclaims all familial ties with the son they have sent out to steal when the boy returns accompanied by a policeman; and, finally, *Caucasian Chalk Circle* reverses all these earlier moments with an unbroken series of successful acts of substantiation, for Azdak's chalk circle legitimization of the Grusha-Michael bond is only the climactic one in a long series initiated and sustained by Grusha herself. Throughout Hardy's novels, the option for self-substantiation comes and goes many times: it is a constant moral occasion. Although for Hardy Tess is not at first "guilty" of anything (not Prince, not Alec, not Sorrow) nor even what would usually be meant by "responsible" for the events of her past, they *are* (as though all three her children) the events of her past; they are not negligible or dismissible.[38] Hardy is stunned by nothing so much as the disowning of one's own or another's body, as when Fitzpiers can simply disown sexual intimacy with Suke, or Angel Clare can conceive of substituting Retty Priddle for Tess. Substitution is often the alternative to self-substantiation. To disown the younger self that rode in a cart carrying beehives one night or rode on a horse a second night is to substitute a different younger self, to replace the sixteen-year-old Tess with another sixteen-year-old girl. The fact that Tess in acknowledging and "owning" the presence of her own younger self at several crossroad collisions must perform that act of "owning" in the presence of someone who, even with her interpretive help ("I was only a child, Angel"), will be incapable of distinguishing "ownership" from "moral causality" and will punish her accordingly, does not by any means mean that she should disown it, for to say that she will be punished for things for which she is guiltless is only to say that self-substantiation has a very high cost which, always the case, is assumed in the term itself: were it not for the cost, Mother Courage would gladly rock Swiss Cheese's dead body back and forth in a lullaby as Jesse, Polly, and Uriah would stand by their companion singing a beautiful, boisterous song about the bounty of friendship, and the Setzuan family would complete the interrupted arm motion of reaching out for the rolls carried by the thieving boy. For Tess, the cost of substantiation is her own more and more severe alteration in the direction of murderess, her movement from not guilty and punished to guilty and punished.

As Tess's footsteps carry assurance of the contiguity and continuity of the changing land, so the narrative, carrying us forward line by line, performs that same act of assurance on behalf of Tess, an assurance that is needed, otherwise it might seem inconceivable that a woman taking an unbroken series of small morally responsible steps to the east could end up many miles to the west in an abyss of guilt and active wrongdoing. So, too, *within* the narrative, within the world of her own relations, her own act of reluctant confession becomes the equivalent of that narration. The confession is her narrative summary of the action: I, the woman standing on this ground, earlier stood here on that ground. . . . Though, like the land, she contains the capacity for radical transformation, she is, like the land, unitary, whole. This is, quite simply, the story Hardy tells, of a woman who is, as her name implies, in the midst of her fragility (for live things always have an acute fragility), as solid as the earth.

The rhythm of owning and disowning again dominates *The Mayor of Casterbridge*. The human being is capable of being wholly immersed in the materials of his work; he is also capable of existing outside the material realm, being immersed in "materials" that are dematerialized, symbolic. While there are modes of work that belong to one or the other of these — as physical immersion might be exemplified by a hay trusser and as separation and the alternative immersion in symbols by a political role such as mayor—there is also a particular form of work, that of the merchant, which hovers between these two, or rather does not simply hover between them as a hybrid that is neither, but instead may literally incorporate into itself both. The merchant's act of buying and selling is an act of owning and disowning the material world, a regular rhythm of taking the materials of the world (not now mine) into one's own personal sphere (now mine), then breaking with them, dismissing them, sending them away (not now mine). Perhaps the more successful merchant, like Farfrae, is a hybrid who stays at all times somewhere in the middle and thus need not experience the psychic reality of either act: never really having been immersed, he never really needs to enact the brutality of disowning, for there is no difficulty of separation; having recognized from the first his separability from his materials, he sheds them as gracefully as he acquired them. But Henchard is a different kind of merchant: in buying, he takes the hay and oats and roots and barley onto himself with all the literalness of one wholly innocent of the fact that a sale will soon follow; and in turn, he disowns the same materials with all the indignation (like an Old Testament father ousting a child — or a wife — from his tent) of one who had never anticipated such a parting and has not a glimmer of any future reunion despite the fact that the very rhythm of his work will require just such a reunion almost immediately. Each beat in the two-beat measure (buying-selling, buying-selling) is entered into as though it were uncompanioned, as though there was only this, to possess, or only this, to dispossess.

Hay trusser-merchant-mayor, Henchard is all three because the life of the merchant contains within itself the embodying activity of the hay trusser and the disembodying role of the mayor. To the familiar recognition that in *every* personal relation in his life (with Susan, with Lucetta, with Elizabeth-Jane, with Farfrae, with Abel Whittle) there is an act of extreme owning (he does not simply like Farfrae, he adores him) and disowning (he does not gradually grow distant but denounces him)[39] one need add nothing except the by now easily anticipated comment that in doing so it is the very rhythm of his work we witness. Every action has a structure made up of buying and selling, owning and disowning, as the selling of his wife is immediately followed by an oath forbidding drinking: it is a complicated disencumbering and encumbering of himself, disowning Susan yet memorializing that act of disowning in a new vow almost as encumbering and as eternal as the marriage vow itself; rum and alcohol are so clearly connected to the grains and grass of his work that it is hay trussing, too, that in shadowed outline is sworn away (as he will later bid adieu to the political realm in a farewell handshake with a royal person). Visible in all his relations with major figures in his life, it is even visible in small acts such as his conversation with the weather prophet where he accepts the mystical premise of the prophet's work, yet will not enter his house, claims he is there for a toothache at the very moment he is there receiving advice, acts on the prophecy, then reverses himself in an agony of attraction now to the world of deep immersion and now to the world wholly "free" of its self-encumbering heaviness. Whether he acts in this way in the personal sphere because of his work, or whether instead the elements of his labor merely objectify what he is elsewhere doing, is an open question; what is incontestable is that the concussive rhythm of the two-part structure of exchange is constantly visible in all spheres of his life. While it is tempting to claim that the cycle of owning-disowning-owning-disowning always comes to rest for Henchard in the "owning" phase — the re-owning of Susan, of Elizabeth-Jane, of Abel Whittle, of the physically immersed part of the tripartite structure of hay trusser-merchant-mayor, it would not be true; for after all his separate acts of reimmersion, his last will and testament disavows all kinship. He is, to the very end, the innocent and brutally literal merchant.

While in each novel the materials of labor make visible the physical and psychic facts of those who work those materials, the attributes projected there are universal: it is not just Giles (or Marty or Old South) who in his limbs and nerve endings and perception and aspiration has the habit of endless reach, nor Tess who alone discovers forms of self-substantiation in the midst of transformation, nor Henchard who is by himself torn by the twin temptations of owning and disowning. But it is Giles as worker-in-trees, Tess as worker-of-the-land, and Henchard as worker-in-the-marketplace who project and objectify in their work the traits that are universal but not universally visible, attributes shared by all but expressed on behalf of all by only some. It is not the attribute but the power to objectify the attribute that belongs to the laborer. Further, though it is appropriate to call these attributes "universally human," the word "human" is here most accurately understood as "the human being as worker," man as creator, man as artificer — where "worker" and "creator" have not the local meaning of a particular form of work but describe the essential nature of the species as an animal capable of creating. Thus the term includes within its expansive reach even those who in the immediacy of their daily lives have a disturbed relation to work whether because, as in the case of Felice, their wealth acts as a surrogate form of will or because of a more overt failure of will as in the instance of Abel Whittle. Over the course of the novels, Hardy recovers certain elementary facts about the creator — that he extends himself out; that in doing so he transforms himself, seeking alteration in the pleasure of transformation and at the same time risking alteration in maiming and wound; that he is capable of deep submersion in the materials of his own making but so, too, is he utterly capable of dissociating himself from the terms and outcomes of his own creation. The kinds of questions raised by Hardy's works are in part moral, for the nature of man as "artificer" carries with it particular kinds of ethical problems: whether the capacities for symbolic thought and for lying can be extricated from one another, for example; whether "loyalty" is possible in the midst of "making"; or whether the capacity for self-substantiation is incompatible with the ability for self-transformation. Important aesthetic questions are almost as directly raised by the works. It should be stressed that the characters' choice between immersion in and extrication from the physical realm would be misread as indicating a split between physical labor and imaginative labor, for the very alteration may itself indicate what it is that occurs in imaginative labor. The rhythm of owning and disowning that appears to be required by the work of economic exchange may, for example, be equally required by aesthetic exchange. It may, for example, be not incidental but wholly central to creation that Zola, who in *L'Assommoir* engages our sympathies to intricately in Gervaise, can write to himself in his working notes with brutalizing self-distance an instruction to create a woman who will want "almost nothing" and will not be allowed to have it ("In the beginning she says: 'I should like a little corner where I might be happy, see my children well settled. Eat bread every day, not be beaten. Die at home, etc.' On the whole give her those modest desires that will never be realized"[40]), or that Dickens who in his wrenching scene of Jo's death in *Bleak House* uses every rhetorical and emotional strategy available for making us feel acutely the vulnerability of the child and the indifference of society, should in his own working notes cover this scene with four words: "Jo — Yes — Kill him."[41]

What the attributes of "imagining" are and which of them are only occasional accompaniments to the process and which are essential are problems whose solutions require the dissolution of our inhibitions about describing directly the nature of creation and require as well the dissolution of a different set of inhibitions we have about attending to representations of work — two sets of inhibitions that we perhaps only appear to arrive at by separate paths. The two require one another because it is by witnessing "making" in its internal and external manifestations that each will be "seen" and understood. Finally, it is a subject on which the antagonism between moral and aesthetic preoccupations may itself dissolve, for whether one begins with representations of workers in order to enter the inner recesses of the structure of artistic creation, or one instead begins to recognize that very structure of activity in the actions of workers and moves from those representations through the only apparent "non-transparency"[42] of the text to their historical equivalent and confronts the actual structures and conditions of work, one is at all moments addressing a pressing set of questions about failed and successful artifice. For, as little as we know on this topic, we at least know that when a poet confesses his inability to "make" out of the "almost nothing" of the raw materials a new image in his mind, it is the stuttering of the imagination that he confesses; as again when he describes his inability to transfer, relocate, the now existing image from the interior of his mind to the external world, it is the breakdown of the imagination that he allows us to witness; as again in the actual historical inability to "make" the needed materials of survival it is the stuttering of the imagination we see; as in the failure to redistribute and relocate the now existing materials of rescue to the world outside their benefit it is the massive breakdown of the human imagination that we watch. The failure to rescue is the first and final manifestation of the failure to invent; so too the reluctance to recognize and name the responsibilities of the imagination may one day be understood as the reluctance of an individual or a profession or a century to participate in an act of rescue.

It is, at last, this thing on behalf of which all rescue occurs, the body, that is Hardy's subject. What is particular to and remarkable about him is not his representation of man as maker (for it would perhaps be the failure to see this as an important subject that would make an artist noteworthy) but instead his representation of man as *embodied maker*. That all human acts take place through and out of his body never ceases to intrigue and quietly amaze him. That the human being should at once be a "body" and a "maker" is for Hardy an astonishing conflation that he is able to objectify in the materials of work precisely because those materials acquire through their contact with the human being exactly the same conflation: they are at one and the same moment the "prolongation of the human body" *and* the latent products of artifice.

In each of the three novels there comes a particular moment when Hardy attempts to objectify this particular conflation in a single image or set of images. In *The Mayor of Casterbridge*, the overlay of bull and finch (made extensions of one another not only by their shared association with Henchard but by the framing of barn and cage) articulate the fact that fluttering through the sheer facticity of matter, the unequivocal space-taking fact of the physical body, is this other delicate, fragile thing — breath, life, the voice, song, in a combination that, were Hardy Thomas Mann, would be lifted out of concrete materials into the rhapsodic abstractions of unstoppable sentences, but that Hardy insists on trying to unfold with the concrete image itself. It is the same conflation that he reaches for when he extends Giles Winterborne's body into twelve tons of wood loaded on a wagon that must be maneuvered (like a big cumbersome body) down a road so narrow as to make backing up or turning around nearly unthinkable: hovering over its weight and shuddering through its density is the light shimmer of bells — faint, only (as the rich lady learns) "almost" ignorable, as audible as light spilling through the underside of shaded leaves, and itself incontestably present. In *Tess*, the heavy sensuous surfaces of the cows suddenly evaporate like quicksilver into momentary cartoon or undergo mystical self-dissolution into the mist, objectifying the nature of live tissue in all its magnificent capacity for self-alteration. But the equivalent of the two earlier images is not in the many-pages-long description of the cows but in that brief image which is prelude to the moment when Angel Clare, acting out of the twin imperatives of desire and rescue, will for the first time not simply touch the human body but hold its weight in his arms. This is, finally, Hardy's most beautiful and haunting image of the human body in this novel. It is the image of the translucent dresses worn by three milkmaids that, already full of light and air, brush against the grass and stir up butterflies that, caught within the layers of the skirts, fly there visible from the outside. One thinks of the sun glowing through the translucent nostrils of Susan Henchard as she walks down the road or shining on Elizabeth-Jane's eyelids as she sleeps. So the gauze-like dresses become the magnified image of this translucent tissue with something — voice, bells, butterflies — something, caught in its meshes and flickering through it like radiant consciousness.

Notes

1. Thomas Hardy, *The Woodlanders*, intro. David Lodge (London, 1974), pp. 143, 296. The *Norton Critical Edition* is used to cite *Tess of the D'Urbervilles* (ed. Scott Elledge, New York, 1965) and *The Mayor of Casterbridge* (ed. James K. Robinson, New York, 1977). Page numbers are given in the text.

2. Much of the power of the Central and South American novel of the twentieth century resides in the ease with which it depicts embodied consciousness (this is perhaps particularly true of Miguel Asturias). When the body enters American and British literature, it tends to enter in the singular and thus relatively narrow form of the erotic. Though desire is an important fact about the body, it is only one of many. In the South and Central American novel, the body in its perceptual, somatic, and psychological complexity routinely enters the text. Growing familiarity with these writings will probably work to re-affirm and amplify our already great admiration for writers like Hardy and Faulkner who are, within their own cultural contexts, exceptional in this achievement.

Studies of Hardy that explicitly attend to the physical include Robert Kiely, "Vision and Viewpoint in *The Mayor of Casterbridge,*" *Nineteenth-Century Fiction* 23 (September 1968), 189–200; Tony Tanner, "Colour and Movement in Hardy's *Tess of the d'Urbervilles,*" *Critical Quarterly* 10 (Autumn 1968), 219–39; and Terry Eagleton, "Thomas Hardy: Nature as Language," *Critical Quarterly* 13 (Summer 1971), 153–62.

Studies assessing the significance of nature in Hardy include David J. DeLaura, "'The Ache of Modernism' in Hardy's Later Novels," *ELH* 34 (1967), 380–99; and Bruce Johnson's "'The Perfection of Species' and Hardy's *Tess*," and John Paterson's "Lawrence's Vital Source: Nature and Character in Thomas Hardy," both in *Nature and the Victorian Imagination*, ed. U. C. Knoepflmacher and G. R. Tennyson (Berkeley, 1977), pp. 259–77 and 455–69.

3. Although all three women passing through the gate belong to the laboring class, they are immersed in it to varying degrees, and both the way paint adheres to them and the way they remove it reflects those varying degrees. Suke Damson is a physical laborer: to remove the paint on her shoulder she lies down and rubs the paint onto the grass. Marty South is a laborer and craftsman: she moves on, wiping away the paint without changing her posture and almost without interrupting her movement. Grace Melbury is the daughter of a laborer-merchant who has been educated out of her class: she anticipates and prevents direct contact with

the paint by using a stick. Presented in the context of the other two, anticipation is seen as the most extreme form of removal, for the grafting of the paint has been wished away, made not to occur by the "artful" intervention of an artifact, a stick capable of erasing the future before it happens.

On the removal of the signs of the physical world from the body, see below pages 52ff and 76–77.

4. Only its uneven appearance in the novels makes it clear that it is a self-conscious form of notation; it is much more densely present in *The Woodlanders* than in either *Tess* or *The Mayor of Casterbridge*. Though some forms of representing the body are constant across the three novels, some are specific to a specific novel. In *Tess*, for example, the repeated emphasis on sleepiness (in the grove, the dairy, the wedding night sleepwalk, and at Stonehenge) is a way of emphasizing embodiedness. For a visual equivalent, see, for example, Millet's astonishingly beautiful *Noonday Rest* where the bodies of the two figures swell to fill the entire canvas (knee, foot, and hand filling the lower lefthand corner; knee, head, and hand filling the upper righthand corner), making visible the evacuation of the world from human consciousness during sleep. On the connection between dazed forms of consciousness and embodiment, see Michael Fried, "The Beholder in Courbet: His Early Self-Portraits and Their Place in His Art," *Glyph* 4 (1979), 85–131. In *The Mayor*, a way of conveying embodiedness, not found in the other two novels, is in the sheer physical magnitude of Henchard, underscored at many points such as in Abel Whittle's final line, "One of the neighbors have gone to get a man to measure him" (254). Hardy has continually measured him; we know his dimensions. The major way of asserting his physical scale is through his breaking of successive frames.

5. There are of course moments when Hardy presents what he intends only as a physical analogue to consciousness (as when he writes "The paternal longing ran on all-fours with her own desire" [315]), but more frequently he is depicting the actual physical manifestation of what we routinely and incorrectly think of as a wholly nonphysical form of consciousness.

6. Thomas Hardy, "The Dorsetshire Labourer," in *The Selected Writings of Thomas Hardy: Stories, Poems, and Essays*, ed. Irving Howe (New York, 1966), p. 124.

7. In respectively Emile Zola, *Germinal*, trans. L. W. Tancock (Baltimore, 1954), pp. 262, 263, 268, 392–93, 396; "The Three Spinners" in *The Complete Grimm's Fairy Tales*, trans. M. Hunt and J. Stern, intro. Padraic Colum (New York, 1972), p. 86; Charles Dickens, *Bleak House*, ed. Norman Page, intro. J. Hillis Miller (Baltimore, 1976), pp. 357, 422.

8. Ronald Blythe, "The Voice of the People," rev. of *William Cobbett: The Poor Man's Friend*, by George Spater, *New York Review of Books* (10 June 1982), 29, 30.

9. Hardy expresses here a literal fact about work: it is the nature of work that raw materials get relocated and that man, conversely, is through his work anchored to one spot. Thus the immobile partner is made mobile and the mobile partner is made immobile.

Again, this emphasis on the reciprocity between man and world, their *shared alteration*, makes it clear that Hardy's main stress is not on work as human will, as it is for a novelist like George Eliot. (Were his interest the will *per se*, it would lead him to depict only the alteration suffered by the world rather than both that suffered by the world and its reciprocal counterpart, that suffered by man.)

10. This description of *The Spinner* is given by Robert Herbert in his catalogue to the 1975–76 exhibition at the Galeries nationales d'exposition du Grand Palais (Paris, Oct. 1975–Jan. 1976) and at the Haywood Gallery (London, 22 January– 7 March 1976). *Jean-François Millet* (London, 1976), p. 100. Robert Herbert makes visible the way the identification between Millet's workers and their world is literalized in the artistic materials: the women in *Faggot-Gatherers Returning from the Forest* are "composed of the same vertical lines that represent the trees" (154); the second and third women in *Women Gathering Wood* are "controlled by the yellow ochre common to each and to the snow-covered earth" (224).

11. The idea of raw materials and tools as an extension of the human body has many different sources: in the nineteenth-century European philosophy of work, in political and economic philosophy, in phenomenology, and in philosophy of perception. The last is implicitly the starting place of all others for it is the actual perceptual experience of extension that gives rise to the idea in its elaborated forms. James J. Gibson, for example, in *The Senses Considered as Perceptual Systems* (Boston, 1966) notes the at-once startling and (once stated) wholly familiar fact that "The man with a walking stick can even feel stones, mud, or grass at the end of his stick," and again that "In use [of a pair of scissors], one actually feels the cutting action of the blades" (112). The idea is most elaborated by and thus most identified with Hegel, Feuerbach, and above all Marx. The phrase quoted "a prolongation of his body" is from Jack Cohen's translation of the Fourth and Fifth Notebooks of Marx's *Grundrisse*, first made available in English under the title *Karl Marx: Pre-Capitalist Economic Formation*, ed. and intro. E. J. Hobsbawm (New York, 1965), p. 89. In Martin Nicolaus's translation of the complete notebooks, *Grundrisse: Foundations of the Critique of Political Economy* (New York, 1973), vol. IV, p. 491, the phrase is given as "his extended body." It is precisely because earth and tools are man's extended body that property, which severs the worker from his extended body, places him in the position of selling not his work but his now-truncated activity of labor: thus the idea is central to *Capital*, though it usually occurs in the more abstract phrasing of "the separation of the worker from the means of production" and as a difference between the capacity to "sell the products of labor" and to sell "labor power" (*Capital: Volume One*, intro. E. Mandel, trans. Ben Fowkes [New York, 1977], p. 951 and *passim*). John McMurtry in *The Structure of Marx's World-View* (Princeton, 1978), p. 64, also recovers Marx's original vocabulary and the idea of body damage by describing property as a dismembering of the worker's external organs. With characteristic sensitivity, J. Hillis Miller (*Thomas Hardy: Distance And Desire* [Cambridge, Mass., 1970]) also remarks on Hardy's sustained absorption with tools and their "intimate" connections with persons (pp. 94, 96).

12. While the emphasis here is on the earth as an extension of the human body, it is also possible to read the relation in the opposite direction and see the human being as the earth's eruption into intelligence onto its own surface. In his continual insistence on the reciprocity of man and the object world, he encourages this reversed reading. Such descriptions as that of the van which "was rather a movable attachment of the roadway than an extraneous object to those who knew it well" (36), tend to invite similar readings of the human beings who move across the earth's surface (though it should again be stressed that Hardy carries us here by the path of reciprocity rather than that of reification). It would not require many steps to see Giles and Marty in the circuit of their work as sentient-

intelligent-movable-attachments. To a large extent, Grace Melbury's relation to Giles is her relation to the forest, and this is for Hardy perhaps the single most important relationship in the novel. Giles is, within a mythical reading of the text, simply the forest's sentient representative. Most scenes between them are as much between Grace and the tree as between Grace and Giles, for Giles is on several occasions invisible. When she walks under the elm in which he is cutting branches, it seems the tree that speaks to her; and again at the end of the novel, Giles is enclosed within a hollow tree trunk, and during their hours together Grace converses with him without seeing him. Her lack of awareness about his precarious state is in part her lack of awareness about the precarious state of the forest. The large, lethal trap placed at the foot of a colossal tree that catches a fragment of her dress is, within this reading, the forest's violent attempt to reclaim her.

13. George Orwell, *Dickens, Dali, and Others* (New York, n.d.), pp. 44–56. Some of Orwell's specific claims (such as Dickens's refusal to specify a character's line of work) are certainly right; others are exaggerated; still others are wrong. But even if all his specific claims were accurate, there are of course many other ways of representing work than those whose absence from Dickens is here attended to.

14. The problem of representation can have at least three sources: (1) a subject may for various reasons be itself difficult to objectify; (2) a subject may instead be easily representable but for some reason be consciously or unconsciously excluded from the art of a particular period; (3) a subject may be both representable and represented in the art of a period but be read out by a later period. Although the problem of work arises from all three sources, the third makes a significant contribution toward its invisibility. This is obviously not to say that the subject is absent from critical writings on the novel, but that it is not a major category of thought, nor a rubric in most indexes, nor a way of perceiving literature taught in the classroom, nor a subject surrounded by a richly elaborated, shared vocabulary like that which surrounds domestic relations in the novel.

15. Bruno Bettelheim, *The Informed Heart: Autonomy in a Mass Age* (New York, 1960), p. 94. Bettelheim is here talking about magazine fiction, but his comment is equally applicable to the fiction of the novel.

16. Colum, viii.

17. For example, "The Cunning Little Tailor," "The Straw, the Coal, and the Bean," "The Valiant Little Tailor," "The Four Skillful Brothers," "The Giant and the Tailor," and "The Tailor in Heaven."

18. Thomas Carlyle, *Sartor Resartus and On Heroes and Hero Worship*, intro. W. H. Hudson (New York, 1973), pp. 20, 31.

19. Based on a tune Handel had heard in a blacksmith shop, Handel's *Harmonious Blacksmith* is an objectification of the space of the forge and of the central argument of *Great Expectations*. The piece is, like thousands of other pieces of music, a theme with variations, but as one listens to the haunting air begin to break into complexity and speed, one hears the fall and lift and drop of the hammer as it becomes increasingly self-confident and graceful: we are allowed to witness the actual moment when work becomes virtuosity; within its four minute expanse, the mysterious passage from craft to art is made audible and thus enterable.

20. On the merchant's closer proximity to overt imaginative invention, see for example, Karl Löwith's famous chapter on "The Problem of Work," which includes an analysis of the distinction Hegel makes in the Jena lectures between farmers, handworkers, and merchants (*From Hegel to Nietzsche: The Revolution in Nineteenth-Century Thought*, trans. David E. Green [Garden City, N.Y., 1967], Vol. II, ii, pp. 260–83). The farmer is by his dependence on the weather and soil, so integrated with nature and accepting of it as a "given" that he is distrustful of overtly created structures such as the law; the merchant who is comparatively separate from those natural "givens," accepts and relies on those same created structures (265).

21. The first two "stores" are in *A Man's A Man* and *Mother Courage* and the last three in *Good Woman of Setzuan*.

22. It is completely appropriate that when Lucetta wishes Elizabeth-Jane absent she sends her to a museum. We should understand the contrast not so much as one between "staying home" and "going out" but as a choice between being at one of two cultural centers, staying at the theatre or going to a museum, staying where objects are utterly unstable and forever transforming themselves or going instead to the building that celebrates the stability of objects. The world of economic and imaginative exchange entails its own brutalities which Elizabeth-Jane feels acutely, as in Hardy's comment that life had come to seem to her not a "series of pure disappointments" but rather a "series of substitutions" (137).

23. The reluctance to place physical and imaginative labor together can originate from either direction. It often arises out of an impulse to protect "imagining," out of the sense that "imagining" will somehow be diminished if seen in its kinship with other forms of making. At other times (though with less frequency) it arises out of an impulse to protect the realm of labor, the sense that it is inappropriate to compare the humanly pressing problems surrounding work with the often safe realm of the imagination. Though both "protective" impulses have legitimacy and generosity in them, both in the end work against the very thing that is being cared for.

24. This is one of two major problems. The second (not immediately relevant to Hardy's representation of the subject) is that work is social, hence not easily located within the boundaries of the "individual," hence not wholly compatible with the nature of "character" as it is conceived and developed in the novel. The complications of this problem will be addressed separately.

25. In many ways the "activity of work" is to "an action" as marriage (repetitive, habitual) is to courtship, and some of the solutions to the problem of representing work thus illustrate by analogy solutions to the representation of the fiction-sustaining capacity of the imagination as entailed in marriage.

26. As the language here ("temporal units," "task units") suggests, the attempts of writers to find a way of subdividing work in order to enter it imaginatively has its parallel in the attempts of economists or factory owners to subdivide and enter it in order to determine appropriate forms of compensation. One brilliantly playful exploration of the difficulty of finding units is Faulkner's "Shingles for the Lord." The story is primarily a parable of how when a man does not own his own tools, he is damned in three or four directions, both compelled to work and excluded from work at someone else's determination, and thus vulnerable to what are shown to be (if carried to their extreme) the twin experiences of slavery and

unemployment. But along the way there are wonderful portraits both of the ultimate wholeness and integrity and non-subdivisibility of work (the church, even as
it falls and is built again, is in its integrity undisturbed) and the humor and near
obscenity of trying to subdivide it into time units, money units, or finally dog-
units, the dominant "coin" of exchange.

27. Often in the nineteenth century it is the worker's ability to work which
must be repaired: Dickens's Richard Carstone, Eliot's Fred Vincy, Hardy's Abel
Whittle are examples of this emphasis which is particularly characteristic of
George Eliot. Adam Bede's workmanship is often displayed in his repair of the
failed work of others: his brother's craft, his father's coffin, Arthur's estate (particularly "the woods" which are the extension of Adam's own wood work in carpentry).

28. There is a form of work that is itself an extended act of repair, detective
work, for it is the legal or social system that has broken down and must be
repaired by being re-understood, restored, and reaffirmed. It is in part because
detective work is repair that a whole subgenre of the novel can grow up around it.
Many of the aspects of work discussed here have their counterpart in detective
work. For example, the inextricability of the worker from the materials of his
work becomes in some detective fiction the complicated relation of the detective to
the corpse, as in Raymond Chandler novels where Philip Marlowe is often standing with the body when the police enter or is, temporarily, believed by his own
clients to have done the murder. So, too, detective work is allied with imaginative
labor (see Steven Marcus's discussion of Dashiell Hammett and the fiction-
generating powers of the detective in "Dashiell Hammett and the Continental
Op," *Representation: Essays on Literature and Society* [New York, 1954], pp. 311–31)
and is also compared with more immediately physical work as when, in *Lady in the
Lake*, Marlowe describes the problem-solving activity of a country detective as
"moving the mind around with the ponderous energy of a homesteader digging
up a stump" (New York, 1972, p. 73).

29. On the eighteenth-century attitude toward invention, see "The Duty To
Invent" in Lewis Mumford's *Technics and Civilization* (New York, 1963), chap. I,
pp. 52–55.

30. Some will no doubt object that this is too generous a description of the
relation of literary criticism to its materials. The moral and intellectual complexity
of the relation between the critic and the art work is, however, accounted for in
the analogy with Hardy's worker. If the lent voice is sometimes damaging to or
intrusive upon the literature, this is only to say (as above) that the relation in both
directions is sometimes wounding, that it entails risks in both directions as it
confers benefits in both directions. That there is self-interest in the worker's association of himself with his materials (Homer, Hardy), if he or she does it in part for
motives of self-magnification, the laborer too is magnified by the elm or hay or soil
that expresses him, and self-enhancement should be unembarrassedly assumed as
a partial motive.

31. The connections between the three acts of (1) disowning the material
"given" of the world, (2) creating, and (3) lying, which Hardy often touches on,
are examined by Hannah Arendt in "Truth and Politics" (*Political Theory and Social
Change*, ed. David Spitz [New York, 1967], pp. 3–37) where she examines the
reasons why deliberate lying so habitually occurs in the realm of politics, and by
Nelson Goodman who in *Ways of Worldmaking* (Indiana, 1978), insists on the

distinction between fictions and frauds (94 and *passim*). For Marx, whose *Capital* is one of the most extended analyses of the nature of "made things," the created object can be either a successful fiction or a fraud: which of the two it is, is determined by the stability of its referential activity.

32. Irenäus Eibl-Eibesfeldt, *The Biology of Peace and War*, trans. Eric Mosbacher (New York, 1979), p. 16.

33. Just as here in the structure of a scene, Hardy may include both a realistic action and a schematic outline of the same action, so on the level of narrative texture there is sometimes this same alternation, and again its effect is to regulate the reader's relation to the outside and the inside of the body. He alternates naturalistic description of objects with abstract renderings of those same objects, which rather than undercutting or breaking the realistic surface (as one might expect), seem to intensify our perception of it. In *Tess*, for example, passages in which the surface of the cows are described as though we are moving across their flanks, udders, distensions, from a distance of only several inches, are sometimes "interrupted" as Hardy switches to a cartoon version: the back of the cow becomes a pendulum hanging down from a circle, or the underside of the cow is described as "their large-veined udders hung ponderous as sandbags, the teats sticking out like the legs of a gipsy's crock" (90). The movement from the minutely described surface to a line drawing of the cow's shape—the pendulum, the gipsy's crock— would seem to carry us to a much more distant viewing position (the way in theatre the introduction of a didactic *Sprecher* figure will distance us from the stage); but so little is the immediate physical surface disrupted that we seem to move closer to, almost inside, the cow. E. H. Gombrich and Julian Hochberg (*Art, Perception, and Reality* [Baltimore, 1972], pp. 35, 74, 78) point out that "cartoon" is the opposite of "camouflage," which makes perception more difficult. Caricature assists perception by providing an internal map of what the body would feel like from the inside. Our inner reading of the body exaggerates, as when a small lump feels from the inside like a large one. Hochberg notes that when a photograph, a line drawing, a tracing of the photograph, and a cartoon of a curled hand are all shown to a person and the person is then asked to reproduce the hand gesture, it is the cartoon that can be reproduced most easily, presumably because it is closer to what the internal experience of curled fingers is like. In these passages in Hardy, the reader is almost made to feel what it is like to have a switching tail or distended underbelly.

34. "The Dorsetshire Labourer," p. 130.

35. Gibson, pp. 101, 106. That the senses are "tentacles and feelers," "ways of seeking and extracting information about the environment from the flowing array of ambient energy" (24) is a central premise of *The Senses Considered as Perceptual Systems*.

36. On the striking characteristics which differentiate the senses from one another—such as the distance from the body, or whether the perceptual object is able to round corners (as is true of auditory information but not visual)—see in addition to Gibson (*passim*), Erwin W. Straus, "Aesthesiology and Hallucinations" in *Existence: A New Dimension in Psychiatry and Psychology*, ed. Rollo May, Ernest Angel, and Henri F. Ellenberger (New York, 1958), pp. 139-69.

37. Dorothy Van Ghent, *The English Novel: Form and Function* (New York, 1968), pp. 201-203. Van Ghent also emphasizes the importance of Tess's confes-

sion. See also Bruce Johnson's striking discussion of geological strata as a characteristic both of the earth and of persons in "'The Perfection of Species' and Hardy's Tess."

38. See above, pages 92ff.

39. J. Hillis Miller, for example, in *Thomas Hardy: Distance and Desire* writes that Henchard has an overwhelming desire to "possess" but that the "object of possession" keeps changing from one person to another (147).

40. "Appendix: Zola's Technique: The Method and Plans" in Matthew Josephson, *Zola and His Time* (New York, 1928), p. 530.

41. "Appendix: Dickens's number-plans for *Bleak House*," in *Bleak House*, p. 947.

42. The term is Goodman's, p. 69.

3

NOUNS: THE REALM
OF THINGS

Six Ways To Kill a Blackbird
(or Any Other Intentional Object)
in Samuel Beckett

This chapter, like many writings about Beckett before it, will attempt to describe the negation and the affirmation, the nothing and the something, of his works. Although the discussion will not be restricted to any one corner of his canon, it will focus on the short stories in *No's Knife*; for these pieces, often ignored by readers, exist as distillations of the author's thought. In their brevity and coherence, they represent what the narrator of *Murphy* would have called "Beckett's account, expurgated, accelerated, improved, and reduced."

Any description of Beckett's works can begin by acknowledging what he himself has named the critical factor in his vision: "The key word in my plays is 'perhaps.'"[1] His works are ambivalent in subject and interrogatory in mood. Even the time-honored tautology is no longer trustworthy, for logic's first principle is Beckett's last principle: the assertion "For all x, $x = x$" exists only as a cruel joke in a world where x is unnamable or, if namable, subject to constant mutation in name. The disintegration of logic has logical ramifications (or would, were there any left to be had): the concept of identity is existentially sterile; the concept of certainty, epistemologically sterile; the concept of commitment, morally sterile. The world, therefore, is defined by uncertainty, ambiguity, and antinomy; the man in that world, by failure, frustration, and impotence. The ironic ambivalence of the plays, novels, and short stories is Beckett's honesty about man and his tribute to man: the pervasive "perhaps" reflects his insistence that we stop reacting to logical absurdity "with a kind of Pythagorean terror, as though the irrationality of *pi* were an offense against the deity, not to mention his creature."[2]

After acknowledging the presence of "all the sad etcetera of the wrong" in Beckett's world, one must assign it to its proper place: paradox is the crucial *given* in his works; it is not the *point* of those works. Consequently, this discussion will adopt the maxim of the character in *The Calmative*: "It is not my wish to labor these antinomies."[3] Beckett's point is not to reveal the tragic void, to evoke or to exorcise contemporary anguish, to recommend salvation or to offer consolation for what can't be salvaged. Rather, he attempts something far more elementary. As W. V. Quine suggests in *The Ways of Paradox*, antinomy "can be accompanied by nothing less than a reputation of part of our conceptual heritage."[4] Given complexity and uncertainty, Beckett, in effect, clears the boards and begins again with those things about which we can be certain. Each of his works isolates and bestows visibility on modes of feeling, thinking, and acting that collectively constitute the central human experience. His method will be demonstrated first by examining briefly the nature of the story setting, the landscapes against which his ideas are presented.

Beckett's landscapes manifest his attempt to articulate the concrete universals of existence. The most particularized setting of any story in *No's Knife* is that in *The Expelled*: we know that the city through which the character travels is the *capital* of, presumably, some country, though which country remains unknown. The more typical Beckettian landscape is described by the "voice" in *Texts for Nothing V*:

> The sky, I've heard — the sky and earth, I've heard great accounts of them, now that's pure word for word, I invent nothing. I've noted, I must have noted many a story with them as setting, they create the atmosphere. Between them where the hero stands a great gulf is fixed, while all about they flow together more and more, till they meet, so that he finds himself as it were under glass, and yet with no limit to his movements in all directions, let him understand who can, that is no part of my attributions. The sea too, I am conversant with the sea too, it belongs to the same family. (92, 93)

Beckett's settings are generic: they consist of sea, sky, earth, a river, a marsh, a mountain. These elements in addition to simple directions such as "toward," "away from," "left of," enable him to chart the movement of his characters, even when they are moving through city streets: "By keeping the red part of the sky as much as possible on my right hand I came at last to the river" (*The Calmative*, 47). Such elemental settings universalize the situation presented and enable us to examine character and idea "as it were under glass": the value of the individual idea is amplified by the lack of particularized detail which would deflect our attention from Beckett's major concern.

Beckett's primary interest, of course, resides not in these exterior landscapes but rather in their equally elemental counterpart, man's psychic and existential landscapes. The way in which he focuses on these elementary states may be described in the language of contemporary philosophy. Contemporary philosophers argue that any intentional act posits an intentional object, and that the structure of consciousness can be better understood by including the object in analysis: consciousness is consciousness of x; desire is desire for y; fear is fear of z. Traditional fiction has automatically included and specified the intentional object: so, for example, the subject of Salinger's *Pretty Mouth and Green My Eyes* is not fear but, rather, a husband's fear of his wife's infidelity. Beckett, in contrast, attempts to eliminate or at least minimize the presence of any intentional object in order to emphasize the necessary universality of the condition itself.

There are four ways in which Beckett evacuates the object from the work. Often, any mention of the object is simply *omitted*. In the following passages, Beckett's interest is not a specific man hoping for x or y but "man hoping" or "man coping with hoping":

No. How one hoped above, on and off.
With what diversity. (*Texts for Nothing* II, 80)

Yes, I don't know why, but I have never been
disappointed, and I often was in the early
days, without feeling at the same time, or a
moment later, an undeniable relief. (*The Expelled*, 13)

More explicit than simple *omission* is Beckett's second technique, the character's self-conscious *rejection* of the object:

Vladimir: Suppose we repented.
Estragon: Repented what?
Vladimir: Oh . . . (*He reflects.*) We wouldn't have to go into the details.
   (*Waiting for Godot*, 8)

Winnie: Fear no more the heat o' the sun. (*Pause.*)
   Did you hear that?
Willie: (*irritated*). Yes.
Winnie: (*same voice*). What? (*Pause.*) What?
Willie: (*more irritated*). Fear no more.
   Pause.
Winnie: (*same voice*). No more what? (*Pause.*) Fear no more what?
Willie: (*violently*). Fear no more!
Winnie: (*normal voice, gabbled*). Bless you Willie I do appreciate your goodness. . . . (*Happy Days*, 26)

In the short stories, as in the plays, self-conscious *rejection* is a major technique:

Over, over, there is a soft place in my heart
for all that is over, no, for the being over . . . (*From An Abandoned Work*,
    147)

I have never in my life been on my way anywhere, but
simply on my way. (*From An Abandoned Work*, 139)

It was none the less the return, to what no
matter, the return . . . (*Texts for Nothing* II, 79)

This method is again operative when, as happens repeatedly throughout
the shorter prose works, a character concludes his tale by assuring us that
the particular story related is without significance: "I don't know why I
told this story. I could just as well have told another. Perhaps some other
time I'll be able to tell another. Living souls, you will see how alike they
are" (*The Expelled*, 24). What is significant is not the *x* or *y* about which
the story is told; it is, rather, the act of telling the story, the act of
communing with a listener, even when one is one's own listener: "Then
babble, babble words, like the solitary child who turns himself into children, two three, so as to be together, and whisper together, in the dark"
(*Endgame*, 70).

The third method of minimizing the object's significance requires that
Beckett allude to the object without defining it. In *Waiting for Godot* it is
irrelevant whether Godot is God, night, death, Pozzo, silence, or a war
agent, for Beckett's interest is expectation or anticipation, that psychic
state which defines one's present in relation to one's future. If Godot were
identifiable, it would suggest that were Godot to come, man would stop
waiting. But if Godot were actually to come in the play, the vagabonds
(now no longer waiting for Godot) would merely wait in the presence of
Godot for something else. The satisfaction of desire transcends our temporal grasp: the moment we attain satisfaction, we simultaneously lose
it, for the old object of expectation is replaced with a new object. In
effect, waiting for Godot means "waiting for Godot, Christmas, lover,
summer, *ad infinitum*" or "waiting for the end of waiting." A more condensed articulation of the same idea occurs in Hamm's final soliloquy in
Endgame:

You CRIED for night; it comes — (*Pause. He corrects himself.*) It FALLS: now
cry in darkness. (*He repeats, chanting.*) You cried for night; it falls: now cry
in darkness. (83)

The object for which one cries may come, but the crying does not cease.
Caliban may dream and dream and dream again, but he will always
wake, and waking, weep. The *ambiguity* of Godot underscores the fact that
however mutable and variable are the objects of human longing, longing
itself remains an unalterable constant.

The three techniques discussed this far—omission, rejection, and ambivalence—share a common dynamic: each is a way of *underexposing* the intentional object in order to minimize its significance in the final picture. The same effect, however, may be achieved through *overexposure*; that is by *littering* the story with concrete objects. This fourth technique is implemented in *The Expelled*. Here, again, a single existential state is objectified: its theme is "man going in and coming out," or, if one prefers a less primitive rubric, "man alternating between security and insecurity," "man moving between the polar miseries of rest and restlessness." The hero's day begins with his forceful, head-first eviction from his residence, a phenomenon which, his comments suggest, has occurred with a certain regularity throughout his life: "It was neither the cradle nor the grave of anything whatever. Or rather it resembled so many other cradles, so many other graves, that I'm lost" (11). He then spends the day getting in and getting out of a horse-drawn cab and going in and coming out of apartments for rent. At evening, the cabman offers him a bed. He goes into the cabman's house. Soon discontented, he comes out of the cabman's house and goes into the cabman's stable. A short time later, he gets into the cab which is in the stable. He then gets out of the cab. Finally, at dawn, he expels himself from the stable: his posture recalls that of his initial eviction on the previous morning, for he exits head-first through the stable window. In this story, the *object* into which the character goes and out of which he comes is made irrelevant by the number of such objects: the object is lost in the *litter* of similar objects. Similarly, the *agent* of his eviction is irrelevant. Another artist might have concentrated on the "they" who forcefully expelled the hero at the story's opening; his theme would be "injustice" or "victimization." In *The Expelled*, the culpability of the "they" is undercut by the subsequent series of entrances and exits. As is made emphatic at the story's conclusion, if "they" don't evict him, he will evict himself—an act that demonstrates less the perversity of this particular character than the painful norm of all humanity. Again, whatever the variables of one's existence, one must necessarily, as the title of one play indicates, "Come and Go."

For Beckett, then, the intentional act is universal and absolute; the object, particular and relative. "Fear of x" and "fear of y" are essentially the same, for the essence of the composite act resides in the fearing rather than in the x or the y. Generic man fears; individual man fears x. Beckett, as shown above, makes emphatic the distinction between essential and non-essential by creating a world in which intentional objects, subject to authorial acts of *omission, rejection, equivocation,* and *alliteration,* have a relatively low survival rate. Furthermore, even those objects which do survive—and some must, a work wholly devoid of objects is an aesthetic impossibility—often do little more than survive; for Beckett frequently includes particular objects in a work while simultaneously neutralizing their effect, preventing their presence from endowing the character with any particularity. Two ways in which the author deprives the object of its "particularizing" function will be briefly examined.

The first technique manifests itself in the relationship between the heroes of two or more works. It there were no objects in the works, the heroes would lack any particularity; no hero would have a discrete, individual identity; each hero would be generic man; all heroes would be interchangeable. But there are some objects in the works; consequently, the objects should bestow individuality on the characters and afford a basis for differentiating one character from another. This law, qua law, tra la, is inoperable in Beckett: his treatment of the object often encourages us to identify one character with another, for there is a *standardization of object* from work to work. The heroes' psychic states are repeatedly defined in terms of a small number of recurring objects such as horizons, stars, flowers, bicycles, greatcoats, bowler hats, and boils. As this list suggests, Beckett's "standard objects" fall into two groups. Those in the first group are elemental: we immediately recognize them as the common property of all persons' subjective worlds. Those in the second group are eccentric: that they are idiosyncratic to Beckett's world only intensifies our awareness of their omnipresence throughout that world. Both universal phenomena and singular phenomena universalized contribute to Beckett's portrayal of generic man's subjective world.

The dynamic of this technique will be clarified by examining specific examples from *No's Knife*. Human beings remember; individual human beings may be differentiated by the x or the y that is the object of their remembering. In Beckett, however, a single x may be the object of two individuals' memory: the heroes of both *The Calmative* and *Texts for Nothing* I recall a tale about "Joe Breen or Breem." Again, all men experience antipathy. In Beckett, the x about which they feel antipathetic is standardized: the characters in both *The End* and *Enough* insist on their aversion to "looking back." In these and many similar instances, the identification of the two characters is explicit. Even more frequently, we experience only a momentary, fleeting impression that the character speaking has participated in the consciousness of a character previously encountered by the reader. When, for example, the hero of *The Calmative* says, "I saw on the horizon, where sky, sea, plain and mountain meet, a few low stars, not to be confused with the fires men light, at night, or that go alight alone" (34), we think momentarily of Murphy and Murphy's end, of Murphy who knew about stars and about fires that go alight alone. Our tendency to see part of each character reborn into the next character is encouraged by their professed familiarity with death: "Dying is such a long tiresome business I always found" (*Abandoned*, 143). In Beckett, reincarnation entails no complicated metaphysic: the person that dies and is reborn into each successive character is generic, an aggregate of intentional states compelled to love, hate, fear, and ache regardless of parochial contingencies of time and space. Beckett makes those temporal and spatial contingencies irrelevant to the reader by standardizing the world of objects from work to work.

Equally important is Beckett's second method of negating the specificity of specific details: the author selects particular objects that function as mirrors reflecting the universal condition itself. The most sustained instance of this technique is *Enough*, a seven-page story that makes the simple assertion, "men come together and go apart," "being human necessarily entails inevitable communion followed by inevitable separation." An examination of the story will demonstrate how consistently the narrative details mirror this one universal fact of human existence.

The narrator of *Enough* moves leisurely back and forth among three areas: his descriptions of his initial union with an aged man; his descriptions of their separation years later; and his descriptions of the interim between the two events, their "long outing" over flowered hills. The causal antecedents of their coming together and their going apart are buried in ambiguity: while, for example, the speaker attributes their separation to the old man's desire, the desire may have originated with the speaker himself, or with both characters, or with neither character:

> One day he told me to leave him. It's the verb he used. He must have been on his last legs. I don't know if by that he meant me to leave him for good or only to step aside a moment. I never asked myself the question. I never asked myself any questions but his. Whatever it was he meant I made off without looking back. Gone from reach of his voice I was gone from his life. Perhaps it was that he desired. There are questions you see and don't ask yourself. (153)

Here, as in *The Expelled*, the question of agency is ultimately silenced by the assurance of inevitability: "The art of combining is not my fault. It's a curse from above. For the rest [and the rest includes their separation] I would suggest not guilty" (154).[5]

Their initial union and final separation exist as a frame within which the phenomenon of union-division is continually reenacted. It is first made visible in their continual clasping and unclasping of hands:

> We advanced side by side hand in hand . . . Sometimes they let each other go. The clasp loosened and they fell apart. Whole minutes often passed before they clasped again. Before his clasped mine again. (154)

Within the single act of hand-clasping, union-division is recapitulated on a smaller scale: at times their hands clasp in naked intimacy; at times, though clasped, they are separated by cotton gloves. These physical acts of union-division have a verbal counterpart, for intervals of silent move-

ment through generic landscapes alternate with intervals of rest in which
the older man speaks to the younger:

> Sooner or later his foot broke away from the flowers and we moved on.
> Perhaps only to halt again after a few steps. So that he might say at last
> what was in his heart or decide not to say it again. (156)

Just as the presence or absence of gloves mirrors in miniature the larger
act of clasping and unclasping hands, so the substance of the verbal communications mirrors the act of alternating between speech and silence,
communication and non-communication:

> One day he halted and fumbling for his words explained to me that *anatomy
> is a whole.* (155, italics mine)

> But he wished everything to be heard including the ejaculations and *broken
> paternosters* that he poured out to the flowers at his feet. (155, italics mine)

"Anatomy," which in isolation connotes division and dissection, here has
for its predicate nominative the concept of wholeness: union is predicated
on separation. Conversely, "paternosters," which in isolation connotes
wholeness or integration, is here qualified by the concept of fragmenta-
tion. *Enough* is, then, iterative in form, for successive structural levels
objectify a single idea: first, there is the initial communion and final
separation; between these terminal acts, union-division is continually re-
enacted both physically and verbally; within the physical act and within
the verbal act, union-division again recurs in the presence or absence of
gloves and in the actual content of the speeches. One additional structural
manifestation of the idea is its explicit articulation at the story's center:

> Other main examples suggest themselves to the mind. Immediate continu-
> ous communication with immediate redeparture. Same thing with delayed
> redeparture. Delayed continuous communication with immediate redepar-
> ture. Same thing with delayed redeparture. Immediate discontinuous com-
> munication with immediate redeparture. Same thing with delayed redepar-
> ture. Delayed discontinuous communication with immediate redeparture.
> Same thing with delayed redeparture. (156, 157)

Here, as throughout Beckett, syntax reflects the structure of existence:
the fact of integration and disintegration remains absolute throughout
mutations of successive rephrasings, throughout mutations of time and
space.

The act of union-division, then, is visible in the large structural outlines
of the story. Within this framework, particular details function as mirrors,
momentarily deflecting our attention from the essential act, ultimately
reflecting the act itself. The act is, for example, mirrored in the characters'

preoccupation with its mathematical correlative, addition followed by subtraction, multiplication followed by division:

> We took flight in arithmetic. What mental calculations bent double hand in hand! Whole ternary numbers we raised in this way to the third power sometimes in downpours of rain. Graving themselves in his memory as best they could the ensuring cubes accumulated. In view of the converse operation at a later stage. When time would have done its work. (155)

> We did not keep tally of the days. If I arrive at ten years it is thanks to our podometer. Total milage divided by average daily milage. So many days. Divide. Such a figure the night before the sacrum. Such another the eve of my disgrace. Daily average always up to date. Subtract. Divide. (158–59)

The mathematical is mirrored in the physical: addition-subtraction is mirrored in the physical terrain, the alternation of hills and holes; multiplication-division, in the simultaneous doubling and halving of the characters' physical proportions. "Bent double heads touching silent hand in hand" (156); operation and converse operation, in the physical movement of characters against land, "The crest once reached alas the going down" (157). The mathematical and the physical are in turn reflected in the astronomical: "He said I had Aquaris hands. Its a mansion above" (154), a mansion symbolizing the dissolution of bonds. Finally, there is an explicit image of the universe as a mirror in which man examines the structure of his being:

> In order from time to time to enjoy the sky he resorted to a little round mirror. Having misted it with his breath and polished it on his calf he looked in it for the constellations. I have it! he exclaimed referring to the Lyre or the Swan. And often he added that the sky seemed much the same. (157)

The Lyre traditionally symbolizes cosmic unity and the Swan, death and separation born of unity attained, desire fulfilled. The astronomical, then, like the other planes of existence, here objectifies the forces of integration and disintegration. Despite the gentle ironies and ambiguities of the story, one essential fact of existence is continually objectified, reflected, and reclarified: total action reveals itself a multiple of a single act continually re-enacted; total imagery, a multiple of a single image of a single act continually re-enacted. In its insistent, reiterative clarification of the essential and its equally insistent dismissal of the non-essential, *Enough* is like its flowers: "It is only fair to say there was nothing to sweep away. The very flowers were stemless and flush with the ground like waterlilies. No brightening our buttonholes with these" (158). There is nothing superfluous.

Notes

1. Tom Driver, "Beckett by the Madeleine," *Columbia University Forum* (Summer, 1961), p. 23.

2. Samuel Beckett and Georges Duthuit, "Three Dialogues," in *Samuel Beckett: A Collection of Critical Essays*, ed. Martin Esslin (Englewood Cliffs, N.J., 1965), p. 21.

3. Samuel Beckett, "The Calmative," in *No's Knife* (London, 1967). References to Beckett's works as given in the text refer to the following editions: *Endgame* (New York, 1958); *Happy Days* (New York, 1961); *Waiting for Godot* (New York, 1954).

4. W. V. Quine, *The Ways of Paradox and Other Essays* (New York, 1966), p. 11.

5. Just as Beckett obscures the "why" of the union and separation, so he obscures the "who." In a letter, John Fletcher has alerted me to the intentional ambiguity of the narrator's sex: "In the definite French text in *Têtes-mortes* Beckett suppresses all verbal agreements which would designate the narrator as masculine or feminine. This is quite deliberate—the earlier version shows an agreement which he blurs later." The narrator, then, may be either man or woman and the love of the two characters, either homosexual or heterosexual. This instance of equivocation once more underscores Beckett's attempt to extract the universal from the distractions of the particular.

4

THE EXTERNAL REFERENT: HISTORY

Untransmissible History in Thackeray's *Henry Esmond*

> Yes, this is Vanity Fair; not a moral place certainly; nor a merry
> one, though very noisy. . . . But the general impression is one
> more melancholy than mirthful. When you come home, you sit
> down, in a sober, contemplative, not uncharitable frame of mind,
> and apply yourself to your books or your business.
>
> "Before the Curtain," *Vanity Fair*

Henry Esmond might have been called *Coming Home After the Fair*: its world differs from that of the fair not in the degree to which its values are fatuous but in the degree to which its fatuousness is funny. The tonal distance separating the two novels reflects the difference in narrative perspective: the man describing the world of Vanity Fair is characteristically an anonymous spectator; the man describing the world of Henry Esmond is Henry Esmond. The vanity that often intoxicates and amuses the first instills in the second sobriety and sadness. Only one can afford the bravado of satiric insight; the other, as he himself confesses, is not given to huzzas.

Like *Vanity Fair*, *Henry Esmond* is a sustained argument against the reality of moral absolutes. Esmond himself does much of the arguing. He is proficient at identifying illusory values and beliefs. His sophisticated scepticism, however, is itself founded on a dedication to one surviving absolute: truth. The very act of writing an autobiography assumes that the truth about oneself is able to be known and transmitted to others. For this particular autobiographer, the assumption is a studied conviction: throughout his memoirs, he continually alerts us to the pains he is taking to describe his world with an accuracy unaltered by beneficence. Esmond's belief in the reality of truth, however, is not shared by Thackeray. Early

101

in the novel occurs an incident in which several sermons are burned; the single passage surviving the fire warns of the disjunction between the tree of knowledge and the tree of life.[1] When the novel, like the fire, is spent, it is again this message that survives. While the narrator "has taken truth for his motto" (81), the author has taken the absence of truth for his theme.

Thackeray has endowed his trusting hero with a particular belief for the purpose of proving that belief untenable. His techniques will be examined in detail after first setting forth the specific definition of truth to which Esmond subscribes. A loyal heir of Cartesian enlightenment, Esmond rejects all authorities external to himself, trusting only his own perceptions. His random comments on truth consistently reveal his distrust of formal abstractions: social ceremony, political principle, religious doctrine, and aesthetic design are all dismissed as falsifications of the single knowable reality, the intimate thoughts and feelings of the individual. To this personal sphere he attributes an integrity as absolute as that which is traditionally, and erroneously, ascribed to canons and creeds: "Our great thoughts, our great affections, the truths of our life, never leave us. Surely they cannot separate from our consciousness, shall follow it whithersoever that shall go, and are of their nature divine and immortal" (383). In effect, Esmond denies the existence of an objective sphere of truth but affirms the existence of a subjective sphere of truth.

Esmond's concept of personal truth has as corollary the concept of personal history advocated in and exemplified by his memoirs. While *The History of Henry Esmond* is like all histories in its attempt to bestow on the future a knowledge of the past, here past and future belong to intimately related individuals: as Esmond emphasizes in periodic asides to his reader, his history records not the past life of the nation but his own private past; his history is to be read not by the public of an anonymous future but by his own private future, his grandsons (203, 267, 273, 350). Here, then, the unit of historical continuity is the family and the proper historical perspective, personal intimacy. If Esmond includes in his private memoirs public events and figures, it is because his life included a personal acquaintance with those events and figures, and he maintains the perspective of personal acquaintance when describing them. We see the part Steele played in Esmond's daily affairs, not Steele's contribution to mankind. We see the War of Spanish Succession only as a fragmented series of military incidents in which Esmond himself participated: he makes no attempt to formulate an objective overview summarizing or clarifying the pattern of issues and events. His portrait of Marlborough, he tells us, is shaped by his subjective response to the man rather than by an impartial, objective estimate of the man's career. In these and many other details, Esmond practices the belief announced in his preface, that a work of history is more valid when ceremony and formality are replaced with familiarity.

Esmond's narrative, then, offers subjective truth as an alternative to objective truth, subjective history as an alternative to objective history. But Esmond's narrative is not Thackeray's novel. Thackeray disables the narrative to demonstrate that personal truths are as elusive and illusory as the objective truths Esmond rejects. This chapter will examine the three basic verbal patterns through which this subversion is accomplished before showing similar patterns visible in the novel's larger structural elements.

I

The first verbal pattern is one that weakens, but does not necessarily destroy, the reader's confidence in subjective truth. Esmond has a peculiar habit of expression with which he inadvertently discredits the very world he wishes to praise. He consistently describes his private experiences in language borrowed from the formal doctrines he has ridiculed. For example, despite his professed hostility to certain religious mythologies (142, 200, 275, 335, 402), he invariably relies upon images from those mythologies when describing his beloved "saint," "goddess," and "angel," Rachel Castlewood. Significantly, those passages in which he scoffs at deities and those in which he deifies Rachel often occur in close succession:

> When [Esmond's] early credulity was disturbed and his saints and virgins taken out of his worship to a rank little higher than the divinities of Olympus, his belief became acquiescence rather than ardour. (104)

> It was [Rachel's] disposition to think kindnesses, and devise silent bounties, and to scheme benevolence for those about her. We take such goodness, for the most part, as if it was our due; the Marys who bring ointment for our feet get but little thanks. (105)

> . . .

> "Dearest saint [Rachel]" says [Esmond], "purest soul, that has had so much to suffer, that has blest the poor lonely orphan with such a treasure of love. 'Tis for me to kneel, not for you." (332)

> [Frank] reminded Colonel Esmond that he too was, by birth, of that church and that his mother and sister should have his lordship's prayers to the saints (an inestimable benefit, truly!) for their conversion. (335)

While a saint need not be a metaphysical reality to be an effective metaphor, Esmond unintentionally deprives sainthood of its metaphorical as well as metaphysical powers.[2] The Ptolemaic system, though itself untrue, can be used metaphorically to express the truth of a personal vision; but the Ptolemaic system will not be an effective metaphor if prefaced with disdainful comments on the idiocy of Ptolemy.

Esmond first divests a particular idiom of its original meaning and authority; he then calls upon the now weakened idiom to bestow meaning and authority on his private world. Brief examples from two additional vocabularies, the political and the aesthetic, will suggest Esmond's fondness for these weakened idioms. While Rachel is described in the language of deceased spiritual deities, Beatrix is described in the language of discarded political principles. In Esmond's estimation, the divine right doctrine—"that monstrous pedigree which the Tories chose to consider divine" (323)—is an arbitrary and empty claim, neither entitling a mortal to rule nor exempting a ruler from his mortality. Yet all that Beatrix is and is not, she is and is not by divine right. The idiom is used in a physical capacity: she is an "imperious beauty," a "lovely queenly creature" (383) who carries "her head with a toss of supreme authority" (362). The idiom is used in a psychological capacity: it explains "the conquering spirit which impels her" (389) as well as the eagerness of others to be conquered by that spirit. Most important, and most disturbing, the idiom is used in a moral capacity: it bestows privileges and immunities on one who, born to rule, "can neither help her beauty, nor her courage, nor her cruelty" (389). The vocabulary of divine right enables Esmond to translate her faults into signs of superior humanity:

> She never at that time could be brought to think but of the world and her beauty, and seemed to have no more sense of devotion than some people have of music, that cannot distinguish one air from another. Esmond saw this fault in her, as he saw many others—a bad wife would Beatrix Esmond make, he thought, for any man under the degree of a prince. She was born to shine in great assemblies, and to adorn palaces, and to command everywhere—to conduct an intrigue of politics or to glitter in a queen's train. (338)

While the idiom is compelling, it is also discomforting: Esmond's repeated insistence that a king is merely a man (17, 420) necessarily disrupts his attempt to convert a mere woman into a queen.

Again, Esmond convincingly demonstrates that whatever virtues reside in formal art, truth is not among them: his own elegy for Nancy Sieveright, he confesses, was inspired by the desire to write a Latin elegy rather than by a sense of loss at the young girl's death (94); the view of the war presented in Addison's "Campaign" is dictated more by the poem's genre than by the nature of the actual events (258, 260). In the opening passage of his memoirs, Esmond protests the inflated formality of dramatic and historical works, and promises that his own life story will be told in a style "familiar rather than heroic" (18). Despite these arguments, protests, and promises, Esmond calls upon a large number of biblical, mythological, and literary heroes, presumably to clarify "the truth" of his personal experiences. Each of the major participants in his life story is, in the course of the narrative, endowed with a repertoire of aesthetic antecedents. Aeneas, Ulysses, Hamlet, Macbeth, Othello, Oedipus, Orpheus, Diogenes, Esau, and Lazarus are a few of the figures to whom Esmond, sometimes facetiously but often soberly, compares Esmond. The discrepancy between his sceptical attitude toward formal art and his reliance on its allusive powers becomes even more emphatic when any one particular allusion is examined. On three separate occasions, for example, he satirizes the painting by Sir Peter Lely portraying Isabella Castlewood as the huntress Diana: if the aging dowager ever resembled the ageless nymph of mythology, time has falsified the relation, once more demonstrating the incompatibility of art and truth (20, 110, 186). Yet the same Esmond who prides himself on this satiric insight eagerly and innocently offers the reader a lengthy description of Beatrix in which he sincerely compares her to "the famous antique statue of the huntress Diana" (136, 137). The aesthetic vocabulary, like the political and religious, is called upon to express after having been deprived of its expressive potential.

Through these discredited metaphors, Thackeray invites us to witness the failure of Esmond's language to support his assertions: Esmond offers personal truth as an alternative to and asylum from the precarious instability of formal truths, but his reliance on the vocabulary of those formal truths arouses in us the suspicion that his subjective perceptions are equally precarious. This suspicion is amplified by the second, far more damaging way in which Thackeray incapacitates Esmond's narrative.

II

Through Thackeray's second technique, Esmond's narrative violates the primary criterion of subjective truth. If Esmond claimed to be the exponent of objective truth, if he claimed his memoirs were an objective record of public history, we might consult other historical records, check his chronology of battle dates, quarrel with his judgment of Marlborough (as did Winston Churchill[3]), and condemn as fantasy his portrait of the Stuart Pretender. External certification is, however, a wholly irrelevant measure of Esmond's truth: in subjective truth the source of consistency or stability resides not in the external object perceived but in the perceiver himself; consequently, the primary criterion of subjective truth is not external certification but internal consistency.

The claim of internal consistency is implicit in the two basic qualities Esmond attributes to his narrative perspective in the memoirs, stability and precision of perception. He has, at the time he is writing, a single stable overview of his life: he is narrating the events not as they occur but "in his old age, and at a distance" (273). This perspective carries with it the assurance of simplicity and serenity:

Now, at the close of his life, as he sits and recalls in tranquility . . . (78)

[Young Esmond was] of a hotter and more impetuous nature than now, when care, and reflection, and grey hairs have calmed him. (158)

We get to understand truth better, and grow simpler as we grow older. (94)

This narrative distance stabilizes his vision without diminishing its accuracy. Convinced that great significance often resides in apparent "trivialities" (92, 136), he demands that his history be precise and detailed in its descriptions: it is with a sense of self-obligation that he specifies the location of a smallpox scar on Rachel's forehead, the existence of a wart on the nose of an anonymous nun, or the occurrence of a dinner party "three days after the fifteenth of November, 1712" (379). According to Esmond, both the stability and the precision of his narrative perspective are made possible by the power of memory. His confidence in the permanence of memory is made explicit in continual, casual reassurances to the reader—

How those trivial incidents and words . . . remain fixed on the memory. (24)

He will remember to his life's end . . . (35)

I have good reason to remember it. (83)

He sees them now (will he ever forget them?). (102)

Esmond minds him well of the date. (379)

—and is made emphatic in studied declarations:

Our great thoughts, our great affections, the truths of our life, never leave us. Surely they cannot separate from our consciousness, shall follow it whithersoever that shall go, and are of their nature divine and immortal. (383)

We forget nothing. The memory sleeps but wakens again; I often think how it shall be when, after the last sleep of death, the *reveillée* shall arouse us forever, and the past in one flash of self-consciousness rush back, like the soul, revivified. (394)

The history of the changes and growth experienced by a young Esmond is, then, being told through the stable perspective of the aged Esmond who has, according to his own self portrait, a matured, fixed identity, an immutable core of remembered facts, feelings, and thoughts. This insistence on the accuracy and the stability of his narrative perspective contains the promise of an internally consistent work of history.

But Esmond's history does not fulfill the promise of internal consistency. Thackeray subverts the narrator's assumptions about subjective truth by allowing him to contradict himself incessantly: the trivial factual details to which Esmond assigns such significance, as well as the "great thoughts and affections" he believes "divine and immortal," tend to collapse in the course of the narrative. The novel is a tissue of small, almost imperceptible contradictions, each in isolation insignificant; collectively, devastating. This pattern of mutation will be demonstrated below with a handful of representative examples. "Truth," the word that tolls throughout Esmond's history, means "open to proof"; "truth" calls for a test.

Question 1: Esmond periodically describes the intricacies of his ancestral lineage. His paternal grandfather, Thomas Esmond, had two brothers. What were their names?[4]

Answer 1: Thomas Esmond had an elder brother, George, and a younger brother, "Francis, in holy orders, who was slain whilst defending the house of Castlewood against the Parliament, anno 1647." (26)

Answer 2: Thomas Esmond had an elder brother, George, and a younger brother, "Edward, who had embraced the ecclesiastical profession, was slain on Castlewood tower, being engaged there both as preacher and artilleryman." (18)

Question 2: As a young child, Henry Esmond lived at Castlewood with Isabella Esmond, Thomas Esmond, and Father Holt. During one period of political upheaval, the child was left at home alone. Was he made happy or sad by his separation from Father Holt?

Answer 1: The chapter devoted to this period (I, 4) opens with a description of young Henry's love for Father Holt, and continues: "After being at home for a few months in tranquility (if theirs might be called tranquility which was, in truth, a constant bickering) my lord and lady left the country for London, taking their director with them; and his little pupil scarce ever shed more bitter tears in his life than he did for nights after the first parting with his dear friend, as he lay in the lonely chamber next to that which the Father used to occupy." (43)

Answer 2: The same chapter (I, 4) concludes: "He liked the solitude of the great house very well; he had all the play-books to read, and no Father Holt to whip him, and a hundred childish pursuits and pastimes, without doors and within, which made this time very pleasant." (49)

Question 3: The first chapter of Esmond's memoirs describes the day on which Francis and Rachel Esmond take possession of the Castlewood estate, previously possessed by Thomas and Isabella. In what year does this event occur?[5]

Answer 1: 1691.

"When Francis, fourth Viscount Castlewood, came to his title, and presently after to take possession of his house of Castlewood, county Hants, in the year 1691, almost the only tenant of the place besides the domestics was a lad of twelve." (20)

Answer 2: 1690.

On the first day of his arrival at Castlewood, Francis mentions the present year when he describes his age in arithmetic riddle: "'I was but two years old [when the Roundheads attacked the clocktower],' says he, 'but take forty-six from ninety, and how old shall I be, kinsman Harry?'" (23)

Question 4: What is the age difference between Esmond and Rachel's son, Frank?

Answer 1: On the day Harry Esmond first meets Rachel's family, Harry is "a lad of twelve years of age" and Frank is "a child of two years old." (21, 23)

Answer 2: "Harry Esmond, who was [Frank's] tutor and eight years his little lordship's senior, had hard work sometimes to keep his own temper and hold his authority over his rebellious little chief and kinsman." (99)

Question 5: Esmond frequently interrupts the flow of the narrative to share with us his vivid memory of physical details, often the details of a beloved person's beauty. At the time the boy Esmond was tutoring the child Beatrix, what color was Beatrix's hair?

Answer 1: "He sees them now (will he ever forget them?) as they used to sit together of the summer evenings—the two golden heads over the page—the child's little hand and the mother's beating the time, with their voices rising and falling in unison." (102)

Answer 2: "And Harry remembered all his life after how he saw his mistress at the window looking out on him, in a white robe, the little Beatrix's chestnut curls resting at her mother's side." (109)

Question 6: Esmond lived his adolescence at Castlewood with Francis and Rachel Esmond. According to Rachel, was it she or her husband who insisted that the child share their home?

Answer 1: "'You were but an orphan child when I first saw you—when *he* [Francis] first saw you, who was so good, and noble, and trusting. He would have had you sent away, but like a foolish woman I besought him to let you stay.'" (170)

Answer 2: "'I always thought . . . that 'twas a pity to shut you out from the world. You would but have pined and chafed at Castlewood, and 'tis better you should make a name for yourself. I often said so to my dear lord. How he loved you! 'Twas my lord that made you stay with us.'" (214)

Question 7: How long prior to his death did Francis Esmond know Henry Esmond was the legitimate heir to the Castlewood titles?

Answer 1: A few months.
"The late lord, my dear patron, knew not the truth until a few months before his death, when Father Holt brought the news to him." (188)

Answer 2: Two years.
"It appeared from my poor lord's hurried confession that he had been made acquainted with the real facts of the case only two years since, when Mr. Holt visited him." (195)

Answer 3: One year.
Rachel quoting Isabella: "'And a proof of this is that a year before your husband's death, when he thought of taking a place under the Prince of Orange, Mr. Holt went to him, and told him what the state of the matter was.'" (331)

Answer 4: Four years.
According to one of Esmond's versions of Francis's dying confession (197), Father Holt's crucial visit was made at the time Sir John Fenwick's conspiracy blew up, an event which occurred in December 1696 (124, 125, 127). Francis Esmond died in October 1700 (155). So the period must have been almost exactly four years.

Question 8: During which campaign, did Esmond serve under General Lumley?

Answer 1: Vigo Bay Campaign, 1702.

Describing the events immediately following the Vigo Bay Campaign, Esmond tells us: "And Esmond, giving up his post of secretary to General Lumley, whose command was over, and parting with that officer with many kind expressions of goodwill on the general's side, had leave to go to London to see if he could push his fortunes any way further." (205)

Answer 2: Blenheim Campaign, 1704.

Describing the events immediately prior to the Blenheim campaign, Esmond tells us: "[Esmond] went immediately and paid his court to his new general, General Lumley, who received him graciously, having known his father, and also, he was pleased to say, having had the very best accounts of Mr. Esmond from the officer whose aide-de-camp he had been at Vigo." (234)

Question 9: After Francis Esmond dies, Rachel and Henry undergo a long period of estrangement, a period that begins with Esmond's imprisonment in Newgate and ends shortly after his participation in the Vigo expedition. An entire chapter, "The Twenty-Ninth December," is devoted to the day of their dramatic reconciliation at Winchester Cathedral. Both Rachel and Esmond find the timing of the event particularly significant. How many years have elapsed during their separation? What is the date on which the reconciliation takes place? At what time of day does it occur?

Part A: How many years have elapsed?

Answer 1: According to the characters' verbal statements, *one year* has elapsed. Esmond says, "The year of grief and estrangement was over" (213). Rachel says, "But last year we did not drink [to your birthday] — no, no. My lord was cold, and my Harry was likely to die, and my brain was in a fever, and we had no wine." (216)

Answer 2: According to a comparison of the two dates on which the separation and reunion occur, *two years* have elapsed: Esmond was imprisoned in October 1700 (155), and it is presently December, 1702 (227).

Answer 3: According to a comparison of Esmond's respective ages, *three years* have elapsed; when imprisoned Esmond was twenty-two (174); prior to his return to Rachel, he is twenty-five (209).

Part B: We know that the reconciliation itself occurs in December. According to Rachel, is it before or after Christmas?

Answer 1: *After.*

"'Do you know what day it is?' [Rachel] continued. 'It is the twenty-ninth of December — it is your birthday!'" (216)

Answer 2: *Before.*

"'I cannot follow [my children] into the great world, where their way lies — it scares me. They will come and visit me; and you will, sometimes, Henry — yes, sometimes, as now, in the Holy Advent season, when I have seen and blessed you once more.'" (217)[6]

Part C: At what time of day does their reconciliation occur?

Answers: Before Esmond even enters the cathedral, he tells us: "The organ was playing, the winter's day was already growing grey, as he passed under the street-arch into the cathedral-yard and made his way into the ancient solemn edifice" (211). It is not until after the evening prayers and a "rather long" anthem that Rachel looks up and sees Esmond. Describing that moment later, Rachel says: "I looked up from the book and saw you. I was not surprised when I saw you. I knew you would come, my dear, and saw the gold sunshine round your head" (216).

Question 10: How was Esmond's play, *The Faithful Fool*, received by Rachel and its audience?

Answer 1: "Mr. Henry Esmond remained in his sickroom, where he wrote a fine comedy that his mistress pronounced to be sublime and that was acted no less than three successive nights in London in the next year." (322).

Answer 2: "But it must be owned that the audience yawned through the play and that it perished on the third night, with only half a dozen persons to behold its agonies. Esmond and his two mistresses came to the first night, and Miss Beatrix fell asleep, whilst her mother, who had not been to a play since King James the Second's time, thought the piece, though not brilliant, had a very pretty moral." (344).

Question 11: Was Frank Esmond wounded at Ramillies?

Answer 1: "I remember at Ramillies, when [Frank] was hit and fell, a great big red-haired Scotch sergeant flung his halbert down, burst out a-crying like a woman, seizing him up as if he had been an infant and carrying him out of the fire." (225)

Answer 2: In that part of Esmond's narrative specifically devoted to Ramillies, he tells us "if he had any anxiety about his boy 'twas relieved at once" (266) that evening, for he finds Frank singing, drinking, and enriched with booty looted during the day's battle. Esmond concludes, "Far more pleasant to him than the victory [of Ramillies], though for that too he may say *meminisse juvat*, it was to find that the day was over and his dear young Castlewood was unhurt" (267).

Question 12: Dick Steele was only four years old when his father died. According to Steele, did he at that early age experience grief or was he oblivious to the death?

Answer 1: "'That was the first sensation of grief,' Dick said, 'I ever knew. I remember I went into the room where his body lay and my mother sat weeping beside it. I had my battledore in my hand and fell a-beating the coffin and calling papa, on which my mother caught me in her arms and told me in a flood of tears papa could not hear me and would play with me no more, for they were going to put him under ground, whence he could never come to us again. And this,' said Dick kindly, 'has made me pity all children ever since, and caused me to love thee, my poor fatherless, motherless lad.'" (74)

Answer 2: "' . . . (grief touches the young but lightly, and I remember I beat a drum at the coffin of my own father) . . . '" (181)

Question 13: According to Esmond, is a person's suffering greatest before, during, or after the painful event? That is, is the anticipation of pain, the immediate experience of pain, or the memory of pain the most difficult to endure? (In all three passages, the painful event referred to is the loss of a mistress.)

Answer 1: The memory of pain is more painful than the immediate experience.

"You do not know how much you suffer in those critical maladies of the heart until the disease is over and you look back on it afterwards. During the time, the suffering is at least sufferable." (176)

Answer 2: The immediate experience of pain is far more painful than the memory.

"Wounds heal rapidly in a heart of two and twenty, hopes revive daily, and courage rallies in spite of a man. Perhaps as Esmond thought of his late despondency and melancholy and how irremediable it had seemed to him as he lay in his prison a few months back, he was almost mortified in his secret mind at finding himself so cheerful." (202)

Answer 3: The anticipation of pain is worse than the immediate experience.

"From the loss of a tooth to that of a mistress there's no pang that is not bearable. The apprehension is much more cruel than the certainty; and we make up our mind to the misfortune when 'tis irremediable, part with the tormentor, and mumble our crust on t'other side of the jaws." (361)

Question 14: Esmond never wins Beatrix. Does he ever outgrow his love for her?

Answer 1: "Her cheek was desecrated, her beauty tarnished; shame and honour stood between it and him. The love was dead within him; had she a crown to bring him with her love, he felt that both would degrade him." (454)

"As [Esmond] looked at her, he wondered that he could ever have loved her. His love of ten years was over; it fell down dead on the spot, at the Kensington Tavern, where Frank brought him the note out of *Eikun Basilikum*. The Prince blushed and bowed low, as she gazed at him, and quitted the chamber. I have never seen her from that day." (459)

Answer 2: "I invoke that beautiful spirit from the shades and love her still; or rather I should say such a past is always present to a man; such a passion once felt forms a part of his whole being and cannot be separated from it." (383)

Question 15: While it is difficult to know with any certainty whether or not Esmond's love for Beatrix dies when he reads her note contained in the *Eikun Basilikum*, we do at least know that he reads her note contained in the *Eikun Basilikum*. Where is Esmond when he receives and reads the note?

Answer 1: In that passage of the memoirs specifically devoted to a description of Frank's delivery of the note, Esmond twice tells us that the event occurs in a tavern called the King's Arms. (449, 451)

Answer 2: "[His love] fell down dead on the spot, at the Kensington Tavern, where Frank brought him the note out of *Eikun Basilikum*." (459)

Throughout the novel, a fact given is a fact that will be repeated, and repeated, contradicted.[7] Thackeray's technique, and its intended effect on the reader, are clarified when contrasted with the approach of Samuel

Beckett, another writer who uses contradictions to make visible the instability of truth. Moran's narrative in *Molloy* begins: "It is midnight. The
rain is beating on the windows." It ends: "Then I went back into the house
and wrote, It is midnight. The rain is beating on the windows. It was not
midnight. It was not raining."[8] The final sentence cancels out the first
and, by implication, all that follows the first: we are given a simple instruction to erase from our minds all we have read. The life span of
particular details is even shorter in *Texts for Nothing* where individual
sentences are immediately self-cancelling: "Suddenly, no at last . . . " (I);
"This evening, I say this evening, perhaps it's morning . . . " (IV); "Dry
it's possible, or wet . . . " (II).[9] For Beckett's narrators, the instability of
truth is a self-evident given of reality; consequently, the contradictions
are presented in overt declarations; they are made immediately accessible
to the reader's attention.

The contradictions in *Henry Esmond* are not part of Esmond's overt,
surface narrative but, rather, part of Thackeray's subversive counternar-
rative. While Thackeray necessarily intends the reader to recognize them,
the mode of recognition required is not the overt, self-conscious act expected of Beckett's reader; they are carefully chosen to disorient and discomfort the reader without necessarily enabling one to specify the source
of discomfort. Thackeray relies on two major factors to obscure the errors.
The first is their location. As was evident in the series of quotations given
above, the two terms of each contradiction are separated by anywhere
from one to several hundred pages of intervening material, a separation
that invariably interferes with our ability to recognize the error. A rare
instance in which both terms of the contradiction occur within a single
sentence will make visible two additional aspects of location that typically
come into play. The contradicted fact is seldom the major clause of the
sentence; it is usually a qualifying phrase embedded deep within the complex sentence structure of Esmond's prose:

> The French began the action, as usual, with a cannonade which lasted three
> hours, when they made their attack, advancing in twelve lines, four of Foot
> and four of Horse, upon the Allied troops in the wood where we were
> posted. (290)

Obscured by its subordinate position in the sentence, the contradiction is
further obscured by the nature of the surrounding subject matter: the
sentence just cited occurs in the fourth of four successive, short paragraphs
which contain a total of twenty-one numbers, numbers which blunt our
sensitivity to Esmond's erroneous computation.[10] The oblique presentation of the contradiction, then, prevents it from being noticed by the
reader; it does not, however, prevent it from affecting the reader. While
we will probably not stop and consciously acknowledge the incompatibility
of "twelve lines" and "four of Foot and four of Horse," neither will we

have a visual image of the battle formation used in the French attack. While, in turn, we will probably not notice our inability to grasp this one isolated image, we will begin to notice that, despite the aura of precision in Esmond's descriptions, we have very few coherent impressions of the world he is describing. So much for logistics.

The second major factor that obscures the contradictions is their asymmetry. Beckett's contradictions are conspicuous not only because of their direct presentation but also because the contradictions themselves are symmetrical: they consist of antithetical pairs such as raining-not raining, evening-morning, suddenly-at last. A small percentage of Thackeray's are equally symmetrical — Frank is both wounded at Ramillies and not wounded at Ramillies (Question 11 above) — and are only made inconspicuous by the oblique mode of presentation. But the majority fall into two classes characterized by different degrees of asymmetry. Those in the first class consist of pairs whose terms, though not strict symmetrical opposites, are mutually exclusive: Esmond throughout his memoirs reckons his age on the birth year of 1679 (20, 138, *passim*) yet without hesitation or qualification relays to the reader Father Holt's description of his birth a few weeks after his parents' marriage in 1677 (197, 275, 276). The more the terms of a contradiction approximate each other while yet remaining contradictory, the more difficult it is to identify the contradiction. It is this phenomenon which makes the contradictions in the second group far more obscure than those in the first. They constitute a class exemplified by Beatrix's golden and chestnut hair (Question 5 above). The discrepancy between the two colors is too small to strike the reader as a contradiction; yet golden and chestnut, while neither symmetrical opposites (white and black) nor even mutually exclusive alternatives (golden and black), are facts which fail to coincide, reinforce, and substantiate each other and, therefore, facts which deprive us of a coherent visual image, facts which undermine our stable participation in the narrative.

The complexity of this second form of mutation is evident in Esmond's references to music:

1. "And Mr. Holt found that Harry could read and write and possessed the two languages of French and English very well; and when he asked Harry about singing, the lad broke out with a hymn to the tune of Dr. Martin Luther, which set [the Catholic] Mr. Holt a-laughing." (35)
2. "[Rachel's] songs did not amuse [her husband], and she hushed them and the children when in his presence. My lord sat silent at his dinner, drinking greatly, his lady opposite to him, looking furtively at his face, though also speechless." (97)
3. "[Beatrix] sang sweetly, but this was from her mother's teaching — not Harry Esmond's, who could scarce distinguish between 'Greensleeves' and 'Lillibullero.'" (102)
4. "Beatrix could sing and dance like a nymph. Her voice was her father's delight after dinner." (122)

5. "Why did [Beatrix's] voice thrill in his ear so? She could not sing near so well as Nicolini or Mrs. Tofts; nay, she sang out of tune, and yet he liked to hear her better than St. Cecilia." (301)
6. "The song yet lay on the harpsichord which Esmond had writ and [Beatrix and Esmond] had sung together." (313)
7. "Mr. Esmond whistled 'Lillibullero,' at which Teague's eyes began to twinkle." (325)
8. "[Beatrix] never at that time could be brought to think but of the world and her beauty, and seemed to have no more sense of devotion than some people have of music, that cannot distinguish one air from another." (338)
9. "[Beatrix] set up a school of children and taught singing to some of them. We had a pair of beautiful old organs in Castlewood Church, on which she played admirably, so that the music there became to be known in the country for many miles round, and no doubt people came to see the fair organist as well as to hear her." (395)

Each of these quotations either states or implies something about the musical ability of Esmond or Beatrix. When read serially, they do not appear strikingly incompatible. Each, however, is slightly out of phase with those it follows, preventing the emergence of any single coherent picture. The fifth reference, when read in isolation, suggests that Esmond's musical acumen surpasses Beatrix's: she sings out of tune; his ear is sensitive enough to detect her faulty intonation and to appraise her talent in relation to a second singer. The third reference is an inversion of the fifth: here Esmond credits Beatrix with the ability to sing and confesses that he himself is tone deaf. The fifth and third are, then, when each is read in isolation, contradictory. When read in conjunction, however, they are strangely compatible: the answer to Esmond's question "Why did her voice thrill in his ear so?" is that an out-of-tune voice is resonating in a tone-deaf ear. The third and the fifth references are, in turn, contradicted by the sixth and the ninth: Esmond's formerly tone-deaf ear now enables him not simply to sing but to compose music; Beatrix's formerly absent musical talent now enables her to teach singing (the power of teaching is specifically denied to the tone deaf in the third) and endows her with a proficiency on the organ admired "for many miles round." Even the more neutral statements, those which neither credit nor discredit the characters, lose their neutrality when juxtaposed with other statements: the seventh reference, for example, would be simply a neutral description of an event were it not that the anonymous Irish stranger immediately recognizes Esmond's rendition of the very song Esmond has earlier named to illustrate his inability to carry a tune. While the quotations collectively credit Beatrix and Esmond with a spectrum of musical talent that ranges from poor to distinguished, the mutation from one statement to the next is almost imperceptible. The method of contradiction is not, therefore, one which invites us to keep tally of the inversions during the process of reading; it is, however, one which ensures that we will emerge from the novel with little or no idea of the characters' musical abilities.

The instability of Esmond's world, and the discomfort that instability instills in the reader, cannot be demonstrated with any single instance of contradiction. Contradiction, in this novel, is never an instance, self-contained and isolated; it is a process, relentless and multidimensional. While all the aforementioned contradictions are occurring, the English victory at Lille, achieved over an enemy "six or seven times greater" (288), is achieved over an enemy "five times" greater (291); the estrangement of Strephon and Cloe, a psychological separation for which neither is exclusively to blame (97), is blamed exclusively on Strephon's physical brutality (119); Sir John Fenwick, executed for his participation in the conspiracy of 1691 (64), is executed for his participation in the conspiracy of 1695 (124); the memory of Nancy Sievewright, filling Esmond with gentle respect for the surprising strength of first love and its "magnetic attraction which draws people together from ever so far" (83, 84), provokes Esmond to an impatient dismissal of first love whose "passions . . . are mostly abortive and are dead almost before they are born" (94); and, far from finally, throughout all this, Esmond is faithfully served by his boyhood friend and lifelong manservant, Job Lockwood, Tom Lockwood, Jack Lockwood, and John Lockwood (49, 344, 357, 242).

While it would be neither possible nor enlightening to enumerate endlessly all instances of contradiction, a crucial part of the novel, not part of the narrative proper, has so far been ignored. Esmond's memoirs are accompanied by his daughter's introductory preface and footnotes appended by his wife, his daughter, and his grandsons. Esmond, as mentioned previously, conceives of the family as the unit of historical continuity: he not only wants to tell the truth about his past; he wants the truth told about his past to be understood by his family. The preface and footnotes provide a measure of the extent to which that desire is fulfilled. As the following examples suggest, the family provides historical continuity only in perpetuating Esmond's custom of contradiction.

1. Despite Esmond's frequent references to his own act of narration, it is difficult to determine the precise time at which he is writing. Most of his comments suggest that he is old, so old that he considers death imminent: "Esmond could repeat to his last day . . . " (94); "To the very last hour of his life, Esmond remembered . . . " (21); "Now, at the close of his life . . . " (78). One particular statement, "My years are past the Hebrew poet's limit" (375), an allusion to Psalm 90 where man's terminal age is given as three score and ten, reveals that *Esmond's age is at least 70 and the date, at least 1750.*

A second set of comments, however, suggests that *Esmond is writing in his early 60s during the early 1740s*; he tells us he is writing 40 years after the Vigo Campaign of 1702 (202); at a later point in the memoirs, he tells us it is 40 years after the Blenheim Campaign of 1704 (383); and still later, he mentions that it is presently 27 years after the political conspiracy of 1714 (402). (While all three comments refer to the early 1740s, the sequence is disconcerting: as the memoirs progress, the year progresses from 1742 to 1744 and then moves back to 1741.)

The contradiction is compounded rather than resolved by information provided in the preface and footnotes. According to Rachel Warrington's preface, Esmond's wife died in 1736 (viii). Presumably his wife was alive during the writing of the memoirs since she has appended footnotes (e.g., 315, 435). Consequently a third set of figures emerges: *Esmond is writing in the early 1730s and is in his early 50s.*

2. According to the chronology given in Rachel Warrington's preface, her two sons were born either after their grandmother died or, at most, six months prior to her death (viii, ix). A footnote written by one of the grandsons, however, indicates that he and his brother were at least several years old before their grandmother died: "And our grandmother used to tell us children . . . " (296).

3. Esmond is, for Esmond, consistent in his condemnation of war's invariably base brutality (238, 266, 287, 321), a brutality so indiscriminate that it makes a mockery of victory celebrations, converts *Te Deum* into a "woeful and dreary satire" (321), and reduces "God is on our side" proclamations into revelations of ignorance. Yet when, lamenting the continual deaths of young soldiers, Esmond exclaims, "What must have been the continued agonies of fears and apprehensions which racked the gentle breasts of wives and matrons in those dreadful days" (315), Rachel responds in an indignant footnote, "What indeed? Psm. XCI: 2, 3, 7" (315). The final verse of the reference reads, "A thousand shall fall at thy side, and ten thousand at thy right hand, *but* it shall not come nigh thee." Thackeray lets Rachel miss the point of Esmond's arguments concerning the true nature of war.

4. Describing Rachel Esmond's complexion after the smallpox epidemic, Esmond writes, "When the marks of the disease cleared away, they did not, it is true, leave furrows or scars on her face (except one, perhaps, on her forehead over her left eyebrow); but the delicacy of her rosy colour and complexion were gone" (92). Rachel Warrington writes in her preface, "My dear mother possessed to the last an extraordinary brightness and freshness of complexion; nor would people believe that she did not wear rouge" (ix).

5. In one of Esmond's passages announcing his allegiance to truth he writes that "he would have his grandsons believe or represent him

to be not an inch taller than Nature has made him" (80). In compli-
ance with the letter rather than the spirit of Esmond's words, Rachel
Warrington notes in her preface that her father "was of rather low
stature, not being above five feet seven inches in height" (viii). But
she misunderstands the spirit of his request, for she goes on to speak
of him in unmeasured praise: she says that he was unequalled in
"grace and majesty of deportment" except by Washington (viii) and
asks, "They say he liked to be first in his company, but what company was there in which he would not be first?" (x).

6. In describing the battle of Ramillies (1706), Esmond praises Marlborough's "intrepid skill" and calls him "the very genius of victory"
   (264). In describing the siege of Lille (1708) Esmond confesses his
   suspicion that Marlborough received a treasonous bribe immediately prior to the battle (287, 288). In a footnote, Esmond's grandson
   tells us of his grandfather's conviction that Marlborough received a
   treasonous bribe immediately prior to the battle of Ramillies (296).

One imagines Esmond's memoirs passed down endlessly from era to era,
with each generation appending its own footnotes, contributing its own
layer of contradiction, compounding the confusion until the last semblance of stability disintegrates. Transmissibility is a key concern. By including prefaces and footnotes, Thackeray does not merely question transmissibility but illustrates its half-life.

This sustained rhythm of statement and counter-statement systemati-
cally erodes the world Esmond is laboring to preserve. The following
section will focus on Thackeray's precise use of language and demonstrate
that the same instability characterizing sets of sentences is visible in individual words and images. Esmond cannot, as he hopes, preserve his world
by committing it to the written word, for the instability is inherent in the
structure of language itself.

III

Typically when a writer reiterates a particular word or image throughout
a work, he limits and controls its connotations, endowing it with a central
core of meaning which, while gaining weight and resonance, remains
essentially stable throughout successive repetitions. The image becomes
not only a vehicle of meaning but a vehicle of stability: in the underlying
coherence of its iterations, it functions as a structural or unifying element
in the work. In *Henry Esmond* the opposite holds. Denying the possibility
that anything possesses an essential or fixed identity, Thackeray endows a
given image with as many disparate connotations as possible, intentionally
depriving it of a stable core of meaning. His imagery becomes a vehicle

of instability, undermining rather than contributing to the structural coherence of the narrative.

Earlier this essay alluded to the incident in which a fire burns a sheaf
of papers, leaving unburned a single passage warning of the disjunction
between life and truth (66). Thackeray's treatment of fire is consonant
with this message, for the image recurs incessantly, its meaning changing
with each new appearance. In the following passage, for example, fire
first embodies the idea of success and then the idea of failure:

> [Addison] was bringing out his own play of *Cato* at the time, the *blaze* of
> which quite extinguished Esmond's farthing candle [his play, *The Faithful
> Fool*]; and his name was never put to the piece, which was printed as by a
> Person of Quality. Only nine copies were sold, though Mr. Dennis, the
> great critic, praised it and said 'twas a work of great merit; and Colonel
> Esmond had the whole impression *burned* one day in a rage, by Jack Lock-
> wood, his man. (344, italics added)

Often, as in this instance, the connotations are paired by antithesis: the
positive and the negative, here success and failure, cancel each other out.
More often, however, even the logic of antithesis is abandoned: in the
majority of passages Thackeray simply moves rapidly and arbitrarily from
one connotation to a second to a third, allowing each to replace the one it
follows until replaced by the one it precedes, thereby preventing the image
from acquiring any solidarity of meaning:

> "*Fire! Fire!*" cries out Father Holt, sending another shot after the trooper.
> . . . "The poor gentleman's horse was a better one than that I rode," *Blaise*
> continues. . . . He read that to himself, which only said, "*Burn* the papers
> in the cupboard, *burn* this. You know nothing about anything." (59, italics
> added)

> "Here is a paper whereon his Majesty hath deigned to commence some
> verses in honour, or dishonour of Beatrix. Here is 'Madame' and '*Flamme*,'
> 'Cruelle' and 'Rebelle,' and 'Amour' and 'Jour,' in the royal writing and
> spelling." . . . "Sir," says the Prince, *burning* with rage. . . . And taking the
> *taper* up and backing before the Prince with very great ceremony, Mr.
> Esmond passed into the little chaplain's room. . . . And as Esmond spoke
> he set the papers *burning* in the brazier. (457, italics added)

As these passages suggest, the creation of a self-effacing image requires
that a given image be repeated as frequently as possible while any given
meaning be repeated as infrequently as possible. This effect of image
scattering can be most quickly apprehended with a catalogue enumerating
the divergent meanings assigned to fire. It is not the particular meanings
themselves, but their number and range that make visible the absence of
a stable center in the connotative activity of the image:

1. Fire as success: "'tis not a masterpiece of wit, but Dick is a good fellow, though he doth not set the Thames on fire" (261, see 344). The expression, "set the Thames on fire," here used metaphorically, is later used in a strictly literal capacity (378).
2. Fire as failure: "Here it was her ladyship's turn to shriek, for the captain, with his fist shaking the pillows and bolsters, at last came to 'burn,' as they say in the play of forfeits" (63, see 344).
3. Fire revealing: "As characters written with a secret ink come out with the application of fire and disappear again and leave the paper white so soon as it is cool . . . " (445).
4. Fire concealing: The burning of conspirational notes, deathbed confessions, marriage certificates, birth certificates (50, 59, 165, 439, 457). Occasionally the same fire simultaneously reveals and conceals. The fire that burns Francis Esmond's dying confession simultaneously illuminates an allegorical mosaic over the fireplace. However, the revealed allegory returns us to the idea of concealing; for it pictures "Jacob in hairy gloves cheating Isaac of Esau's birthright" (166).
5. Fire as agent of illegality: The burning of documents, see above.
6. Fire as agent of legality: "The sentence, as we all know, in these cases is that the culprit lies a year in prison, or during the King's pleasure, and is burned in the hand" (173).
7. Fire coupled with genius: "The fire and genius, perhaps, he had not (that were given to baser men), but except these he had some of the best qualities of a leader" (401).
8. Fire as beauty: "Esmond looked at Beatrix, blazing with her jewels on her beautiful neck" (415, see 36).
9. Fire as disease: "The St. Anthony's fire broke out on the royal legs" (425). "Your lordship would be much better if you took off all that flannel—it only serves to inflame the toe" (147). While the passages coupling fire with disease focus on the feet, "the fire of the Foot" (288) refers to the gunfire of the infantry.
10. Fire as security: The domesticity and safety implicit in the fireside hearth (84, 85, 118, 140, 141). While the fireside hearth usually connotes comfort and safety, several incidents emphasize its perils: "I daren't leave the child lest he should fall into the fire" (378, see 126).
11. Fire as danger: The guns of war. Book II, *passim*. In contrast to the "seriousness" inherent in the destructive fires of war, there is also the destructive fire of caprice: among the schoolboy pranks which eventually result in Frank's expulsion from Cambridge is his attempt to "set fire to Nevil's Court" (248).
12. Fire as mortal passion: Anger and desire: "With her illness and altered beauty my lord's fire for his wife disappeared" (121); "Hot as a flame at this salute" (369); "Cries the doctor in a great fume"

(378); "A burning blush flushed over her whole face" (385); "Burning with rage" (457).

13. Fire as immortality: Fire as a test of sainthood (69).

    Fire as punishment of hell (330).

    Fire of sacred love: "From that day until now, and from now till death is past, and beyond it, he prays that sacred flame may ever burn" (234, see 120).

14. Fire as flame, the color: "Flame-coloured brocade" (38).

    Fire as flame, a lamp: "There were flambeaux in the room lighting up the brilliant mistress of it" (385).

15. Fire in the names of unrelated people and places: Blaise, Tyburn, Ashburnam, Halifax, Firebrace, Boyle; and to add fuel to the fire, Castlewood, Lockwood, Marwood, Harwood, Rookwood, Woodstock, Holt, Berwick, Fenwick, Lodwick, Lowick, Warwick, and Hampton Wick.

This constant, deliberate mutation of meaning argues that truth, which posit the existence of a stable core of meaning, is an *ignis fatuus*.

Fire is not the sole instance of the self-effacing image. Equally unstable, for example, is the idea of the connective bond, its most positive connotations always threatening to collapse into its most negative. The dissonant images that spin forth from the idea include the household head's "purse strings" (31), the child's "lines for eels" (49), the coquet's "nets and baits" (341), the priest's "authority to bind and to loose" (218), the "mother's apron strings" (128), the domineering wife's "leading strings" (391), ornaments connoting love or attachment such as a "string of diamonds," a locket, a velvet bracelet, and a gold button from a military jacket (368, 164, 396, 463), "matrimonial chains" (399), an impotent religious medal (200), the honorable order of the "Garter" (361), the "garter" with which one hangs oneself (421), the rope with which one is hanged (20), colorful ribbons adorning a young girl's beauty (219), military ribbons connoting honor (359), military ribbons connoting dishonor (267), ribbons designating royalty (458), the silk-weaving profession of Henry's foster parents (277), beautiful tapestries (37), "spun smocks" as an image of demeaning servility (375), hair woven together as an image of family intimacy and affection (409), the "web" of bedding (409), the "web of coquetry" (351), the "snare" of deceit (456), Ealing, Bates, Knightsbridge, Tunbridge, Brace, Bracegirdle, Armstrong, Cheyne, Lock, Lockit, Lockwood, Scurlock, Bullock, Button, and Webb.

In contrast to the complexity of these images, there are also much simpler manifestations of the instability of words.[11] The image of the rose is made an ineffective vehicle of meaning by its indiscriminate application to such diverse figures as Rachel (92, 181, 219, 355), Beatrix (136, 221, 454), Isabella (30, 306), Nancy Sievewright (93), Rosamond, the tipsy painted mistress of Francis (100), Rosaria, the "country lass endowed with every virtue" in Esmond's play (344), the "Rose," a London tavern (159, 209), and the *Rose*, a Spanish ship (226). Again, honorific titles such as "his Majesty," "my lord," "my mistress," and "our general" are deprived of single, stable referents: during the course of the narrative each is given so many antecedents that in any given instance it is often not immediately clear about whom Esmond is speaking. For example, describing the events which occur on the night Francis dies defending his wife's honor, Esmond writes, "My lord had a paper of oranges, which he ate and offered to the actresses, joking with them" (160). While "My lord" may refer to Francis Esmond, it may instead refer to "my lord the Earl of Warwick and Holland," mentioned in the sentence immediately preceding the sentence cited; then again, it may refer to "my Lord Mohun," mentioned in the sentence immediately following the sentence cited. As a result, the reader can never know whether or not Frank busied himself flirting on the night of his fatal mission. In addition to single words, images, and titles, many multi-word expressions are also deprived of meaning by their occurrence in two or more dissonant contexts. At one point in the narrative, Esmond announces:

> Now it was, after this, that Lord Castlewood *swore his great oath* that he would never, so help him Heaven, be engaged in any transaction against that brave and merciful man [King William]; and so he told Holt when the indefatigable priest visited him and would have had him engage in a farther conspiracy. (125, italics added)

When this sentence is read in isolation, "swore his great oath" seems a solemn expression: the weighty tone of the sentence implies that Frank's swearing of the oath is a singular event attended by significant political consequences. When the sentence is read in its narrative context, however, its potential impact is lost; for up to this point the expression "swore a great oath" has been consistently used to introduce the blasphemies accompanying Frank's frequent fits of merriment, impatience, or anger (87, 90, 96, 106, 122). Once more the ground suddenly shifts beneath the reader.[12]

In the midst of this constant verbal mutation there is one recurring image which has the semblance of stability. It is the image of Castlewood. Esmond repeatedly prefaces his descriptions of the old estate with the insistence that Castlewood has a permanent hold on his memory. Furthermore, his new estate in America is named after the old, strengthening the impression that "Castlewood" is emblematic of the underlying unity of experience. One of Thackeray's most acute readers claims that the image sustains "the novel's memory-motif," that its various "modalities are all aspects of permanence," and that "the persistent recurrence of the image is as timeless as memory itself."[13] Because the motif has this aura of permanence, it deserves special attention here: as will be shown, Castlewood is an example of rather than an exception to Thackeray's reliance on disorienting imagery.

The Castlewood motif is in part a composite of several recurring images which, unlike the novel's other images, do not change when repeated. While, however, each remains stable from its first to its final occurrence, each from its first to its final occurrence connotes instability. At the heart of Castlewood, "plashing away in silence," is the fountain—a time-honored image of fluidity and flux (37, 40, 52, 152, 153, 392). Mentioned almost as frequently as the fountain is the "great army of rooks"—rooks that never fly unattended by connotations of deceit and fraud (23, 36, 37, 40, 453). Castlewood's sundial—time measured in the passing of a shadow, a shadow passing over the inscription *memento mori*—is a third image of the insubstantial and the transient (152, 394). Esmond's most vivid memories of Castlewood are typically of events occurring at dawn or dusk—moments, once more, of transition and flux (23, 36, 37, 40, 393, 453). Finally, in most instances three or four of these images occur simultaneously within a single passage: the idea of instability inherent in each is compounded and reinforced by the presence of the others.

Those aspects of Castlewood that remain consistent throughout successive repetitions are, then, images in which the concept of instability is inherent. Conversely, those aspects of Castlewood in which the concept of instability does not inhere are inconsistent in their repetitions: they are subjected to the contradiction and mutation elsewhere at work in the novel. If any aspect of Castlewood should convey stability and solidity, it is the structure of the mansion itself, the fortress-like architecture with its ancient towers, gables, and buttresses. The locations of the building in relation to the surrounding land and the locations of particular rooms in relation to one another prove, however, to be as fluid as the fountain.

Esmond's descriptions confound the compass points. According to one passage, Castlewood is located on a hill and has two courts: the eastern court is the fountain court; the western court is the clock-tower court destroyed by the Roundheads in 1647. To the east lie the river, the road to London, and Castlewood village. To the west lie the hills from which enemy gunfire destroyed the western court (40). Approximately half of Esmond's other descriptions coincide with the description above, from which the other half depart. While, for example, it is reassuring that Esmond watches the dawn rise over Castlewood village (393), it is disconcerting that standing in the western court facing the sunset he sees Castlewood village (23). Again, when as a child Henry first comes to Castlewood with Father Holt, they are approaching from the east facing west; for they have come from London by the London road and enter by the front gate at the fountain court. Yet Esmond comments on the flaming reflection of the sunset in the windows, a reflection that he would only see if the sunset were behind him—if he were approaching from the west facing east (36). Again, throughout Book I of the memoirs, the woods where the rooks roost is located "behind" the house; that is, in the hills to the west of Castlewood (23, 37, 40). Returning to Castlewood in Book III, however, Esmond passes by the elms on the Castlewood village green and comments that "the rooks were still roosting" there (453).

Just as Castlewood's relation to the landscape shifts, so the rooms within Castlewood shift. The Queen Elizabeth room, with its tapestries and stained glass windows, is occupied first by Isabella and years later by Beatrix. While the room is usually located in the western or clock-tower court (23, 455) on at least one occasion it is located immediately above Holt's and Harry's rooms (37), rooms that are consistently situated in the eastern court. While Harry's bedchamber and Holt's bedchamber and study are consistently located near one another in the eastern court, the precise arrangement of the three rooms periodically shifts: on one occasion, Harry's sleeping closet is within Holt's study (44); on another occasion, Harry's room and Holt's study are separate but adjoining chambers (392); on a third occasion, Harry's room and Holt's study face each other on opposite sides of a corridor (50). Again, the terrace-walk is usually located in the western court (23, 40, 41, 394). Yet one day when Rachel faints on the terrace, she is quickly revived with water from the fountain—which is in the fountain court, half a mile away (151, 453). The sundial, too, roams from the eastern (152) to the western court (394). Finally, Esmond tells us that on his penultimate visit to Castlewood, he lay awake "for many hours as the clock kept tolling (in tones so well remembered)" (392). The tones so well remembered may well not be remembered by the reader, for while we have heard the cawing of the rooks, the tolling of the church bells, and the babbling of the fountain, we have never heard a sound from the clock-tower, which was partially destroyed by the Roundheads in 1647 and never restored (23, 40). Esmond's vividly remembered Castlewood, the bastion of stability and tribute to the power of memory, seems at times to be located on a rotating hill and to have migrating rooms and a clock that re-materializes during the sleepless nights of sentimental visitors. The Castlewood motif, like the novel's other images and idioms, disorients rather than orients the reader.

The instability introduced into the narrative by these disorienting images and rapid shifts in word meanings is compounded by one additional factor, the intentional inconsistencies in grammar. No coherent logic, for example, underlies Esmond's rapid alternations between first and third person. It is simply not the case, as various readers have suggested, that "I" is reserved for the Esmond who narrates and "he" for the younger Esmond whose actions are described. Nor is any other intelligible principle at work:

> Now, at the close of *his* life, as *he* sits and recalls in tranquillity the happy and busy scenes of it, *he* can think, not ungratefully, that *he* has been faithful to that early vow. . . . But few men's life-voyages are destined to be all

prosperous, and this calm of which *we* are speaking was soon to come to an end. (78, italics added)

Prometheus *I* saw, but when first *I* ever had any words with him . . . *I* disliked this Mr. Swift, and heard many a story about him, of his conduct to men and his words to women. He could flatter the great as much as he could bully the weak; and *Mr. Esmond*, being younger and hotter in that day than now, was determined, should he ever meet this dragon, not to run away from his teeth and his fire. (374, 375, italics added)

Esmond desired *my* landlord not to acquaint Mistress Beatrix with *his* coming. (437, italics added)

We travelled through the night, *Esmond* discoursing to *his* mistress of the events of the last twenty-four hours. (460, italics added)

Finally, even that part of grammar devoted to the external form of words is subjected to mutation. In Esmond's imitation *Spectator* paper, Jocasta's trick to elicit her suitor's name springs out of her complaint about the absence of consistent rules in English orthography, the arbitrary relation between sound and spelling (347). On another occasion, Esmond remarks that "spelling was not an article of general commodity in the world then" (185); and periodically, with bemused detachment, he comments on the poor spelling abilities of Isabella (185), Marlborough (185), the Chevalier (457), young Frank Castlewood (334), and Frank's wife, Clotilda (334). Esmond himself, however, also practices the slippery English orthography. Although modern editions correct many of the original inconsistencies in spelling, a few survive: there is Sieveright (49) and Sievewright (83), Hexton Castle (70) and Hexham Castle (393), Brussels (280) and Bruxelles (403), Marshal (324) and Mareschal (324), Montagu (83) and Montague (308) and Aimes (164) and Aymé (438).

The instability of grammar, the instability of spelling, and, above all, the instability of imagery and word meaning conspire to create a language that is often as much a barrier between Esmond and the reader as it is a vehicle of transmission, a language in which both meaning and tone repeatedly shift, rapidly alternating between coherence and incoherence. While it is not possible to chart the disruptive effect of this linguistic instability, a brief contemplation of one passage will begin to suggest the dislocation and discomfort it generates. Book III focuses on Esmond's attempt to win Beatrix's love by his participation in a political conspiracy. After recounting the failure of the conspiracy and his loss of Beatrix, Esmond summarizes the remainder of his life story with three concluding paragraphs in which he announces his marriage to his beloved mistress, Rachel. The overt tone of this final passage is one of serenity and joy: Esmond calls his marriage "the great joy of my life" (462) and describes their life together in America as one of sustained tranquility (463). Many nineteenth- and twentieth-century readers, however, have found them-

selves unable to share Esmond's attitude toward his fate. Their uneasi-
ness is in part attributable to the language itself, for the passage is a
paradigm of the many modes of ambivalence that have been examined
here. An analysis of a few representative sentences will suggest how consistently and artfully Thackeray operates on his reader in these final moments.

Esmond makes his transition from Beatrix and his past aspirations to
Rachel and his future reality in a startlingly abrupt summation:

> With the sound of King George's trumpets, all the vain hopes of the weak
> and foolish young Pretender were blown away; and with that music too, I
> may say, the drama of my own life was ended. That happiness which hath
> subsequently crowned it cannot be written in words; 'tis of its nature sacred
> and secret, and not to be spoken of, though the heart be ever so full of
> thankfulness, save to Heaven and the One Ear alone—to one fond being,
> the truest and tenderest and purest wife ever man was blessed with. (461,
> 462)

The first sentence provides a curious opening for a passage in which
Esmond will describe his fate as one enriched with gifts from God, for it
is suffused with the sense of loss: the expression "the drama of my own
life was ended" is almost funereal. On the surface, the tone of the second
sentence immediately redeems the first; if Esmond has died, he has also
gone to heaven. However, the sentence contains several disconcerting
elements. Attempting to describe his happiness in the superlative mode,
he uses the word "crowned." This word, like many others in the passage,
is an example of the unstable image. Throughout Book III it continually
occurs in conjunction with the Chevalier's aspirations to the English
throne and with Esmond's longing for the queenly Beatrix. In this final
passage, then, the word is more likely to evoke the name of Beatrix than
that of her mother. Furthermore, by this point in the narrative the word
has acquired pejorative connotations. Rejected by Beatrix, Esmond has
bitterly rejected the concept of the crown. In the passage immediately
preceding the final passage, Esmond, anxious to show Rachel's other-
worldly superiority to the worldly Beatrix, praises her disdain for crowns:
"*She* wasn't thinking of queens and crowns" (460). After asserting that the
remainder of his life has been "crowned" with great happiness, he must
explain why, in that case, he is ending the memoirs now, why he will not
share the story of that happiness with the reader: it is, he tells us, too
"sacred and secret." Both adjectives are troubling. While Esmond has
previously argued that the proper subject of a history is the personal, the
familiar, the intimate, here intimacy becomes a reason for silence. In
addition, as was shown earlier, the religious vocabulary, used not only in
this sentence but throughout the entire passage, is a discredited idiom.
The focus of our discomfort is the grammatical ambiguity at the end of the

sentence. No longer satisfied to designate Rachel a mere saint, goddess, or angel, Esmond here comes perilously close to identifying her with God, for the two are placed in apposition: his story is not to be spoken of "save to Heaven and the One Ear alone — to one fond being, the truest and tenderest and purest wife."[14]

The instability of these complex sentences is equally visible in far simpler statements. Toward the end of this first paragraph, Esmond writes:

> In the name of my wife I write the completion of hope, and the summit of happiness. (462)

"In the name of my wife" is a figurative expression that does not necessarily demand that Esmond utter Rachel's name. But figurative language derives its stability from its basis in or compatibility with the literal fact. The occurrence of this expression in a passage from which Rachel's name is conspicuously absent is, consequently, troubling: the presence of the expression heightens our awareness of the absence of her name, heightens our awareness of Esmond's reliance on titles such as "my mistress," titles which have not, during the course of the narrative, been exclusively reserved for Rachel. Furthermore, while the phrase "the completion of hope" means "the fulfillment of hope," it is similar to "the drama of my own life was ended," for it carries with it the faint suggestion of "the end of hope."

In the second paragraph of this passage, Esmond confides to the reader:

> We had been so accustomed to an extreme intimacy and confidence, and had lived so long and tenderly together, that we might have gone on to the end without thinking of a closer tie; but circumstances brought about that event which so prodigiously multiplied my happiness and hers (for which I humbly thank Heaven), although a calamity befell us which, I blush to think, hath occurred more than once in our house. (462)

In the first half of the sentence Esmond asserts that he had not previously considered marrying Rachel and in making that assertion, reminds the reader that he had, in fact, previously proposed to Rachel: Esmond has forgotten that when he returned to England after the Vigo Bay expedition, he asked her to leave Europe and live with him in America until death (217). The first half of the sentence, then, describes an event, overtly denies the existence of an historical antecedent, and thereby reminds the reader that such an antecedent exists. Conversely, the second half of the sentence alludes to an unspecified event, asserts that the event has antecedents in the Castlewood family history, and wrongly assumes that the reader will remember those antecedents. Unless Esmond is suggesting that he and Rachel — like Henry's own parents (see above, page 113) and like young Frank and Clotilda (327, 328) — have conceived a child out of wedlock, it is not clear what he means by "the calamity . . . which, I blush to think, hath occurred more than once in our house." Esmond's "blush" of shame also disconcerts. Six sentences later he will use the expression "blushes of love" to describe the way in which Rachel accepted his marriage proposal. The one disrupts our reading of the other: the shame of the first intrudes upon the tenderness of the second.

Later in the same paragraph, Esmond writes of Beatrix:

> I know not what infatuation of ambition urged the beautiful and wayward woman whose name hath occupied so many of these pages and who was served by me with ten years of such a constant fidelity and passion, but ever after that day at Castlewood when we rescued her, she persisted in holding all her family as her enemies, and left us, and escaped to France, to what a fate I disdain to tell.

The most volatile element in this sentence is the phrase, "who was *served* by me with ten years of such a *constant fidelity*." Three sentences later, describing Rachel's situation immediately prior to their marriage, Esmond tells us she was "alone but for one *constant servant* on whose *fidelity*, praised be Heaven, she could count." The asserted fidelity to Rachel is undermined by the assertion of fidelity to Beatrix. Throughout the passage, he describes Rachel in the language of superlatives, creating the surface impression that she is above and apart from all other humanity. For Rachel to share any given vocabulary with Beatrix would disrupt this impression, but the repetition of this particular vocabulary is especially unhappy since "fidelity" itself contains the concept of exclusiveness. Furthermore, our discomfort is compounded by the sentence that immediately follows the repetition. Up to this point, the repetition has contained one potentially positive idea: Esmond's fidelity to the Castlewood family as a whole supersedes his devotion to any one woman in the family. The next sentence, however, dismisses as merely pathetic such family allegiance: "'Twas after a scene of ignoble quarrel on the part of Frank's wife and mother (for the poor lad had been made to marry the whole of that German family with whom he had connected himself) that I . . . " (463). The parallel between Frank's situation and Henry's is unmistakable. One additional linguistic coincidence makes Esmond's description of the heartless Beatrix painful. In specifying the length of his devotion as "ten years," his complaint recalls an almost identical complaint made against Rachel during his imprisonment: "Not that [Esmond's] fidelity was recompensed by any answering kindness, or show of relenting even, on the part of a mistress obdurate now after ten years of love and benefactions" (179). While Esmond devotes much of the energy of his final passage to praising Rachel's virtue, the complaint against Beatrix reminds us of that long period of time in which Rachel seemed most cruel. Finally, the conclusion to the sentence, "to what a fate I disdain to tell," recalls to the reader one of Esmond's major criticisms of historical works, their artificial propriety: in his introduction to the memoirs, he protests, "The Historical Muse turns away shamefaced from the vulgar scene and closes the door" (19). The dignity of "to what fate I disdain to tell" carries with it the indignity of a shamefaced retreat from the vulgar scene.

Toward the end of the passage, Esmond presents a brief picture of his life with Rachel in America:

> In our transatlantic country we have a season, the calmest and most delightful of the year, which we call the Indian summer; I often say the autumn of our life resembles that happy and serene weather, and am thankful for its rest and its sweet sunshine. (463)

When read in isolation, this is surely one of the most beautiful sentences in the novel. But its aura of tranquility and fulfillment, largely generated by the controlling image of "Indian summer," is subverted by the presence of the word "Indian," which is, in its antecedent uses, an explosive image. In the preface to the memoirs, we learn that Rachel dies of a nervous breakdown following a violent attack on their home by the Indians (ix). Equally untranquil is the second reference. Describing the suffering he endures at the hands of Rachel while in prison, Esmond writes: "Esmond thought of his early times as a novitiate and of this past trial as an initiation before entering into life—as our young Indians undergo tortures silently before they pass to the rank of warriors in the tribe" (176). On another occasion, Esmond confesses to Beatrix his inability to withstand the longing he experiences while in her presence and the consequent necessity of his separation from her: "I am thinking of retiring into the plantations, and building myself a wigwam in the woods, and perhaps, if I want company, suiting myself with a squaw" (358). Finally, in the paragraph that immediately precedes this concluding passage, Indians appear in conjunction with Father Holt, the character in the memoirs most explicitly associated with unintentional inaccuracy as well as intentional disguise and deception: "I am not sure that he did not assume the hatchet and moccasins [in America], and attired in a blanket and war-paint, skulk about a missionary amongst the Indians" (461). The Indian image, then, is associated with violent death, with torture, with the reluctant desire for companionship amidst the isolation of unrequited love, and with semicomic attempts at deception—associations that make it difficult for the image to function in this final passage as a vehicle of serenity and purity.

Finally, there is the concluding sentence of the passage, the climactic statement of the memoirs:

> Our diamonds are turned into ploughs and axes for our plantations, and into Negroes, the happiest and merriest, I think, in all this country; and the only jewel by which my wife sets any store, and from which she hath never parted, is that gold button she took from my arm on the day when she

visited me in prison, and which she wore ever after, as she told me, on the tenderest heart in the world. (463)

Even leaving aside the moral responsibility for the lighthearted accommo- dation to slavery,[15] the passage in its many other details slides out of control. Throughout Book III, diamonds are associated with Esmond's futile longing for Beatrix. The underlying movement of this final sentence is its transition from the image of the diamonds to that of the gold but- ton—on the surface, a graceful emblematic statement of the difference between Beatrix and Rachel, between the compelling worldly splendor of the first and the unworldly simplicity and virtue of the second. Several factors, however, conspire to discomfort the reader. The phrase "I think" by this point in the narrative discredits rather than makes creditable the assertion in which the phrase is embedded. The phrase "as she told me" is grammatically unsteady. Its position in the sentence fosters two interpre- tations: the dominant reading, "She told me she wore it ever after on her heart," is unavoidably attended by a second, slightly embarrassing read- ing, "She told me hers was the tenderest heart in the world." But the major source of instability is the image of the gold button itself. There is only one previous occasion on which the button is mentioned. While Harry is in prison, the keeper's wife visits him and relates to him the news of Francis Esmond's funeral and Rachel's interview with the King. Esmond then writes:

Such were the news, coupled with assertions about her own honesty and that of Molly, her maid, who would never have stolen a certain trumpery gold sleeve-button of Mr. Esmond's that was missing after his fainting fit, that the keeper's wife brought to her lodger. (172)

Far from suggesting simplicity and virtue, the "trumpery" button is here surrounded with connotations of deceit. Even the grammatical structure of the sentence is deceitful, for it may wilfully mislead the reader into thinking that the keeper's wife returns the missing button. The word "that" in the final phrase, "that the keeper's wife brought to her lodger," is unsta- ble in its antecedent. It may either be read as "the news that the keeper's wife brought" or as "the button that the keeper's wife brought." The reader who emerges from this complex sentence believing that the button has been restored to Henry will be unable to understand the final sentence of his memoirs.

The final image of the button, then, acquires its most uneasy associa- tions from the specific sentence in which it is originally mentioned. But it is also troubling in its evocation of the more general context, its evocation of the prison incident as a whole. Here, in the climactic statement, we are not only reminded of Rachel's former cruelty, we are reminded that the ostensible cause of that cruelty was illusory. Her grief and rage had appeared to be inspired by her love for her dead husband. Instead, as the final passage makes emphatic, she was obsessed with love not for Francis but for Harry. The reversal is charted in the displacement of one icon by another. Shortly before dying, the repentant Francis asks Harry to carry a small, heart-shaped locket to his wife. It is as Francis reaches into his breast for the locket that he falls unconscious from the wound he has just received (164). The concluding sentence of the narrative informs us that during that prison meeting between Henry and Rachel immediately following Francis's death, Rachel takes and begins to wear on her heart not Francis's locket but Henry's button. The charm of the button is tarnished by the poignancy of the forgotten locket. The morality of the reversal is less striking, however, than the simple fact of the reversal: the displacement of Francis by Harry in Rachel's heart is less disheartening than the displacement of Francis by Harry in our understanding of Rachel's love motives during the prison incident. This reversal, like the scores of similar reversals, makes visible the continual confusion and uncertainty that surround human thoughts and affections, the human thoughts and affections that Esmond believes "divine and immortal." Nor does the uncertainty ever resolve itself into any final certainty. It was Rachel who during the prison incident tells Henry that she is grief-stricken by her love for her lost lord. Now it is Rachel who tells Henry about the button and its significance. Given the instability of her previous "telling," there is perhaps no reason to trust her final words.

Esmond intends this final passage to be unequivocal in its praise of Rachel and of the happiness she bestows on him: "Let the last words I write thank her, and bless her who hath blessed [my home]" (463). On the surface his language is characterized by its conviction and its commitment to the superlative mode, but its primary characteristic is its instability, an instability unable to accommodate unequivocal superlatives, an instability that converts single-minded conviction into half-hearted assertion. By the time readers emerge from the final passage, they feel uncertain whether the grace with which Esmond abandons Beatrix and embraces Rachel reflects the serenity of a newly matured man or only the fatalistic stoicism of one whose repertoire of maxims includes, "If the palace burns down, you take shelter in the barn" (98) and "I can't but accept the world as I find it, including a rope's end, as long as it is in fashion" (20) and "There is no fortune that a philosopher cannot endure" (261). In the end, the two incompatible possibilities survive. If there were only the surface serenity, the reader would simply share Esmond's serenity; if the underlying despair were wholly able to eclipse the surface serenity, the reader would simply feel despair. As it is, the reader feels neither serenity nor despair but unending unease.

The instability found in the final passage is present throughout the memoirs. The reader consistently encounters the language of dislocation, a language in which it is difficult to ascertain the narrator's meaning and tone, a language in which the denotative and connotative activities of a given word are so unrestricted that its possible sphere of meaning expands to accommodate polar opposites. At one point, in the midst of a conversation with Beatrix, Esmond perceives and consciously exploits the instability of language to extricate himself from an embarrassing moment: as he confesses to the reader, he tells Beatrix "a truth which [is] nevertheless an entire falsehood" (354). Esmond's confession, while immediately descriptive of a single statement made to Beatrix, is also descriptive of Thackeray's entire narrative.

IV

The instability of truth evident in these complex language patterns is also evident in the novel's large, immediately visible structural elements. By locating its source of stability in the subject rather than the object of perception, subjective truth credits the concept of identity, assumes in the individual an underlying unity of self. This assumption, the implicit premise of any autobiography, is made explicit in the motto Esmond affixes to his memoirs: "*Servetur ad imum / Qualis ab incepto processerit, et sibi constet.*" Esmond's life story, however, is dominated by events that continually call into question the validity of this premise. A simple enumeration of incidents will recall the extent to which the overt plot, in both its general outlines and its details, is saturated with problems of recognition.

Esmond lived in a period of English history notable for sustained confusion in both its international and domestic policies. Internationally, England was engaged in the War of the Spanish Succession: the unnecessary length of the war—it lasted from 1701 to 1713—is usually attributed to the fact that its participants had a stable definition of neither the issues nor the lines of allegiance. The instability generated by England's foreign policy was amplified by the confusion in its internal affairs, a confusion that centered on the dissension over the identity of the proper heir to the English throne.

Like England's international and domestic history, Esmond's life story in both its public and private dimensions is dominated by confusion. His public identity—as revealed in the relation between his religious, military, and political careers (Books I, II, and III respectively)—is a composite of incompatible allegiances. His military ambition, for example, is dedicated to England's triumph over France; yet a major cause of England's animosity toward France is the latter's support of the Stuart claim to the English throne, a claim Esmond himself actively supports. In turn, his support of the Stuart claim is incompatible with his religious and social sympathies, which are Anglican rather than Catholic, republican rather than divine-right authoritarian. Esmond's personal identity is equally unstable: until the end of the memoirs, the identity of his parents, the legitimacy of his birth, and his status within the Castlewood family hierarchy are questions continually asked and unanswered.

In its most general outlines, then, *Henry Esmond* consists of two spheres, a historical background and an autobiographical foreground, each dominated by its confrontation with the undefined. But it is in the novel's details even more than in its general outlines that we see this obsessive concern with personal coherence.

The relevant details occur in conjunction with major characters and incidents as well as with characters and incidents so minor and isolated that they appear to exist almost solely to reinforce the theme of identity. In addition to the sustained counterpoint of disguise and counterfeit dress surrounding both Father Holt (Holtz, von Holtz, Holton) and the Chevalier in his attempt to establish his "true" identity as James III, the novel contains such isolated fragments of masquerade as Esmond's encounter with "Captain James," a disguised Duke of Berwick (124, 401); his meeting at Cambridge with a Jesuit priest who presents himself as a French Protestant refugee (116); and his contact in France with a deserter from the Irish army masquerading as a French soldier, a masquerade whose transparency Esmond finds "infinitely amusing" (325). Again, in addition to the psychological resonance of the episode in which Rachel mistakes Harry Mohun for Harry Esmond (80, 151) and the complexity of confusion arising from the affinity between young Frank Castlewood and Henry Esmond, there are such brief incidents as that in which Esmond, delirious with smallpox, is unable to recognize Rachel (170) and that in which Esmond, delirious with a wound received at Blenheim, mistakes a surgeon's assistant for Beatrix (242). At times the confusion in identity results from a conscious act of deception that carries with it the moral disapproval of the narrator: it is uncertain whether Marlborough's primary efforts are committed to England or to England's enemy, France (287, 288); Thomas Esmond conceals his true identity from his first wife, Gertrude Maes, and, by abandoning her and marrying Isabella, virtually denies her existence and that of her son (278). But for the most part such acts seem so omnipresent that they appear a given of reality, whether presented humorously, as in Isabella's attempt to obscure her physical identity with paints and wigs (45); painfully, as in Trix's constant play of deceptive coquetry; or compassionately, as in the description of Rachel, who "amongst her other feminine qualities had that of being a perfect dissembler" (398).

Almost without exception, the letters and other written articles that Esmond records in his memoirs use language to disguise their writer's meaning. Three conspiratorial notes, for example, have messages embedded in code. They are intended to be comprehensible to a few, incomprehensible to most. The degree of obscurity ranges from the naïve transparency of Thomas Esmond's code in which the Prince of Orange is designated as "the P. of O." and King James as "the K." or *"you know who"*

(65) to Father Holt's more sophisticated code in which the political idiom is replaced by an economic idiom (64) and finally, to Henry Esmond's code in which the key is so deeply concealed that the reader can only take Esmond's word that one exists (405). Equally, if not intentionally, obscure is a letter Esmond receives from Isabella written in a "strange barbarous French" that converts "Mohun" to "M. de Moon" and "Warwick" to "M. le Compte de Varique": as is clear to any reader who has worked his or her way through that barbarous French, Esmond's comments following the letter reveal that he himself has misunderstood its meaning, that he has misread her reference to Lord Blanford, Lady Marlborough's son, as a reference to Prince James (185, 186). Again in Esmond's imitation *Spectator* paper (345–49), duplicity is visible on three levels: first, its subject is deception, the deception in Beatrix's coquetry; second, that subject is obscured, embedded in a parable rather than presented overtly; third and most important, the presentation of the paper itself is deceptive, for its effect on Beatrix requires her ignorance of the author's true identity. Many additional pieces of writing that Esmond describes but does not record *verbatim* also demonstrate the failure of language to act as a vehicle of honest communication: Mohun's seductive notes to Rachel (157), Beatrix's deceptive note to her mother at Kensington (452), Frank's untruthful letters to his mother (322), Rachel's letters to Esmond lost or stolen by a privateer (317), Esmond's play to which, when published, he refuses to sign his name (344), and the Gazette that credits Cadogan rather than Webb for the English victory at Wynendael (294).

The incoherence of persons, brought about both by conscious acts of deception and by mere chance, recurs everywhere in Esmond's life story.[16] *Henry Esmond*, however, is not only a life story but a love story; and in one sense, all the random instances of confusion enumerated above are tangential to the overriding complexities of the central love triangle, or what would be a triangle were it not too insistently equivocal to be defined by geometric design. While Esmond's two mistresses are on the surface polar opposites — one dark, the other fair; one tall, the other short; one worldly, the other unworldly — their two identities repeatedly merge, emerge and separate, only to merge once more. The intricacies of this sustained confusion ultimately involve a mother-mistress interchange whose incestuous implications have been immediately apparent to both nineteenth- and twentieth-century readers. Only two points, obvious but unacknowledged, need be emphasized here.

The first involves the relationship between Esmond's autobiography and his daughter's preface. In the autobiography proper, the theme of incest occurs only on the psychological plane, never the physical: while Rachel is emphatically a mother figure, she is not Esmond's biological mother. Even the smaller manifestations of the incest theme stay safely within the realm of the nonphysical. Sometimes it emerges as metaphor: it is in the guise of Beatrix's brother that the Chevalier attempts to seduce

Beatrix. At other times, its appearance is reduced to mere mistake: Esmond at one point incorrectly identifies Isabella as "his father's wife and . . . his grandfather's daughter" (187); depending on whether one reads the antecedent of the second "his" as Henry or Thomas, Isabella has married either her brother, her nephew, or her son. If, however, in the autobiography proper the incestuous implications are confined to the psychological, metaphorical, and mistaken, they are grounded in biological reality in Rachel Warrington's preface. We there learn that she and her father, Henry Esmond, became widow and widower in the same year (ix), after which they shared a happy and intimate life-long union. More important, we learn that Warrington's death occurred prior to the birth of his wife's children (viii, ix). These factual details do not rule out the probability that Warrington did beget his wife's sons; they merely invite the possibility that he did not. Thackeray has selected details calculated to arouse for a moment the worry that Esmond, fulfilling his desire to "found a family" in the new world (358), fathered his own grandsons. This worry is amplified by Rachel Warrington's impassioned descriptions of her father: they convey an intensity of affection and admiration that makes even her simplest assertions vulnerable to *double entendre*:

> I am sure that [my sons] love me, and one another, and him above all, my father and theirs, the dearest friend of their childhood, the noble gentleman who bred them from their infancy in the practice and knowledge of Truth, and Love, and Honour. (viii)

> I know that, before [my mother], my dear father did not show the love which he had for his daughter; and in her last and most sacred moments this dear and tender parent owned to me her repentance that she had not loved me enough, her jealousy even that my father should give his affection to any but herself; and in the most fond and beautiful words of affection and admonition she bade me never to leave him and to supply the place which she was quitting. With a clear conscience and a heart inexpressibly thankful, I think I can say that I fulfilled those dying commands . . . (ix)

These implications of physical incest in the preface are far less innocent than the theme in the autobiography itself.

The second point that warrants attention is the reason for Thackeray's inclusion of the incest theme in the novel. While he, like his readers, may have found the subject fascinating in and of itself, it seems certain that he selected the theme for its participation in the larger theme of misrecognition. Esmond's autobiography is a sustained attempt at self-definition, an attempt in which he relies heavily on relational terms. As the memoirs progress, these terms undergo rapid, unpredictable changes: Rachel is Beatrix's mother, Rachel is Beatrix's elder sister (328), Beatrix is Rachel's elder sister (303), Esmond is Isabella's son (317), Esmond is Isabella's son-in-law (187), Esmond is Rachel's son (251, 252, 315), Esmond is Beatrix's brother (385), Esmond is Rachel's brother (386), Esmond is elder brother and father of Rachel, Frank, and Beatrix (358, 359). The very fluidity of the terms reveals their instability, an instability made more dangerous by the presence of the incest theme. A recognition of the incestuous impulse requires a rejection of the concept of fixed, relational identities: the familial is no longer exclusive of the sexually intimate; mother-son, father-daughter, and brother-sister are no longer stable, definitive terms.

Esmond's surface narrative, then, in its major outlines as well as its details, its historical background as well as its personal foreground, is saturated with confusions in identity. The dominance of such confusions in the overt events of the story is twofold in its purpose. First, it announces the novel's central concern, designates as a major problem Esmond's belief in subjective truth. Second, and more important, after designating the problem, it dismisses the problem, creates the hope that the problem does not exist. Despite the sheer number of confusions, despite the fact that Esmond himself is often their temporary victim, he ultimately appears to be in control of them by virtue of the very fact that he is writing about them. If he is a participant he is also the narrator: his act of describing an instance of identity interchange necessarily entails the act of differentiating an erroneous perception from its accurate counterpart, an act that carries with it the assurance that the dislocated can be relocated, that the confusion can be clarified, that ignorance finally yields to the perception of a stable, knowable reality. Within the overt surface of the story, Esmond's concept of subjective truth is threatened but simultaneously salvaged— only to be obliterated on a second, deeper level where, as shown earlier, Esmond's narrative, and with it his identity, are subjected to a sustained and systematic process of erosion. While Esmond is calmly assuring us that physical disguises can be penetrated, psychological interchanges explained, people's identities identified, Thackeray is busy demonstrating the ultimate inaccessibility of personal identity: by the end of the novel, we do not know the first thing about our autobiographer, not the simplest fact, the date of his birth, not the simplest thought, his ideas about pain, not the simplest emotion, his feeling for Rachel.

Thackeray's act of refuting on a second level what he has superficially affirmed on the first is not simply a gratuitous act of irony at Esmond's expense. Although ultimately illusory, the surface affirmation is crucial to the author's central argument. He is trying to show that subjective truth— a stable core of facts, feelings, and thoughts—is an impossibility *per se*, not merely an impossibility for Esmond. If the disintegration of subjective truth is to be attributed to an instability inherent in the concept itself rather than to an instability peculiar to a particular character, Thackeray must absolve his hero of personal responsibility by convincing us that were reliability possible, Esmond would be reliable; were there a truth to be told, Esmond would tell it.

Four major factors contribute to Esmond's absolution. The most important is his rejection of objective truth, a rejection that makes his acceptance of subjective truth appear more trustworthy, less capricious: it assures us that he is not an eager idealist randomly affirming all dimensions of all possible realities; he is, instead, one who has tested reality before becoming the exponent of the single realm his testing proved sound. Second, not only is objective truth rejected but, as this section of the discussion has shown, subjective truth is itself tested on the surface of the story: the narrator is interested in and capable of disentangling the ordinary confusions arising from physical disguise and psychological affinity. As important as these two factors that encourage us to trust Esmond are two other factors which, once we realize the failure of Esmond's narrative to substantiate our trust, assure us that the failure was not Esmond's to avert. While he is devastatingly unreliable, it is notable that nowhere in the novel is the possibility of reliability affirmed: as was suggested in the second section of this discussion, all the characters in the narrative as well as those who supplement the narrative with preface and footnotes share the hero's habit of contradiction. Esmond's final absolution resides in that factor examined in the third section of the discussion, the structure of language itself. The instability characterizing the narrator's assertions is equally characteristic of much smaller grammatical units such as individual words and images. As a result, the problem of instability is dissociated from Esmond: it penetrates language so deeply that it appears to be beyond his control, out of his hands. In his espousal of subjective truth, then, Esmond is the dupe of dreams, but he is not the agent of the dream's disintegration. While he is assuredly the victim of Thackeray's irony, he is also the victim of a larger irony in which Thackeray, too, plays victim.

V

The overall structure of *Henry Esmond* is based on an ironic formula familiar to readers of *Vanity Fair*. In both novels, the surface narrative poses a question and offers the illusion of two alternative answers, one of which is made to appear strong, the other, weak. In both novels the argument presented in the surface narrative is refuted by a counter-narrative in which the antithesis is proved illusory, the two alternatives equally inviable. On the surface, *Vanity Fair* questions the source of value and virtue and proposes, in response, the Amelia life style against the Becky life style, an opposition erased on a second level where the polar life styles collapse and merge in their shared absence of value. On the surface, *Henry Esmond* questions the source of truth and proposes, in response, the subjective realm of existence against the objective, an opposition erased on a second level where the first disintegrates into the instability of the second.

Although *Vanity Fair* is more overtly cynical in tone, the transition from the earlier novel to the later represents a movement toward a deeper pessimism, for the focus shifts from the ethical to the epistemological, from the impotence of the distinction between "good and bad" to the impotence of the distinction between "true and false." While the first questions the validity of assigning moral labels to facts, the second denies our ability even to know the facts to which we cannot assign the labels. But if Thackeray's pessimism deepened, so did the artistry of the techniques he used to present the surface alternatives in the two novels. In *Vanity Fair*, he explores the resources of plot, dramatizing the opposition in life styles by simply doubling the plot-line. In *Henry Esmond*, he explores not plot but genre, converting the two spheres implicit in "historical-romance," the public and the private, into the two spheres where the potential existence of truth might be examined. In rejecting both spheres he calls into question major assumptions the nineteenth century held about the distinction between history and fiction.

The essential dynamic of *Henry Esmond*, however, resides not in the relationship between the novel and the author's earlier works, nor in the relationship between the novel and its genre, nor in the relationship between the novel and nineteenth-century assumptions, but in the relationship between the novel's author and its hero, a relationship epitomized in a single sentence describing Esmond's portrait:

[Dowager Isabella] must have his picture taken; and accordingly he was painted by Mr. Jervas, in his red coat, and smiling upon a bomb-shell, which was bursting at the corner of the piece. (300)

Despite the brevity of its description, Esmond's portrait is emblematic of his entire life story: Esmond's surface narrative is dominated by the tone of serene conviction, but immediately beneath this glacine surface is the restless energy of Thackeray, ever threatening to explode in the smiling face of the self-assured narrator and instilling in us a permanent state of cognitive unease.

Notes

1. William Thackeray, *The History of Henry Esmond, Esq.* (New York: Signet, 1964), p. 66. All subsequent references to *Henry Esmond* are to this edition. Page numbers will be given in the text.

2. Henry's application of the religious idiom to Rachel is further discredited by the fact that he himself acknowledges its inapplicability, yet after that admission continues to use it. Immediately prior to his reunion with Rachel at Winchester, Esmond writes: "[Rachel] had been sister, mother, goddess to him during his youth—goddess now no more, for he knew of her weaknesses . . . but [she was]

more fondly cherished as woman perhaps than ever she had been adored as divinity" (213). On the basis of this quotation, some readers believe that Esmond eventually outgrows his reliance on the religious idiom (see, for example, John Loofbourow, *Thackeray and the Form of Fiction* [Princeton, 1964], p. 137). The same chapter (II, 6) in which Esmond makes this assertion, however, concludes with a paragraph in which, embracing Rachel, he says, "I think the angels are not all in heaven" (218). Nor does he abandon that idiom until the memoirs themselves have ended.

3. Walter Allen, "Afterword," in *Henry Esmond*, p. 475.

4. I would like to thank Marc Warner for locating and alerting me to this instance of contradiction as well as several others included in this essay.

5. In this instance of contradiction, as in many others, one or both terms of the contradiction are embedded in statements made by characters other than Esmond. Depending on whether we assume that Esmond is or is not quoting the character correctly, the character himself may or may not be responsible. In either case, however, Esmond himself is always responsible. Whenever a contradiction occurs and Esmond records it, we can assume that he is himself unaware of the contradiction, for when he records a character's statement that he knows includes an inaccuracy or contradiction, he hurriedly relays this information to the reader (32, 40, 92, 127, 214, 270, 273, 278, 284).

Two instances in which we are warned about inaccuracy are of particular interest. Esmond at one point cautions us about Holt's "trifling blunders" (270). A few pages later, Holt in turn confides to Esmond about Thomas Esmond's habit of inaccuracy (278). It remains for the reader to complete the circle: just as Henry's words about Holt are echoed in Holt's words about Thomas, so the reader can apply Holt's words about Thomas to Henry himself. Were it not that Thomas's inaccuracies are intentional and Henry's unintentional, the description of Thomas would provide an excellent description of Esmond's narrative: "His tales used to gather verisimilitude as he went on with him. He strung together fact after fact with a wonderful rapidity and coherence. It required, saving your presence, a very long habit of acquaintance with your father to know when his lordship was l_____ (telling the truth or no)" (278).

6. As the term indicates, Advent ends with the coming of Christ, December 25.

7. Most readings of the novel do not take note of these contradictions and essentially agree with Walter Allen's judgment that "[Esmond] is the one clear-sighted character in the novel" ("Afterword," p. 476).

There are, however, at least three exceptions in the history of Thackeray scholarship. The contradictions were noted by Samuel Phillips in "Mr. Thackeray's New Novel," a review in *The* [London] *Times*, Dec. 22, 1852. Phillips, however, seeing only isolated instances of contradiction, attributed it to the author's carelessness rather than his craft: "That Steele should be described as a private in the Guards in the year 1690, when he was only 15 years old and a schoolboy at the Charter-house, is, perhaps, no great offence in a work of fiction; but a fatal smile involuntarily crosses the reader's cheek, when he learns, in an early part of the story, that a nobleman is 'made to play at ball and billiards by sharpers, who take his money;' and is informed some time afterwards that the same lord has 'gotten a new game from London, a French game, called a billiard'" (quoted in *Thackeray: The Critical Heritage*, ed. Geoffrey Tillotson and Donald

Hawes [London, 1968], p. 156). Second, included in the collected letters of Thackeray is a letter from Anne Procter noting two small instances of contradiction (*The Letters and Private Papers of William Makepeace Thackeray*, ed. Gordon N. Ray [Cambridge, 1946], III, 128). Thackeray nowhere responds to her comments. In a footnote, the editor dismisses Anne Procter's comment, suggesting that the quotations she finds contradictory are not at all incompatible. More recently, John Sutherland has noted several instances of contradiction: for example, Webb promises Esmond his majority after Wynendale, a promotion Esmond has already received after Oudenarde. Sutherland, like Phillips, attributes such contradictions to rapid and careless composition ("The Inhibiting Secretary in Thackeray's Fiction," *Modern Language Quarterly*, 32 [1971], 175–88; "*Henry Esmond* and the Virtues of Carelessness," *Modern Philology*, 68, No. 4 [May, 1971], 345–54).

The fact that Thackeray occasionally contradicts himself in other novels is sometimes invoked to suggest that the contradictions in *Henry Esmond* are (as in the other instances) unintentional. But the nature and frequency of the contradictions elsewhere are simply incomparable to the extraordinary linguistic events taking place in *Esmond*. Because reviewers and friends made Thackeray aware of his own carelessness, it is completely plausible that in *Esmond* he decided to take what had formerly been an unpreventable accident and convert it into a controlled argument—the argument that compositional consistency is unachievable. The speculation is compatible with his announcement concerning *Esmond*, "I've got a better subject for a novel than any I've yet had" (*Letters*, II, 706), as well as with his repeated references to the unprecedented labor of composition (*Letters*, III, 27, 38, 47, 91) and with his continual description of the book's contents as "sad," "dull," "frightfully glum" and, most accurately, as possessing a "cutthroat melancholy" (*Letters*, II, 811; III, 24, 37, 91).

Finally, although only a small number of readers explicitly acknowledge the contradictions, many (including Charlotte Brontë and Virginia Woolf) speak of it as among the most unpleasant or uncomfortable books they have ever read. The dissolution of the narrative, the sense that no claim retains its substance, explains the unusual discomfort produced by the book better than does the book's psychological contents (such as the love triangles) which, however unhappy, do not seem especially remarkable in the spectrum of novel subjects.

The ambient distress reported by Charlotte Brontë and Virginia Woolf reappears in the richly philosophic distress of Stephen Bann and J. Hillis Miller (whose essays I had not yet encountered when first publishing this). Neither of the two attends to the capacious phenomenon of contradiction: Miller, for example, repeatedly notes that Esmond "remembers seemingly 'trivial' details with extraordinary vividness" and holds that "Henry's narration is based on a claim of total memory, as Thackeray's must be, and as the reader's interpretation must be too" (*Henry Esmond*: Repetition and Irony," *Fiction and Repetition* [Cambridge, Mass., 1982, pp. 91, 114]). Yet both Bann and Miller argue that this book—sometimes received as "le plus beau roman historique jamais ecrit" (Bann, "L'anti histoire de Henri Esmond," 9 *Poetique* [1972], 63)—essentially disappears before our eyes; and they both provide intriguing accounts of the processes by which they believe this comes about.

8. Samuel Beckett, *Three Novels* (New York, 1965), pp. 92, 176.

9. Samuel Beckett, *No's Knife* (London, 1967), pp. 71, 88, 79.

10. Even when the two terms of the contradiction are separated, it is often possible to locate the specific piece of subject matter Thackeray has inserted in the intervening narrative in order to obscure the contradiction. For example, the first time Harry meets Francis Esmond, Francis is rescuing Harry from the assaults of another lad who had called Harry a "bastard" (48). Later, recounting his first encounter with Francis to Dick Steele, Harry not only omits the fact that Francis was the rescuer, but asserts that it was Francis who called him a bastard (73). But between the two terms of this contradiction we have seen one of Father Holt's letters in which Holt says that Francis referred to Harry as a "bastard" (65), a piece of information that interferes with our ability to recognize the contradiction when it occurs. Again, at the beginning of the smallpox incident Esmond reports to us that Dr. Tusher brings the news that one of the maids at Three Castles has smallpox; three pages later, summarizing the incident, Henry writes, "When, then, the news was brought that the little boy at Three Castles was ill with the smallpox . . . " (86). Between the two terms of this contradiction Harry has realized that Nancy Sievewright's small brother, whom he had just seen complaining of a headache, is probably coming down with smallpox (84).

11. Included among Thackeray's working notes for *Esmond* is the following note in which he seems to be preparing for an instance of ambiguous reference or disintegrating image: "*Exchange* — There be many Exchanges in London, besides markets and the Royal Exchange — as that stately building called the New Exchange and Exeter Change, both in the Strand, where all attire for ladies and gentlemen is sold." (Quoted by Anne Thackeray Ritchie, "Introduction," *The Works of William Makepeace Thackeray* [New York, 1899], VII, xxix.)

12. It might be argued that the wide range of incompatible connotations surrounding single images and phrases is not the intentional result of Thackeray's craft — that, for example, the many meanings assigned to "fire" might crop up in any long novel of the period. This argument might be tenable if Thackeray nowhere showed his interest in controlling and limiting an image's connotations; but in *Vanity Fair* he had already shown extreme skill in such control and limitation. Again, the argument might be tenable if the instances of disintegrating images in *Henry Esmond* were an exception rather than the rule, but Thackeray is consistently inconsistent throughout. Most important, these disintegrating images occur in a novel whose key question concerns the validity of subjective truth; as will be shown, even Esmond himself calls attention to the instability of verbal communications.

13. John Loofbourow, *Thackeray and the Form of Fiction*, p. 171.

14. As Alexander Welsh has shown in Part Three of *The City of Dickens* (Oxford, 1971), the equation of female figures with some form of divinity occurs throughout Victorian novels. The omnipresence of this equation does not make its occurrence in *Esmond* any less ironic, however, since Thackeray has specifically discredited the equation within the novel.

15. This reference to slavery probably must be assigned to Thackeray rather than to a narrator who can be comfortably decoupled from the author. Thackeray's attitude to race has been probed by John Sutherland ("Thackeray as Victorian Racialist," *Essays in Criticism* 20 [1970], 441–45) and by Deborah A. Thomas ("Bondage and Freedom in Thackeray's *Pendennis*," *Studies in the Novel* 17:2 [1985],

138–57). Sutherland documents Thackeray's threefold denial of the central abolitionist question: "Am I not a man and a brother too?" Two of these occur in a letter to his mother: "They are not my men and brethren. . . . Sambo is not my man and my brother" (13 Feb. 1853). The third comes in the 1862 novel *Philip* where Thackeray reworks the abolitionist question into a crude slogan: "VOTE FOR ME! AM I NOT A MAN AND A BRUDDER?"

16. There is one form of confusion in identity not included in the text of this section of the discussion because it is not immediately visible in the overt events of the plot. Thackeray continually allows Esmond to describe two different characters in the same words, or allows two different characters to utter almost identical sentences. Esmond and Steele describe young Frank Castlewood in the following way: "[Esmond] never beheld a more fascinating and *charming* gentleman [than Frank]. Castlewood had *not wit so much as enjoyment*. 'The lad looks good things,' Mr. Steele used to say; 'and his laugh *lights up* a conversation as much as ten *repartees* from Mr. *Congreve*.'" (249, 250, italics added). A few pages later, Esmond describes Steele in these words: "There was a kindness about him and a sweet playful fancy that seemed to Esmond far more *charming* than the pointed talk of the brightest *wits*, with their elaborate *repartees* and affected severities. I think Steele *shone* rather than sparkled. Those famous *beaux esprits* of the coffee-houses (Mr. William *Congreve*, for instance, when his gout and his grandeur permitted him to come among us) . . . " (253). The reader interested in this form of confusion should compare Esmond's description of Lord Cutts (240) with his description of Colonel Webb (245, 281); Esmond's description of Webb's pride in his lineal descent (245) with Frank Castlewood's assertions about his lineal descent (227, 229), and again with Isabella's similar comment (55); Esmond's comment on the significance of trivialities (92) with an almost identical comment he attributes to M. Massillon (136); Esmond's descriptions of Marlborough as a god (238, 239) with Addison's (259); Rachel's complaint about the way women are treated in literature (101, 102) with Esmond's (120). One of the areas in which this phenomenon most frequently occurs is in Esmond's descriptions of Beatrix and Rachel.

5

THE EXTERNAL REFERENT: COSMIC ORDER

The Well-Rounded Sphere: Cognition and Metaphysical Structure in Boethius's *Consolation of Philosophy*

I saw on the horizon where plain, sea, and mountain meet, a few low stars, not to be confused with the fires men light at night or that go alight alone. . . .

It is as though you were looking at the squalid earth and the heavens in turn; by the very law of sight you seem to be in the midst now of mud, now of stars. . . .

I say unto you: One must have chaos within to give birth to a dancing star. I say unto you: You still have chaos within.

Beckett, Boethius, Nietzsche

The possibilities of the human soul manifest themselves along a vertical axis: at the lower terminus is the phenomenon of chaos; at the higher, a dancing star. Although master of all movement along this axis, a human being may come to believe it is impossible to leave the nether pole. Recognizing one's capacity for destruction, one despairs. Despairing, one relinquishes control over all moral and psychic energies. The dance of a star, still latent within, is forgotten. The person forfeits what had been the most cherished possibility.

Boethius refused the forfeit. His *Consolation* is an attempt to release those in pain into a sphere where they can participate in the realization of the human spirit. A large body of personal testimony suggests that there was, in fact, a time when the concrete effect of the *Consolation* coincided with its author's intention. Today its consoling power has diminished: St. Jerome's momentary cry, "Deus Absconditus," has become for many an abiding Absence and this Absence in turn often becomes a solid barrier separating the medieval author from his modern reader. If today the *Consolation* is to console, our susceptibility to its power can originate in a reverence (if not for God then) for the attempt of a passionate intelligence to reckon with the mud lest it eclipse the stars. While the validity of the *Consolation*'s argument may have diminished, the honesty of its underlying impulse has not. The intensity of that moral impulse is made visible in the aesthetic excellence of the work; however, that aesthetic excellence itself, though visible, is often unseen.

The structure of the *Consolation of Philosophy* reflects and sustains the idea of the work. The circular relation of form and content is immediately suggested by the title. *Philosophy* originally *consoles* Boethius (book 1) so that he will be receptive to *philosophy*, by means of which he may eventually attain *philosophy* and so be *consoled* (book 5). Rapidly summarized, the ingenuity might seem mere linguistic virtuosity.[1] Philosophy is the cause of its own consummation; philosophy is the cause of the consummation of consolation; consolation is the cause of its own consummation; consolation is the cause of the consummation of philosophy. Knowledge and happiness are one in the co-incidence of form (cause) and idea (end). The extraordinary measures Boethius takes to ensure that form recapitulates idea is the subject of this chapter.

Certainly Boethius did not intend this circularity as a gratuitous act of craftsmanship. On the contrary: the structure of the *Consolation* mirrors his conception of the first and final cause of the universe. For Boethius, God's perfection, His divine simplicity, consists in the coincidence of substance, *id quod est*, and form, *esse* (*Quomodo Substantia*). In book 3, prose 10, Lady Philosophy demonstrates the unity of end, origin, and cause (*summa, cardo, causa*) in the coterminous realities of God, Happiness, and Goodness. A crucial "corollarium" — a word that denotes both "corollary" and "gratuitous gift" — then follows (1.83): man becomes happy by acquiring happiness; happiness is divinity; therefore, man becomes happy by acquiring divinity. The identification of form and content in the *Consolation* is, then, an aesthetic corollary to the metaphysical reality of God: it is Boethius's attempt to attain the gift of godlikeness by participating in a simple unity of form and substance.

Further assurance that a rigorous identification of form and content was crucial to Boethius is found in book 3, prose 12. Both Boethius and Philosophy attempt to define the nature of God's government. Predictably, the first fails and the second succeeds. But, as Boethius himself realizes, what differentiates the two contestants is less the content of their respective explanations than the form, the mode of argument and articulation (11. 65–68). Boethius's beloved Plato had argued in the *Theaetetus* that one approaches knowledge only when the content of belief is attended by *logos*, the verbal image, rational explanation, and differentiating principle of the idea (208 C,D; see also *Timaeus* 29 B). Appropriately, book 3, prose 12 concludes: "You have no cause to marvel at what you have learned from Plato's teaching, that language must be cognate with the subject about which one is speaking." Throughout the *Consolation* Lady Philosophy explicitly links her mode of presentation with that which is presented: "'It cannot be doubted that there is some solid and perfect [*solidam perfectamque*] happiness.' 'Thou hast,' quoth I, 'concluded most firmly and most truly [*Firmissime, verrissime*]'" (3.pr.10. 20–23); "Then taking as it were a new beginning [*alio orsa principio*] she discussed [*disseruit*, both "to argue" and "to plant"] in this manner, 'The generation [*generatio*] . . .'" (4.pr.6.21, 22); "You bind [*astringas*] me to the word necessity [*necessitatis*]" (5.pr.6.97, 98). Philosophy's insistence on the necessity of a form cognate with the idea, present throughout the *Consolation*, becomes most explicit and self-conscious at that point where the idea itself is the identification of God's form and substance (3.pr.10–12).

This identification in the *Consolation* is visible not only in isolated sentences and passages but also in the work as a whole. As a result there emerges the degree of emphasis on aesthetic form found in Plato's dialogues such as the *Republic, Symposium*, or *Phaedrus*, in which the philosophical argument is carried as much by intricacies of structure as by overt statement. But while Plato is Boethius's earthly model and teacher, God is his ultimate model and teacher. Because Boethius conceives of the *Consolation's* structure as a potential vehicle to godlikeness, the extent to which structure coincides with substance is the extent to which he, as author, approximates divine simplicity and participates in the happiness of God's goodness. His success will be demonstrated here by first summarizing the central idea of the *Consolation* and then showing the ways in which that idea manifests itself in the formal structure of the work.

The central idea of the *Consolation* is the definition of man as knower. If Boethius is to regain his humanity, if he is to become man, he must by definition know man, for man's being resides in man's knowing man's being: "Such is the condition of human nature that it surpasses other classes only when it knows itself, but is reduced to a rank lower than beasts when it ceases to know itself" (2.pr.5. 85–88). Book 5 clarifies the nature of man as knower by presenting the hierarchy of cognitive faculties in both its human and cosmic manifestations. That hierarchy, articulated in the final three prose sections of the work, can be summarized as follows:

	COGNITIVE FACULTY	MANIFESTATION WITHIN CREATION	PROPER OBJECT OF EACH FACULTY
(Passive)	1. Sense	Lower Animals: animals without motion (e.g., sea slug)	Material Particular
	2. Imagination	Higher Animals: animals with motion	Immaterial Particular
	3. Reason	Man	Immaterial Universal
(Active) Here cognition and will are identical.	4. Insight	God	Simple idea: all aspects simultaneously seen

All moral and metaphysical questions are ultimately answered with reference to these hierarchies. As is clear from the opening of the *Consolation*, the exile grasps both the concept of universal order and the concept of man as a rational animal: his difficulty originates in his inability to comprehend their relation (1. m.5, pr.6). Consequently, the *Consolation* attempts to articulate this relation between the hierarchy of cognitive faculties within man and the hierarchy of cognitive faculties without man, a relation that in its final formulation entails the two apparently antimonous terms, *man's will* (knowledge and motion) and *God's foreknowledge* (knowledge and stillness).

This concept of graduated cognitive levels determines the structure of the *Consolation*. The idea of the hierarchy generates three distinct patterns. The first is linear and static: the four faculties are reflected in those technical elements of structure, such as the dual media of prose and verse, which are common to all five books. The second pattern is linear and dynamic: there is a steady upward progression from the realm of sense in book 1 to the realm of Insight in book 5. The third pattern is geometric: book 3, verse 9, the physical center of the *Consolation*, is the center of a circle whose circumference is defined by the remainder of book 3, and book 3 is the center of a sphere whose circumference is defined by books 1, 2, 4, and 5. After each of the three patterns has been examined in isolation, the final and single shape of the *Consolation* will begin to emerge.

Technical Elements of the *Consolation*'s Structure: Personification, Verse, Prose, Book Divisions

Because man is knower, the answer to the question "What is man?" requires an answer to the question "What is knowledge?". Here knowledge itself becomes an object of knowledge. Consequently, like any other object of cognition, it is knowable in four aspects: the sensitive or material particular, the imaginative or immaterial particular, the rational or immaterial universal, and the Simple Idea or all aspects simultaneously seen. If the concept of knowledge is not first made knowable in its limited aspects, it can never be known in its ultimate form; for, as Boethius repeatedly asserts, "it is from particulars that all our comprehension of universals is taken" (*Contra Eutychen*, 3.35,36). Boethius attempts to accommodate the four aspects of knowledge in his selection of the *Consolation's* basic structural elements: knowledge is given (a) "sensitive" representation in its personification as Lady Philosophy, (b) "imaginative" representation in its manifestation as poetry, (c) "rational" representation in its manifestation as prose, and (d) representation as "all aspects grasped simultaneously" in that structural element which grasps all structural elements simultaneously, the *Consolation* as a single entity — an entity whose "singularity" and "simultaneity" are made visible in the work's internal bonding: the division into five books, and the multiple bonds by which they are bound.

This section will examine each of these four elements as aspects of knowledge or modes of thought irrespective of particular subject matter. Here, for example, it will be irrelevant that one verse has for its subject the realm of sense (e.g., 1.m.1) and another, the realm of Insight (3.m.9): both are poetic articulations of their subjects; consequently, it will be argued, both here represent the imaginative mode of thought. What matters is the fact of personification rather than what that persona says in any given instance, the fact of the verse medium, prose medium, or book divisions rather than the content of a particular verse, prose section, or book.

Personification: Knowledge as Material Particular

Certainly Lady Philosophy is not without literary antecedents: Homer, Plato, Cicero, Lucretius, Seneca, Augustine, Symmachus, Claudian, and Prudentius have all been credited with contributing to her portrait.[2] Recognition of her participation in a tradition, however, should not deflect attention from her specific function in the structure of the *Consolation*. She is not simply a mechanical response to the author's prolonged immersion in the classics. Although Boethius was sensitive to the antique charm of personification, he was equally sensitive to its inherent epistemological significance.

Heretical interpretations of Christ's *nature* and *person* had provoked the writing of *Contra Eutychen*, Boethius's attempt to provide clearly articulated definitions of the two terms. There *person* is defined as "the individual substance of a rational nature" (3.45): Boethius argues that the term can be applied only to the particular Cicero or Plato and not to the universal species of rational animal, an argument familiar from the traditional distinction between the particular person, Socrates, and the universal quality, wisdom. Sanction to infer the author's concept of "personification" in the *Consolation* from his definition of "person" in a theological treatise is provided by his explication of that definition. He locates the origin of the term in the *persona* of ancient comedy and tragedy; he explains its etymology as "mask," "sound," and, in combination, "the larger sound necessarily produced through a hollow mask"; and he concludes that the dramatic meaning of *persona* is consonant with his theological definition (*CE* 3. 6–25). Even in this theological treatise, then, the concept of person has an aesthetic referent.

Boethius and the reader are not at the opening of the *Consolation* immediately confronted with philosophy; rather, they are confronted with Lady Philosophy. The persona of philosophy is the materialization of philosophy, the "individual substance of a rational nature." By her bodily presence in the prisoner's cell, Lady Philosophy is knowledge as it manifests itself in the material particular, the concept of knowledge made accessible to the senses. When she first enters (1.pr.1), the author emphasizes her physical immediacy: she is neither specter nor apparition but *mulier*, a woman. If he deprives her of tear glands and blood beneath the flesh, he endows her with burning or passionate eyes (1.4, *oculis ardentibus*) and coloring that is "fresh and suggestive of inexhaustible vigor" (1.6). Her acts are physical: she sits by the prisoner's bed (1.pr.1.48), wipes his eyes with her robe (1.pr.2.15), and lays her hand upon his breast (1.pr.2.13). Her relation to the prisoner is physical: he is a sick man with white hair and sagging skin (1.m.1); she is his nurse, his physician (1 passim). Her idiom is physical: she will ascertain the source of his difficulty by "touching" and "stroking" his mind (*tuae mentis attingere atque temptare* [1.pr.6.1]).

Certainly this initial emphasis on the physicality of the persona diminishes as the work progresses. As the prisoner graduates to higher modes of cognition, he approaches the abstract form of knowledge that is only symbolized or materialized in the *mulier*, Lady Philosophy. The function of physical nurse, for example, is transferred from Philosophy in book 1 to Fortune in book 2, where Philosophy herself becomes the spiritual nurse, "the nurse of all virtue" (2.pr.2.9–13; pr.4.1). The artistry with which Boethius charts the details of this progression will be looked at in a later section. For now, it is important to stress that the persona remains an element of structure throughout the *Consolation*. While references to Lady Philosophy's material aspect are concentrated in the opening book, there is nothing to suggest that she gradually grows frail and finally evaporates out of the prison cell. Since higher modes of cognition apprehend objects of sense without using the faculty of sense (5.pr.5), higher books in the *Consolation* need no longer stress the presence of the persona. That her physical appearance is the *sensory* manifestation of knowledge clarifies what might in the later books seem some unphilosophic, if ladylike, moments of behavior. Despite, for example, her continual injunction "Look skyward!", she is seen "for a while looking steadfastly at the ground" (3.pr.2. 1). Repeatedly the author's love for his subject is betrayed in the care with which he selects such details. One instance is the detail chosen for the final reference to Philosophy's physical countenance: it is the slight smile on her lips as she confesses the impossibility of apprehending Simple Unity through a perspective grounded in temporal multiplicity (4.pr.6.5). It is the archaic smile, the smile on the face of the sphinx, calmly acknowledging the inevitable discrepancy between what is and what can be known.

The Meters: Knowledge as Immaterial Particular

The *Consolation* is written in alternating sections of verse and prose. It is the poems, or meters, that represent the imaginative mode of cognition. Perhaps this assertion requires no evidence, since for Boethius, as for his twentieth-century reader, there is a natural association between art and the imagination. In his attempt to differentiate imaginative forms from intellectual forms in *De Trinitate*, Boethius illustrates the former by first alluding to a piece of sculpture before extending the sphere of reference to include nonaesthetic examples (2.19–28). The Latin language itself reflects the association. In the *Consolation*, for example, the concept "paintings" is designated by the word *imagines* (1.pr.1.16). While there is for Boethius an assumed intimacy between art and the imagination, it will be helpful to make the nature of that intimacy explicit by specifying what he meant by that sometimes equivocal term *imagination*, and then showing how the songs conform to that definition.

While the sensitive faculty apprehends the matter of the material particular, the imaginative faculty apprehends its form (5.pr.4). Here a linguistic ambiguity arises, for the higher cognitive powers, reason and Insight, also have form as their object. In *De Trinitate*, the author insists on the importance of avoiding the ambiguity: "We misname the entities that reside in bodies when we call them forms [*formas*]; they are mere images [*imagines*]" (2.53, 54). Consistently throughout the *Theological Treatises* and the *Consolation*, form as the imagination perceives it in the particular is designated by the words *figura*, *imago*, or *forma* qualified and specified by the context, such as *forma corporis*, *forma materia*, *forma imaginis*.

The imagination is intermediate between sense and reason. Like sense, and unlike reason, its object is the particular rather than the universal; like reason, and unlike sense, its object is form rather than matter. While sense is passive, acting only as the recipient of a sensory stimulus, the imagination is active, able to sustain the figure or image of the particular after the sensory stimulus is no longer present (5.pr.6.111–15). It is from the imaginative retention of particular figures that reason derives the form of the universal (5.m.4). The primary function of the imagination is, then, its active mediation between the material world of the senses and the immaterial world of reason, a function celebrated in the penultimate meter of the *Consolation*.

Boethius's conception of the imagination can be summarized as follows. First, its object is the immaterial particular, the "figure" of the material particular. Second, it is an active power: in the hierarchy of creation, imagination first manifests itself in animals capable of external and internal movement, capable of motion and emotion (5.pr.5). Third, its function is to mediate between sense and reason. That structural element of the *Consolation* which represents the imaginative mode of cognition must accommodate these three defining characteristics.

The two basic elements of poetic language, imagery and rhythm, are identical with the first two characteristics of the imagination, its connections with the realm of the immaterial particular and with the capacity for mood and movement. Poetic images or figures belong to the realm of the immaterial particular: as Aristotle explains in *De Anima*, "Images are like sensuous contents except in that they contain no matter" (3.8).[3] While the images in the songs depict particulars rather than abstract concepts, they themselves are immaterial—they are not, as Lady Philosophy is, physically present in the prisoner's cell. The way in which the songs fulfill the second criterion of the imagination is also immediately apparent: rhythm and meter are as essential to song as movement and mood are to the imagination. So intimately related are music and motion that in *De Institutione Musica* Boethius can argue that a music of the spheres, although inaudible, must necessarily exist, since those spheres undergo constant and rapid rotation: "How indeed could the swift mechanism of the sky move silently in its course? And although this sound does not reach our ears (as must for many reasons be the case) the extremely rapid motion of such great bodies could not be altogether without sound" (1.2). Just as music is caused by motion, so it in turn causes motion, motion within the soul of the listener. *De Musica* opens with a chapter devoted to the effects of music on mood and moral growth. Throughout the *Consolation*, the changes in the prisoner's psychological disposition are repeatedly attributed to the meters: they have the power to mollify and make calm (1.pr.5.38–44), to refresh weary minds (3. pr.1. 4–6), to inspire delight (4. pr.6.17–20), and to excite (4. pr.2.2,3).

The first two defining characteristics of the imagination—its connections with the realm of the immaterial particular and its capacity for mood and movement—are, then, visible in the imagery and rhythm so essential to the meters. The third characteristic of the imagination, its function as a mediating power between the faculties of sense and reason, is identical with Boethius's conception of the function of song: "What human music is, anyone may understand by examining his own nature. For it is that which unites the incorporeal activity of reason with the body" (*De Musica* 1. 2).[4] In the *Consolation*, the importance of music's mediating function is visible in the apparent ambivalence of Lady Philosophy's attitude toward music. The first words she utters are an angry dismissal of the prisoner's poetic muses, his "seducing mummers" (1. pr.1,30). The next words she utters are in verse (1.m.2). Her apparent inconsistency is instead a coherent distinction between songs that "do kill the fruitful crop of reason" (1.pr.1.33) and songs that serve philosophy (1.pr.1.40, 41; 2. pr.1.23) — between music that grounds the individual in the sensitive realm and music that leads the individual out of the sensitive into the rational realm. The distinction is a classical one: it occurs throughout Plato (e.g., *Timaeus* 28 A, B; 47 D; *Republic* 401 D); it appears again in Augustine, who is plagued by the fear that he has allowed the sensory beauty of music to become an end in itself rather than a vehicle to God (*Confessions* 10.33); and it emerges once more in Dante, whose Cato chastises the pilgrims when, entranced by song, they linger to rest rather than continuing their upward climb (*Purgatorio* 2.115–23). Boethius's treatment of the meters in the *Consolation* reflects his emphasis on the mediating function of music and the imagination. It is clear why the meters are placed between prose sections, mediating between one argument and the next. It is also clear why each of the final meters in the five books contains a warning to look not toward the ground but toward the sky.[5] Finally, it is clear why the fifth book does not, like the previous four, end with a meter: music, the exponent of the imagination, is not an end in itself but a vehicle to a higher faculty, a faculty that in the *Consolation* is represented by the medium of prose.

Prose: Knowledge as Immaterial Universal

Nowhere in the *Consolation, De Musica, Tractates,* or *De Arithmetica* does Boethius explicitly designate prose the proper medium of rational thought. Nor does Plato, Aristotle, Cicero, or Augustine provide any explicit assurance that Boethius would have associated the two. Nor is there any authority in Whitehead's tardy assertion that prose makes possible the "rationally coordinated" verbal system through which the suggestive resonance of poetry becomes the self-evident truth of philosophy.[6] Assurance that Boethius intended the prose of the *Consolation* to represent the rational manifestation of knowledge is, however, visible in the way he presented that prose. In addition to the obvious and crucial fact that the rational arguments occur in the prose sections, several other factors encourage the identification of reason and prose.[7]

That prose stands for the rational mode of cognition is suggested by the fact that it is presented as a higher, more demanding medium than poetry. At the opening of book 3, the prisoner who has just experienced the refreshing and comforting power of music (pr. 1, 3–6) but whose eyes are clouded with *imagines* (19) is told that he is ready for remedies that are "bitter to the taste, but being inwardly received wax sweet" (13, 14). At a later point Philosophy explains, "Time is short . . . but if the sweetness of verse delight thee, thou must forbear this pleasure for a while, until I propose unto thee some few arguments" (4. pr.6.14-20). The superior power of prose, acknowledged in Lady Philosophy's explicit comments, is also visible in the spatial relations of the media. While there is a continual alternation of poetry and prose throughout the entire work, the ratio of poetry to prose gradually diminishes as one progresses to the higher books: in book 1 the ratio is approximately one to two; in book 5, one to five.

The nature of the relationship between poetry and prose is also suggested by the etymologies of the two works. *Prosa* is derived from *prorsus*, a compound of *pro* and *vorsus*. It is, then, like *versus*, derived from the root *verto* or *vorto*. Verse or *versus* is so named because it entails turning: it requires of its writer and reader the repeated act of turning back to begin a new line.[8] This requirement dissolves when the prefix *pro* is added: while *versus* means "turning," *prorsus* means "forward" or "straight ahead." One begins to wonder whether it is only coincidental that just as verse denotes a continual alternation between forward and backward movement, so the imagination must continually move back and forth between the material world of the senses and the immaterial world of reason; that just as prose denotes a free and forward movement, so "there can be no reasonable nature, unless it be endowed with free will" (5. pr.2.5,6). The other Latin terms for prose also denote the ideas of straightforward movement (*oratio recte*) and freedom from metrical restraint (*oratio soluta, verba soluta*), a freedom whose importance is stressed by Aristotle's *Rhetoric*, which argues that meter destroys the reader's trust and diverts his attention (3.8). Prose is, then, the higher medium: its movement is straightforward rather than back and forth; its flow is directed by logical connectives rather than restricted by meter; its content describes mental acts rather than material objects; its words are the immaterial universals of abstract definition rather than the immaterial particulars of images. Prose makes possible the semantic conception of truth that is inaccessible to poetry.

The identification of prose with reason is evident not only in its ability to accommodate those aspects of knowledge inaccessible to poetry but also in its inability to accommodate that aspect of knowledge which belongs to the sphere of Insight. The point in the *Consolation* where the subject becomes the simplicity and simultaneity of the divine presence is also the point where the final inadequacy of prose is acknowledged: "The cause of which obscurity is that the motion of human discourse cannot attain to the simplicity of divine knowledge" (5. pr.4.6-9). Just as reason is able to move relentlessly forward through deductive arguments without turning back to the material universe, so the great strength of prose is its ability to move relentlessly forward. But its strength is also its weakness. Its multiple truths can be presented only sequentially, not simultaneously. Like reason and unlike Insight, it tries to approximate by moving the plenitude it cannot comprehend by staying (5. pr.6.54,55).

Book Divisions: Knowledge as Insight

The highest power of cognition, that which God alone possesses, is Insight. It is that faculty which subsumes all other faculties, comprehends all but is comprehended by none, contains but is itself uncontained (5. pr.4.92–104; 5. pr.5.55,56). Accordingly, in the *Consolation* it is represented by that which contains all the previously examined structural elements, that which binds but is itself "enclosed within no bounds" (5. pr.5. 55–56), the work as a whole.

The *Consolation* approximates the simplicity and simultaneity of Insight through the book divisions and the multiple bonds by which they are bound. It will not be possible to demonstrate the nature of this binding until the final section of this discussion. For the moment, however, Insight can, on a much more elementary plane, be understood to be represented by each individual book—each a single entity containing persona, verse, and prose, each a single unity comprehending the sensory, imaginative, and rational manifestations of knowledge.

The preceding discussion has shown the way in which Boethius's selection of the *Consolation*'s basic structural elements accommodates the four cognitive faculties. This first manifestation of the cognitive hierarchy is a static one: persona, verse, prose, and book divisions are all consistently present throughout the entire work. The following section will focus on the second manifestation of the hierarchy, the steady upward progression from the realm of sense in book 1 to the realm of Insight in book 5. While the first pattern was static, the second is dynamic. An understanding of the way in which the work simultaneously accommodates both the static and the dynamic requires a recognition of the internal complexity characterizing Boethius's use of the technical elements.

As has been shown, persona is the sensitive manifestation of knowledge; poetry the imaginative manifestation; prose the rational; and each book, Insight. But each of these technical elements represents not simply *knowledge* as it manifests itself in one particular aspect, but *each aspect of knowledge* as it manifests itself in that one particular aspect. Lady Philosophy is not simply the sensitive manifestation of knowledge, but the sensitive manifestation of the sensitive, imaginative, and rational aspects of knowledge. Boethius's initial presentation of his persona proceeds according to this hierarchy. He first describes her physical vitality and great age (1. pr.1.1–9)—the sensitive aspect of knowledge as it manifests itself in the material particular. He then moves to the imaginative aspect of knowledge as it manifests itself in the material particular: he describes her stature (the *figura* or form of the material particular and, therefore, its immaterial particular), which alternates between the height of humanity and the height of heaven, mediating between the material and immaterial realms. He then presents the rational manifestation of knowledge as it manifests itself in the material particular, her robe with its indissoluble weave and its abstract symbols. Significantly, of these three aspects, it is only the first – her health and age, the sensitive manifestation of the sensitive aspect of knowledge – that is wholly intelligible to the prisoner. His lengthy first sentence of description (1–9) sustains a tone of conviction until the final phrase, *statura discretionis ambiguae*, her stature uncertain and ambiguous; the sensitive manifestation of the imaginative aspect of knowledge eludes his grasp. It is only in the poetry that he will comprehend the imaginative aspect of knowledge: the imagination's intimacy with the realm of the immaterial particular, unintelligible when presented in the persona's figura, becomes intelligible in the imagery of the meters; the imagination's mediation between the material and immaterial spheres, unintelligible when presented in the persona's changes in height, will become intelligible in the mediating power of the meters. Similarly, the sensitive manifestation of the rational aspect of knowledge is equally inaccessible to the prisoner: the weave of the persona's robe is both torn and darkened, obscured by duskiness like pictures in a smoky room (16, 17). It is only in the prose that he will comprehend the rational aspect of knowledge: reason's intimacy with the sphere of the immaterial universal, unintelligible when presented in the obscured abstract symbols on the persona's robe, becomes intelligible when presented as the vocabulary of logical definition in the prose; the indivisibility of universals, unintelligible when presented in the weave of the persona's robe (*texuerat, intextum* [16, 19]) becomes intelligible as the "weave" of rational arguments (*contexo rationes* [4. pr.6.20]; *inextricabilem labyrinthum rationibus texens* [3. pr.12.83]) in the prose. While, then, the persona represents the sensitive manifestation of the sensitive, imaginative, and rational aspects of knowledge, it is only the sensitive manifestation of the sensitive aspect that can be fully comprehended here, for "the superior force of comprehending embraceth the inferior but the inferior can by no means attain to the superior" (5. pr.4. 91–93).

Just as the persona represents the sensitive manifestation of the various levels of the cognitive hierarchy, so the poetry represents the imaginative manifestation of those various levels: which level is represented at any given moment depends upon the content and meter of a given verse. So, too, the different prose sections, through their changes in content, represent the rational manifestation of the different cognitive levels. The controlled complexity of the *Consolation*'s structure begins to emerge. While, for example, the stature of the persona is the sensitive manifestation of the imaginative aspect of knowledge, the opening meter – in which the prisoner-philosopher describes the physical effects of his illness and old age – is the imaginative manifestation of the sensitive aspect of knowledge. Again, while Lady Philosophy's robe is the sensitive manifestation of the rational aspect of knowledge, that prose section devoted to her physical description (1. pr.1) is the rational manifestation of the sensitive aspect of knowledge. It is this internal complexity of the technical elements that makes possible the progression through the work, for while each book represents Insight, the content of a given book determines which level of the cognitive hierarchy is there perceived by Insight. As the following section will suggest, the books of the *Consolation* move from Insight's grasp of the realm of sense in book 1 to Insight's grasp of the realm of Insight in book 5.

The Five Books of the *Consolation*:
Progression through the Cognitive Hierarchy

The *Consolation* contains two explicit definitions of man. The first is given by Boethius in the opening book; it is the inadequacy of this definition that alerts Lady Philosophy to the seriousness of her patient's sickness. The second and correct definition is enunciated by Lady Philosophy in the final book. The two definitions are as follows:

Man is an animal rational and mortal. (1. pr.6.36, 37)

Man is an animal rational and biped. (5. pr.4.108)

There is, of course, a logical basis for Philosophy's quarrel with her student's definition: the fact that man dies does not differentiate his species from other species while the fact that he is biped does. But the displacement of the first definition by the second has metaphorical significance that goes beyond its logical validity. In the transition from the first to the second, man is stripped of his mortality and endowed with two feet, changes that stress his capacity to carry himself toward immortality.

The *Consolation*, like so much of the medieval literature that would follow it, has as its central focus a journey or pilgrimage, a sustained movement toward immortality. While this movement is partially conveyed through metaphors of physical movement, it is primarily a mental journey, a journey toward understanding and philosophic insight. The progression does not evolve from changes in subject matter, for in its subject matter the *Consolation* is very repetitious. The same questions — what are good, evil, fate, and free will? — are reiterated throughout the entire work. The progression evolves instead from the changing perspectives through which that subject matter is viewed. As Philosophy herself counsels, "All that is known is not comprehended according to the force which it hath in itself, but rather according to the faculty of them which know it" (5. pr.4.75–77). As will be shown, the five books of the *Consolation* progress through successive levels of the cognitive hierarchy. Those issues that are viewed through the faculty of sense in the opening book are in the final book viewed through the faculty of Insight.

This section will show the progression of the cognitive faculties from sense in book 1 to imagination in book 2, reason in book 4, and Insight in book 5. But before looking at that progression, it is first necessary to explain the relation of book 3—missing in the sequence just given—to this structural progression. While the other four books follow one another through successive levels of the cognitive hierarchy, through successive levels of the created material world, the central book of the *Consolation* is lifted out of and above the material world of creation. The relation of book 3 to the other four books can be represented visually (Figure 30).[9]

Book 3 is divided into two parts of almost equal length: the two differ by about one hundred lines. Sections 1 through 9 recall all that has been said in books 1 and 2; sections 10 through 12 anticipate all that will be said in books 4 and 5. Sections 1 through 9, like books 1 and 2, deal with and ultimately dismiss the false forms of happiness, while sections 10 through 12, like books 4 and 5, deal with the true form of happiness. Implicit in this distinction between the false forms and the true form is the distinction between finite diversity and divine unity, a distinction reflected in the differing treatments of the false and true forms. In the first half of the *Consolation*, each of the false forms of happiness—sufficiency, power, respect, fame, and pleasure—is examined in isolation despite the fact that in each case the argument given is almost identical to the others. In the second half, an argument about one form is considered

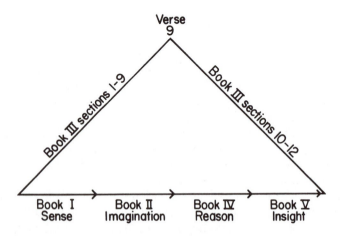

FIGURE 30. Relationship of book 3 of Boethius's *Consolation* to books 1, 2, 4, and 5.

necessarily valid with reference to all forms: if, for example, Philosophy arrives at a truth about sufficiency or power, she will then simply say, "And we may conjecture the same of respect, fame, and pleasure" (3. pr.10.122,123; see 3. pr.10.102 and 3. pr.11.14). Eventually, however, even these individual terms are completely displaced by single and all-embracing terms for happiness, goodness, unity. This distinction between diversity in the first half of the *Consolation* and unity in the second half is, in turn, reflected in the numerical divisions of book 3: the first half is composed of nine sections and the second half of three; the second is, then, the square root of the first.

While book 3 thus recapitulates and anticipates the contents of the other four books, it does so in a way that distinguishes it from those four books. The central book is raised out of and above the progression[10] by the perfection of its reasoning, by the "inextricable labyrinth of arguments" with which Philosophy creates a "wonderful circle of divine simplicity" (pr.12.82-86). Sections 1 through 9 proceed inductively; a conclusion — unity is good, division evil — is reached in prose 9; this conclusion then becomes the first premise in 10 through 12, where the reasoning becomes deductive. The perfection of Philosophy's weave of arguments is matched by the perfection of Boethius's ability to assimilate those arguments. Not once here does he falter, protest, or backslide as he occasionally will even in book 4 (4. pr.1.1-19; 4. pr.4.1-5, 31-33, 91-94; 4. pr.5.3-22; 4. pr.7.12-16); here he becomes *o alumne laetor* in whom his teacher rejoices (3. pr.11.17,18).

The central book, then, is a retreat from the world into the "most secret seat of the mind" (3. pr.2.1,2), where Philosophy and her student attain the sight of God, after which they return to earth (books 4 and 5) to confront with new vision the apparent paradoxes of the mortal realm: their journey "Now lifts its head to highest things,/ Now down to lowest falls again,/ Now turning back unto itself/ False things with true things overthrows" (5.m.4.22-25; see also 11. 35-40 and m.3.28-31). As one reads the books sequentially, the central and perfect book is flanked on both sides by books that, even at their height, are capable of only a lesser perfection, flawed by their participation in the created world. This arrangement reflects the picture of the universe celebrated in the *Consolation*'s central and climactic meter (book 3, verse 9), the picture of the created encircling the uncreated, Plotinus's "dance of the imperfect around the perfect."[11] The relationship between books 1, 2, 4, and 5 and book 3 is analogous to the relationship between time and eternity; for just as time is a moving image of eternity (5. pr.6.29-31), so books 1, 2, 4, and 5 provide a moving or sequential image of all that is contained in stillness and simultaneity in book 3. It is well that Boethius placed this book at the center rather than at the end of the *Consolation*. Dante took his pilgrim to heaven but did not, at the end of the *Commedia*, bring him back to earth again. Boethius did. That he did, assures us that the final vision of the *Consolation* is one attainable by mortals on earth.

One additional aspect of book 3's relation to the other four books, implicit in the visual illustration above, concerns the bonds between book 1's verse 1, book 3's verse 9, and book 5's conclusion, prose 6—the three vertices of the triangle. Book 3, verse 9, the pinnacle, is a direct inversion of book 1, verse 1, the lowest point in the *Consolation*, the point where Boethius bitterly protests Death's deafness to his pleas for life to end. Book 3, verse 9, in contrast, is a prayer, not a complaint; its preoccupation is not Death, the personification of man's mortality, but God, the realization of man's potential immortality. The bond between book 3, verse 9, and the conclusion of book 5, prose 6—the second, though different climax of the *Consolation*—is equally important. Book 3, verse 9, a hymn to God, a prayer to discover "the source of the supreme good" (3. pr.9.102), is uttered in order to prepare a "proper foundation" for the endeavor: this answered prayer makes possible all subsequent understandings attained in books 3, 4, and 5. These understandings, in turn, climax in the final understanding of book 5, prose 6, the final understanding of the *Consolation*, the understanding that the relationship between man and God is one that carries the assurance that prayer is not vain. The relation between book 3, verse 9 and the end of book 5, prose 6 is, then, circular: the prayer to see ultimately enables Boethius to see that prayer, immediate communication with God, is actual.

This, then, is the nature of the structural relationship between book 3 and the four books that surround it. It now remains to show the progression through the cognitive hierarchy in books 1, 2, 4, and 5, a progression that begins when Boethius's teacher converts his plea of political innocence into the charge of philosophical ignorance. Some evidence of this progression has already been encountered in the examination of the *Consolation*'s technical elements in the first part of this essay: the references to the physical countenance of Philosophy, to Boethius, and to their surroundings grow far less frequent as one progresses to the higher books; so too the ratio of poetry, the exponent of the imagination, to prose, the exponent of reason, diminishes. These two details are symptomatic of the sustained and coherent movement from one faculty to the next as one moves through successive books.

As noted earlier, the different prose sections, through their changes in content, represent the rational manifestation of the four cognitive levels. Their changing content and the resulting progression are immediately visible in the changing remedies or modes of argument used by Lady Philosophy. Book 1 represents Sense, for here Philosophy's higher talents are diverted by the necessity of chasing mummers, chastising and comforting the prisoner, and making the diagnosis of his illness that will allow her to go on to higher remedies. In book 2, the mode of argument is

Imaginative: here Philosophy's two remedies are what she herself repeatedly designates as "music and rhetoric" (2. pr.1.21,23; pr.3.5,6; 3. pr.1.5).
The bond between music and the imagination has already been shown.
The bond between rhetoric and the imagination is equally strong. Rhetoric is credited for its "power of sweet persuasion" (2. pr.1.21,22), its ability
to give arguments a "fair form" (2. pr.3.4,5), and its power to comfort (3.
pr.1.6); but it is explicitly differentiated at the opening of book 3 from
inward arguments, arguments addressed exclusively to the rational faculty
(3. pr.1.1-14). Like the imagination and like music, rhetoric mediates
between the material realm of the body and the immaterial realm of
reason, for it is by appealing to the emotions that it leads its listener to
the truth of its argument.[12]

The arguments in book 4, by contrast, are devoid of emotional appeal.
In fact, Boethius is here not always immediately able to assimilate Philosophy's teachings; here he is like the young Socrates in *Parmenides* who is not
wholly willing to accept the "necessary conclusion" to which the logic of the
argument relentlessly leads (4. pr.4.33-39, 91-110). Philosophy's mode of
argument, now far more demanding, has moved from the Imaginative to
the Rational, from rhetoric to reason. While the rational mode is superior
to the imaginative, it is still necessarily flawed by its participation in the
temporal world. Philosophy acknowledges the difficulty of attaining a
vision of unity through the perspective of temporal multiplicity. She explains that their investigation of good and evil requires that they follow
two separate paths, moving back and forth between them (4. pr.2.1-11;
pr.3.32 ff.); at another point she confesses that their subjects of inquiry
are multiple, and, because they cannot all be pursued simultaneously, as
soon as "one doubt has been removed, countless others spring up in its
place, like the Hydra's head" (4. pr.6.7-9). However, the problems of
multiplicity and temporality dissolve in the transition from book 4 to book
5, for now Reason yields to Insight as the mode of argument graduates
from the logical to the analogical. In the early part of the *Consolation*,
analogical movement between the temporal and the eternal is considered
impossible: Philosophy cautions her student that "limited things can be
compared among themselves but the infinite in no way admits comparison
with the limited" (2. pr.7. 57-60). The infinite does begin to admit comparison with the limited, however, as one progresses through the books.
Analogies appear and become more frequent until, by the final book,
analogy resides at the very heart of Philosophy's discourse.[13] Man's temporal existence now becomes the metaphorical ground for the exploration of
eternity. Philosophy presents to her student the description of the cognitive hierarchy and shows him how an understanding of the relations
among the three lowest faculties makes possible an understanding of the
relation between those finite three and the infinite fourth. In this fifth
book, Philosophy has exhorted Boethius, "Let us raise ourselves to that

height where reason will perceive what it can't itself perceive" (5. pr.5. 50–53)—let us see the unseeable. Analogy bestows visibility on the invisible by permitting that mental leap from the created world to the uncreated mind of God.

The intimacy between Insight and analogy can be seen by contrasting the analogical mode of argument here with the deductive logic that dominates book 4. Deduction belongs to the temporal world in which events necessarily follow one another *sequentially*:

A is B.
B is C.
∴ C is A.

While the final term is built on the first two, it *follows* from and replaces them in our attention. In contrast, analogy—

A:B::C:D

—is like Insight; for just as Insight grasps all aspects of knowledge simultaneously (5.pr.4.100–104), so the analogical phrase grasps all its terms simultaneously, requires that all terms be simultaneously present in the mind. Analogy, reenacting the simultaneity of Insight by illuminating things in the immediacy of their identification with other things, affirms the consistent repetition of a single pattern throughout the created and uncreated worlds, affirms the unity of divine consciousness.

While analogy is the dominant manifestation of Insight in book 5, four additional factors signal the transition to a perspective characterized by simultaneity. First, the deductive "It follows," which recurs throughout book 4 (e.g., 4. pr.2.35,68; pr.4.73,74,88,127; pr.7.1) is almost totally absent in book 5, where it is usually displaced by the definitive "It is" (5. pr.4, p.6 passim). The sequential future has become the assertive present. Second, simultaneity is on several occasions explicitly attributed to the ideas or actions of Philosophy or Boethius:

"There is no fear [that I will not be able to finish the direct journey]," quoth I, "for it will be a great ease to me to understand those things in which I take great delight, and *simultaneously*, when thy disputation is fenced in on every side with sure conviction, there can be no doubt made of anything thou shalt infer." "I will," quoth she, "do as thou wouldst me have," and *simultaneously* began in this manner. (5.pr.1.13–18; italics mine)

Significantly, the single other time that the adverb *simul* is used in the *Consolation* to describe the actions of Philosophy occurs at the physical midpoint of the work, in the transition from book 3, prose 9, to the climactic verse 9. The aura of having escaped the confines of the temporal is further reinforced by Philosophy's apparent foreknowledge of her student's thoughts; for like Beatrice in the *Paradiso*, Philosophy toward the end of book 5 anticipates Boethius's questions and objections. The reader repeatedly encounters phrases such as "Here if thou sayest . . . I will grant . . . but I will answer" (5. pr.6.95,98,100), "But thou wilt say . . . " (pr.6.136), and "But yet thou wilt inquire" (pr.6.145)—phrases that create the impression that what is time-future to Boethius and the reader is time-present to our teacher. Finally, simultaneity is visible in the concluding affirmation of prayer, for prayer not only confirms the immediacy of the relation between man and God but also allows man to participate in God's everlasting present and thereby indirectly participate in his own future. The transition from Reason in book 4 to Insight in book 5 is, then, primarily visible in the displacement of the sequential by the simultaneous, a displacement signaled by the presence of analogy, assertion, anticipation, and prayer.

The progression through the cognitive hierarchy in books 1, 2, 4, and 5, visible in Lady Philosophy's changing remedies, is also visible in her patient's changing condition. In book 1, Philosophy's mode of argument is grounded in the sensory because her patient is grounded in the sensory. There are repeated allusions to the fact that his senses are impaired: he is tongue-tied and dumb (1. pr.2.20; pr.4.131); his sight is blinded by tears (1. pr.2.15–18; m.2.1–3; pr.1.44,45); his hearing, too, is affected (Philosophy asks him if he is an "ass deaf to the lyre" [1. pr.4.5]). As one progresses to subsequent books, Boethius's difficulties are no longer located in the sensory mode of cognition. His growth can be seen by focusing on the concept of blindness. In the opening book the cause of his blindness is physical; his vision is obstructed by tears (pr.1.44,45; pr.2.15–18; m.2.1–3). In book 2, the cause of blindness is no longer the material particular but the immaterial particular, for Boethius's vision is said to have been dimmed by *imagines* (3. pr.1.21). In book 4 it is the nature of reason itself that limits vision, for man is "penned in by the narrow space of time" (pr.6.16), confined to a perspective that converts the singular and simultaneous into the multiple and sequential. In the final book Philosophy demands that Boethius transcend his mortality, the ultimate source of blindness (5. m.3.8), and let reason "see what she can not behold in herself" (5. pr.5.52,53), that is, God's "providence or 'looking forth'" (5. pr.6.70–72). The *Consolation*, then, moves from the physical cause of Boethius's blindness in book 1 to the beneficent reality of God's vision in book 5.

The progression visible in the concept of blindness is again visible in the concept of movement. Sense, the reader is told in book 5, is the faculty of animals incapable of movement.[14] Accordingly, at the opening of book 1 Boethius is described in images of inertia. He complains that "life drags out its wearying delays" (1. m.1.20); he is surrounded by images of chains (m.2.25; m.4.18; m.7.29–31), lethargy (pr.3.12), weight (m.2.26), and men lying prostrate on the ground (pr.4.169, 170; m.5.32,33). Imagination, explains Philosophy in book 5, first manifests itself in animals capable of movement. The imagery of inertia in book 1, consequently, gives way to the imagery of movement in book 2. But it is not yet the controlled, self-willed, rational movement that will be found in book 4; here it is precarious and erratic. While the idea of erratic movement finds its primary manifestation in the image of Lady Fortune (book 2 passim), it is also present in many other images describing movement dictated not by man's will but by an external and arbitrary force (2. pr.1.55, 56; m.1; m.2 passim), as well as in Philosophy's exhortations to hold firm, to seek stability (pr.4.30–36; m.4.14–22). In the transition from book 2 to book 4, the concept of movement changes not only from the erratic to the controlled but also from the physical to the mental (4.pr.1.35–38; m.1): what was previously the physical course of a journey now becomes the mental paths of the argument (4. pr.2.9-11,71–73) and the ethical "paths of high example" (m.7.33–35). When images of physical movement do occur, their function is no longer descriptive, as in book 2, but analytic. For example, when attempting to convince her student that the good are more powerful than the wicked, Philosophy demonstrates the superiority of natural over unnatural acts by comparing walking on one's feet to walking on one's hands (4. pr.2.55–62); shortly afterward, the image of running a race is used analogically to clarify the nature of reward and punishment (4. pr.3.4-8). While in book 5 there again appear images of physical movement that function analytically,[15] as well as images of mental movement that function descriptively, the dominant manifestation of movement is almost wholly divorced from any imagistic content or capacity. Just as the imagery of vision ultimately climaxes in the investigation of "pro-vidence," so the imagery of movement ultimately climaxes in the second great issue of book 5, the metaphysical correlative of physical and mental movement, free will. The concept of movement, then, progresses from images of inertia in book 1, to images of erratic movement in book 2, to images of mental and controlled movement in book 4, to an exploration of the metaphysical and moral reality of man's capacity for free will in book 5.

Finally, the changing cognitive perspectives, visible in Philosophy's changing remedies and in the imagery surrounding Boethius's changing condition, are also visible in the progression in subject matter. While the same questions are reiterated throughout the *Consolation*, the nature of any given subject changes as the perspective through which it is viewed changes. One subject is the nature of man. As suggested at the opening of this section, a comparison of the two explicit definitions of man (1. pr.6.36,37; 5. pr.4.108) reveals that he begins in book 1 as a mortal creature and ends in book 5 as an immortal being. The distance between these two definitions is mediated by a more gradual progression in the conception of man as one moves through the cognitive hierarchy.

In the final books Philosophy explains that "Man himself is beheld in different ways by sense-perception, imagination, reason, and intelligence" (5. pr.4.84, 85; see also 11. 85–91). Accordingly, man is beheld in different ways in the four books. In the opening book, man is seen through the sensitive faculty, as he manifests himself in the material particular—not man the species but the particular person Boethius. The movement through subsequent books is a movement away from the particular toward the universal. This progression was implicit in the preceding discussion of the imagery: images of blindness and movement, initially introduced as expressions of Boethius's condition, are increasingly divorced from him in the higher books.

A second manifestation of this progression is the decreasing emphasis on biography. The dominant interest of book 1 is in Boethius's present circumstances and their immediate cause. While one again encounters biography in the first half of book 2, the nature of the biographical allusions has changed. While book 1 focused almost entirely on Boethius's present, now that focus expands to include his past; while in book 1 his prosperity was measured solely by his own isolated successes and failures, now his identity becomes partially contingent on his participation in a larger humanity, for Philosophy demands that he measure his prosperity not only by his own successes and failures but also by those of his wife, his sons, and his father-in-law. By the middle of book 2 the biographical allusions begin to dissolve (pr.4.41 ff.). Because Philosophy no longer addresses herself exclusively to her student, the antecedent of "you" ceases to be Boethius and becomes "you mortal men" (2.pr.4.72), "you creatures of the earth" (2. pr.6.14, 15). With the exception of one oblique reference to Boethius's exile (4.pr.5.4–7), books 4 and 5 are completely devoid of biographical allusion.[16]

Perhaps the most important manifestation of the evolving conception of man is its movement through different planes of existence. The opening book is dominated by references to Boethius's physical well-being. The physical is displaced by the psychological in book 2, which examines the multiple sources of mortal pleasure and pain. The psychological, in turn, yields to the moral in book 4, where man's capacity for good and evil is explored. Finally, in book 5 the dialogue transcends moral categories and becomes metaphysical, examining man in the immediacy of his relation with God.

The sequence of stages through which this conception of man evolves— from the physical through the psychological and moral to the metaphysical—is equally descriptive of other subjects in the *Consolation*. While, for example, Philosophy proves that evil has no existence (3. pr.12.80,81,96, 97), in each book there emerges an apparent evil that must be dealt with and dismissed. In the central book, book 3, the essential definition of goodness is given: goodness is unity. Its opposite, evil, is division or disjunction (pr.9.45–49). In each of the other four books, a particular form of disunity appears. In the opening book the apparent evil is physical. It is the distance between Boethius's illness and desired health, the distance between his place of exile and his home:

> "Doth the cruelty of fortune's rage need further declaration, or doth it not sufficiently appear in itself? Doth not the very countenance of this place move thee? Is this the library which thou thyself hadst chosen to sit in at my house. . . . Had I this attire or countenance when I searched the secrets of nature with thee?" (pr.4. 7–15)

In book 2 the apparent evil is psychological: it is the emotional pain that results from the perception of change, the perception of the discrepancy between what fortune gives at one moment and what she gives at the next (2. pr.1.3–6, 15–18). It is in the fourth book that evil becomes explicitly moral: this is the only book of the four in which the term *evil* consistently recurs, for it has become a rationally articulated category. Furthermore, man is here not only a potential victim of evil, as in books 1 and 2, but also a potential agent. The "chiefest cause of [Boethius's] sorrow" (pr.1.9,10), however, and therefore the major source of apparent evil, is not the existence of wicked men but the discrepancy between vice and virtue on the one hand and punishment and reward on the other (pr.1.9–19). In the fifth book the disjunction is metaphysical or epistemological, for there is an apparent "enmity between two truths" (m.4.2,3), the truth of God's Providence and the truth of man's free will.

A third instance of the progression in subject matter is the evolving conception of the coincidence of knowledge and power. In book 1 the idea is given sensitive representation in the objects carried by Philosophy, her books (knowledge) and her scepter (power). In book 2 the idea is given imaginative representation in the imitation or impersonation of Fortune (power) by Philosophy (knowledge). The idea is given rational representation in book 4 where, through reasoned discourse, Philosophy proves the truth of Plato's words in the *Gorgias* "that only wise men can do that which they desire" (4. pr.2.140–42; see also pr.3. 15,29–32). Finally, the coincidence of knowledge and power is represented in the fifth book by the climactic recognition that God's foreknowledge and man's free will are harmonious truths.

But the single most crucial progression in subject matter is the changing conception of cosmic order. Throughout the *Consolation* recur the problematic terms *chance, fortune, fate,* and *Providence.* Certainly these concepts are not unrelated. Repeatedly a discussion focusing on one of the terms will, without explanation or hesitation, slide over to focus on a second term. In the midst of a passage investigating the nature of chance, for example, Boethius suddenly asks, "Is there nothing that can rightly be called chance or fortune?" (5. pr.1.33,34). The relation implied by this repeated act of cross-reference is made explicit in three passages at the close of book 4 and the opening of book 5, where the dialogue openly addresses itself to the relation between fate and Providence (4. pr.6.21–101), fortune and Providence (4. pr.7.1–55), and, finally, chance and Providence (5. pr.1.4–57). Only in the first of these passages is the precise nature of the relationship articulated: what Insight in the purity of its vision sees as Providence, reason in the limitation of its temporality and multiplicity sees as fate (4. pr.6.78–82). While the next two passages are less explicit, there is a clear implication[17] that just as fate is providence viewed from below, so fortune is fate viewed from below, and chance is fortune viewed from below. That is, just as fate is Providence as it manifests itself to the rational faculty, so fortune is Providence as it manifests itself to the imaginative faculty, and chance, Providence as it manifests itself to the sensitive faculty.

That this hierarchical conception of cosmic order corresponds to the four cognitive faculties is suggested by the disposition of the four terms in the *Consolation*. The term *chance* occurs most frequently in book 1,[18] *fortune* in book 2, *fate* in book 4, and *Providence* in book 5. More important, the correspondence is suggested by the nature of the faculties themselves. The faculty of sense is capable only of perceiving the material particular: unlike the imagination, it is incapable of sustaining the image of the particular after the particular is no longer materially present. It is an atemporal faculty. Throughout book 1 Boethius is so overwhelmed by his immediate present (literally, "prae-sens," that which is before the senses) that he suffers from the loss of memory (1. pr.2.13,14; pr.3.31–34; pr.6.25,26, 34,42,46,47). Because the sensitive faculty, capable of perceiving only a series of unrelated moments each eclipsed by its successor, is incapable of perceiving time, it is also incapable of perceiving cause. It becomes, therefore, a victim of chance, a word that denotes the absence of causation, the absence of any principle of cosmic order.[19] The perception of time originates with the imaginative mode of cognition, for the power to sustain the image of the particular after the particular is no longer materially present is the power of memory. Accordingly, it is in book 2, the book that represents the imaginative faculty, that Boethius learns "It is not sufficient to behold that which we have before our eyes" (pr.1.45,46) and begins to regain his memory (pr.1.9–12; pr.3.14–44; pr.4.3,4). The power of memory, in turn, makes possible the perception of cause, the perception of a connection between anterior and posterior events. Unlike reason, however, the imagination expresses its perception of agency not in the language of abstract universals but in the language of the immaterial particular, not in the vocabulary of causal sequence but in a *figura*, the figure of Lady Fortune.

The progression through the four conceptions of cosmic order is, finally, accompanied by a progression in imagery. The sensitive faculty, incapable of perceiving pattern, sees only chance, the absence of pattern.

Consequently, the concept of chance is unaccompanied by any single, coherent image in the *Consolation*. The imagination is capable of perceiving pattern: its conception of cosmic order is represented by an imaginative object, Fortune's wheel. In the transition from imagination to reason, from fortune to fate, the image of the wheel is displaced by the image of multiple and moving concentric circles (4. pr.6.65–78). While both Fortune's wheel and this new image involve the idea of a circle, the displacement of the first by the second represents a progression from a material object to an abstract geometric figure, as well as a progression from a dependence on the precarious reversibility of "up" and "down" (2. pr.2.31–33) to a dependence on the predictable measure of distance between "center" and "circumference" (4. pr.6.73–76). In the transition from fate to Providence, such distinctions as *up* and *down* and *center* and *circumference* dissolve and are replaced by absolute unity and consistency, "for such is the form of the Divine substance that it is neither divided into outward things, nor receiveth any such into itself" (3. pr.12. 102–4). While the idea of the circle residing in the image of fortune and in the image of fate is carried forward into the image of Providence, the multiplicity, motion, and two-dimensionality of "the multiple and moving circles of fate" are replaced by the singularity, the stillness, and the three-dimensionality of that shape considered by Parmenides and Plato to be of all shapes the most perfect: "a sphere well rounded on all sides" (3. pr.12.106). As the concluding section of this discussion will show, the final shape of the *Consolation* is also "a sphere well rounded on all sides."

Before examining that final shape, it will be helpful to summarize and clarify the relation between the two manifestations of the cognitive hierarchy already examined, the hierarchy visible in the technical elements and the hierarchy visible in the progression of content from book 1 to book 5. Both the similarity and the difference between the two can be articulated in terms of time. As this section of the discussion has suggested, the progression through the cognitive hierarchy in books 1, 2, 4, and 5[20] is accompanied by a progression in temporal perspective. Book 1 represents the limited atemporal, for it is grounded in the present; book 2 represents the recovery of the past, the power of memory; book 4 represents sequential time—past, present, and future; and book 5 represents the simultaneity of the eternal present. There is a parallel progression within the technical elements: *persona*, the concept of knowledge made immediately accessible to the senses, is atemporal; *verse* represents the emergence of the retentive faculty, for in its imagery it reflects and sustains the content of the previous prose sections;[21] *prose* represents sequential time, the free and forward movement from past to present to future; and each *book*, containing persona, verse, and prose simultaneously, represents the eternal present. While, then, there is a parallel progression in temporal perspectives within each of the two hierarchies, the two can also be differentiated on the basis of time. The technical elements are a static manifestation of the cognitive hierarchy, a static manifestation of temporal progression. Persona, verse, prose, and book divisions all remain consistently and unchangingly present from the opening to the close of the *Consolation*; persona, for example, represents the present at the beginning as at the end; prose represents sequential time at the beginning as at the end. The technical elements are, therefore, atemporal. The progression from book 1 to book 5, in contrast, represents sequential time, for as the reader progresses from the opening to the close of the *Consolation*, so the cognitive and temporal perspectives progress. Finally, as will be shown, there is a third manifestation of the cognitive hierarchy, one that subsumes and unifies all previous hierarchies through analogical binding, one that binds but is itself unbound, one that represents simultaneous time, the fullness and perfection of God's eternal present.[22]

The Analogical Binding of the *Consolation*

The verse that resides at almost the exact spatial center of the *Consolation* and that is unanimously applauded as the finest poem of the work is book 3, verse 9, at once a prayer to discover the ultimate principle of cosmic order and a hymn praising that order. The antecedents of the poem in the first half of Plato's *Timaeus*, which have long been recognized, have great significance in the final structure of the *Consolation*. Lines 6–12 of Boethius's climactic poem speak of the elemental binding of hot and cold, wet and dry, fire and earth—the proportions with which God creates cosmic harmony. These lines are an allusion to *Timaeus* 31C and 32A, the passage in which Plato describes proportion and the nature of the most perfect bond:

> In beginning to construct the body of the All, God was making it of fire and earth. But it is not possible that two things alone should be conjoined without a third: for there must needs be some intermediary bond to connect the two. And the fairest of bonds is that which most perfectly unites into one both itself and the things which it binds together; and to effect this in the fairest manner is the natural property of proportion. For whenever the middle term of any three numbers, cubic or square, is such that as the first term is to it, so is it to the last term,—and again, conversely, as the last term is to the middle, so is the middle to the first,—then the middle term becomes in turn the first and the last, while the first and last become in turn middle terms, and the necessary consequence will be that all the terms are interchangeable, and being interchangeable they all form a unity. Now if the body of the All had had to come into existence as a plane surface, having no depth, one middle term would have sufficed to bind together both itself and its fellow-terms; but now it is otherwise: for it behooved it to be solid of

shape, and what brings solids into unison is never one middle term alone but always two. Thus it was that in the midst between fire and earth God set water and air, and having bestowed upon them so far as possible a like ratio one towards another—air being to water as fire to air, and water being to earth as air to water,—he joined together and constructed a Heaven visible and tangible. For these reasons and out of these materials, such in kind and four in number, the body of the Cosmos was harmonized by proportion and brought into existence. These conditions secured for it Amity, so that being united in identity with itself it became indissoluble by any agent other than Him who had bound it together.[23]

Plato goes on to define the solid shape generated by this perfect binding as that of "a sphere, equidistant in all directions from the center to the extremities, which of all shapes is the most perfect and the most self-similar" (33B). This is the shape that Boethius attributes to Providence.

The creation of an indissoluble bond from four analogical and interchangeable terms is as descriptive of Boethius's *Consolation* as it is of Plato's world-body. Boethius's four analogical terms are not, of course, Plato's earth, water, air, and fire, but the four cognitive faculties, as manifested in the technical elements and in books 1, 2, 4, and 5. The mathematics of this binding[24]—the mathematics through which the work is "harmonized by proportion and brought into existence"—will make it easier to apprehend the corresponding analogy of ideas. The total number of prose and verse sections in book 1 is thirteen; in book 2, sixteen; in book 4, fourteen, and in book 5, eleven.[25] These numbers yield the following set of analogies, each of which can be read forward or backward.

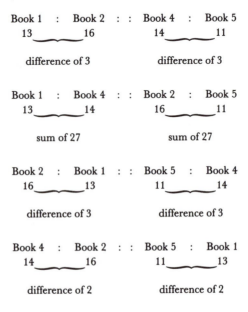

Book 1 : Book 2 : : Book 4 : Book 5
  13 _____ 16   14 _____ 11

difference of 3   difference of 3

Book 1 : Book 4 : : Book 2 : Book 5
  13 _____ 14   16 _____ 11

sum of 27   sum of 27

Book 2 : Book 1 : : Book 5 : Book 4
  16 _____ 13   11 _____ 14

difference of 3   difference of 3

Book 4 : Book 2 : : Book 5 : Book 1
  14 _____ 16   11 _____ 13

difference of 2   difference of 2

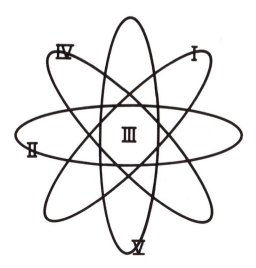

FIGURE 31. Spherical structure of the books of Boethius's *Consolation*.

Because each of the books can occupy any position in the analogical phrase, the single and fixed reading sequence, 1, 2, 4, 5, is displaced by the indissoluble weave of all possible sequences: 1, 2, 4, 5; 1, 4, 2, 5; 5, 2, 4, 1; 4, 2, 5, 1; 2, 1, 5, 4; and so forth. Books 1, 2, 4, and 5 are interchangeable, and hence the result is not a one-dimensional and one-directional sequential line but a sphere on which these books can occupy all possible points (Figure 31). On this sphere all four books are equidistant from and revolve around their common center, book 3.

Boethius's inclusion of a fixed and central book conforms to rather than disrupts Plato's conception of creation. After describing the generation of the body of the world, Plato writes:

> [According to this plan] He made it smooth and even and equal on all sides from the centre, a whole and perfect body compounded of perfect bodies. And in the midst thereof He set Soul, which He stretched throughout the whole of it, and therewith He enveloped also the exterior of its body; and as a Circle revolving in a circle He stablished one sole and solitary Heaven, able of itself because of its excellence to company with itself and needing none other beside, sufficing unto itself as acquaintance and friend. And because of all this He generated it [so perfect as] to be a blessed God. (34B)

Book 3, like the world-soul, is fixed in the centre of the surrounding books yet simultaneously stretches to their circumference, for, as was shown earlier, book 3 recapitulates and anticipates all that is contained in books 1, 2, 4, and 5. Its relation to the other books is visible in the relation between its own internal numerical structure — its division into two halves, the first half consisting of nine prose and verse sections, the second of three — and the numerical structure binding the other four books.

Book 1 : Book 2 :	: Book 3 first half: Book 3 second half : :	Book 4 : Book 5
13 ___ 16	9 ___ 3	14 ___ 11
difference of 3	quotient of 3	difference of 3

Book 1 : Book 4 :	: Book 3 first half: Book 3 second half : :	Book 2 : Book 5
13 ___ 14	9 ___ 3	16 ___ 11
sum of 27	product of 27	sum of 27

Book 2 : Book 1 :	: Book 3 first half: Book 3 second half : :	Book 5 : Book 4
16 ___ 13	9 ___ 3	11 ___ 14
difference of 3	quotient of 3	difference of 3

Book 4 : Book 2 :	: Book 3 first half: Book 3 second half : :	Book 5 : Book 1
14 ___ 16	9 ___ 3	11 ___ 13
difference of 2	power of 2	difference of 2

The third book at once participates in the analogical binding and is differentiated from it. In each instance the numerical bond defining the relation between the first and second halves of book 3 is identical with the numerical bond uniting the four books, but those four books achieve their bond through addition and subtraction while book 3 achieves its bond through the higher-order processes of multiplication and division.

The centrality of the third book is again suggested by a second dimension of the analogical binding. While the numerical bonds between books 1, 2, 4, and 5 can be based on the total number of prose and verse sections within each book, they can also be based on the numbers of the books themselves:

Book 1 : Book 2 :	: Book 4 : Book 5
difference of 1	difference of 1

Book 1 : Book 4 :	: Book 2 : Book 5
difference of 3	difference of 3

Book 2 : Book 1 :	: Book 5 : Book 4
difference of 1	difference of 1

Book 4 : Book 2 :	: Book 5 : Book 1
sum of 6	sum of 6

When the numerical bonds based on the book numbers are juxtaposed with the numerical bonds based on the prose and verse sections, a new numerical bond is generated. It is always the number three.

Books 1, 2, 4, and 5: Bonds based on book numbers		Bond between two bonds	Books 1, 2, 4, and 5: Bonds based on prose and verse	
1 : 2 :: 4 : 5 diff. 1 diff. 1		quotient of 3	13 : 16 :: 14 : 11 diff. 3 diff. 3	
1 : 4 :: 2 : 5 diff. 3 diff. 3		power of 3	13 : 14 :: 16 : 11 sum 27 sum 27	
2 : 1 :: 5 : 4 diff. 1 diff. 1		quotient of 3	16 : 13 :: 11 : 14 diff. 3 diff. 3	
4 : 2 :: 5 : 1 sum 6 sum 6		product of 3	14 : 16 :: 11 : 13 diff. 2 diff. 2	

The two modes of analogical binding—that based on the total number of prose and verse sections and that based on the book numbers—generate a single shape, a sphere well rounded on all sides. The bond defining the relation between the two modes of binding, and hence the bond responsible for the conversion of the two into the single and simple shape, is always the number 3. Like Plato's soul, book 3, fixed at the center, simultaneously reveals itself in all surfaces of the All, all surfaces of the sphere formed by books 1, 2, 4, and 5.[26]

The seriousness of Boethius's attitude toward this numerical binding, implicit in his reverence for Plato, Pythagoras, and Euclid, is made explicit in his assertion, in *De Arithmetica*, that *"Omnia quaecumque a primaeva rerum natura constructa sunt, numerorum videntur ratione formata"* (1.2): All things whatsoever that have been constructed by the primeval nature of things appear to have been formed according to a system of numbers. Far from being an ingenious game, the numerical proportions of the *Consolation* were for the author a reflection of a universe far less wonderful for its "space, firmness, and speedy motion" than for its governing mathematics (*Consolation* 3. pr.8.17–20).

The numerical binding of the work, beautiful in and of itself, simultaneously alerts one to the corresponding and equally beautiful analogy of ideas binding those books, a binding based on the progressive levels of the cognitive hierarchy. Just as in the *Timaeus* the hierarchy of elements (earth, water, air, fire) ultimately makes possible a set of precise analogies in which the middle terms (water, air) become the outer terms and the outer (earth, fire) become the inner—

$$\text{earth} \ : \ \text{water} \quad :: \quad \text{air} \quad : \quad \text{fire}$$

$$\text{air} \ : \ \text{water} \quad :: \quad \text{fire} \quad : \quad \text{air}$$

$$\text{water} \ : \ \text{earth} \quad :: \quad \text{air} \quad : \quad \text{water}$$

—so Boethius's hierarchy of cognitive faculties ultimately makes possible a parallel set of analogies.[27]

$$\text{sense} \ : \ \text{imagination} \quad :: \quad \text{reason} \quad : \quad \text{Insight}$$

$$\text{reason} \ : \ \text{imagination} \quad :: \quad \text{Insight} \quad : \quad \text{reason}$$

$$\text{imagination} \ : \qquad \text{sense} \quad :: \quad \text{reason} \quad : \quad \text{imagination}$$

This pattern of analogical binding is applicable not only to the cognitive faculties themselves, but to each part of the *Consolation* where those faculties are present. Since, for example, book 1 is sense, book 2 is imagination, book 4 is reason, and book 5 is Insight, the single and fixed reading sequence—1, 2, 4, 5—is displaced by an "indissoluble" weave of sequences.

$$\text{Book 1} \ : \ \text{Book 2} \quad :: \quad \text{Book 4} \quad : \quad \text{Book 5}$$

$$\text{Book 4} \ : \ \text{Book 2} \quad :: \quad \text{Book 5} \quad : \quad \text{Book 4}$$

$$\text{Book 2} \ : \ \text{Book 1} \quad :: \quad \text{Book 4} \quad : \quad \text{Book 2}$$

Again, because the cognitive hierarchy is present in the *Consolation*'s persona, verse, prose, and book divisions, what at first seem to be separate technical elements are actually an inseparable unity.

$$\text{persona} \ : \quad \text{verse} \quad :: \qquad \text{prose} \ : \ \text{book divisions}$$

$$\text{prose} \ : \quad \text{verse} \quad :: \quad \text{book div.} \ : \ \text{prose}$$

$$\text{verse} \ : \quad \text{persona} \quad :: \qquad \text{prose} \ : \ \text{verse}$$

Again, chance (sense), fortune (imagination), fate (reason), and Providence (Insight) are not discrete realities. They are ultimately all inextricably bound up with Providence.

chance : forturne :: fate : Prov.

fate : fortune :: Prov. : fate

fortune : change :: fate : fortune

Here, as in each of the earlier sets and in conformity with Plato's description of the world-body, the analogy contains four terms and produces three sequences. The outer and inner terms are interchangeable; the bond is perfect; a sphere is generated.

There is an alternative and condensed way of depicting these analogical patterns. Boethius's emphasis on the cognitive faculties enables us to see that what often appear to be isolated and disparate phenomena are instead a single phenomenon viewed through multiple perspectives.

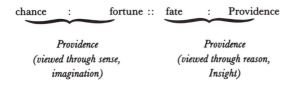

chance   :   fortune :: fate   :   Providence

Providence   *Providence*
(viewed through sense,   *(viewed through reason,*
imagination)   *Insight)*

In this example, the single reality made multiple by four modes of cognition, the common denominator of each pair of terms, is Providence. The weave of analogies can, then, be written in a form that comes close to being an equation, an equation in which Providence equals Providence, one equals one. According to Augustine, equality is the most perfect of all proportions and exists in its absolute form only in God (*De Musica* 6.11).

This process of analogical binding is visible in almost all aspects of the *Consolation*. The following analogies are based on ideas presented in the first two sections of this discussion. In each instance, four apparently unrelated concepts are shown to be in reality a single concept seen from multiple cognitive perspectives. While in each instance only a single arrangement of terms is given, those terms can in every instance be written as a sequence of three interwoven analogies.

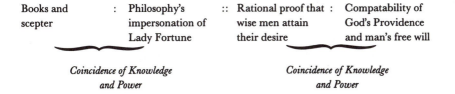

| Books and scepter | : | Philosophy's impersonation of Lady Fortune | :: | Rational proof that wise men attain their desire | : | Compatability of God's Providence and man's free will |

Coincidence of Knowledge   *Coincidence of Knowledge*
and Power   *and Power*

Distance between Boethius's home and place of exile	: Discrepancy between what Fortune gives at one moment and the next	:: Discrepancy between vice and virtue and punishment and reward	Discrepancy between two truths, Providence and free will

Illusory Evil   *Illusory Evil*

Atemporal present	: Memory of past	:: Sequential past, present, future	: Simultaneity

Eternity   *Eternity*

Stroking the mind	: Rhetoric and music	:: Deductive logic	: Analogy

Modes of Consolation   *Modes of Consolation*

Medium of prose in book 2	: Sequential time in book 4	:: Definition of Man in book 5	: Weave of Persona's robe in book 1

Reason   *Reason*

Image of erratic movement in book 2	: Lady Philosophy's changes in height, book 1	:: Subject of Fortune in book 4	: Verse form,[28] book 5

Imagination   *Imagination*

Chance, fortune, fate, and Providence	: No pattern, wheel, concentric circles, and sphere	:: Persona, verse, prose, and book divisions	: Books 1, 2, 4, and 5

Cognitive Hierarchy   *Cognitive Hierarchy*

Persona's health, stature, robe, and all aspects viewed simultaneously	: Persona in book 4, verse in book 5, prose in book 1, and book division 3	:: Atemporal present, memory of past, sequential time, and simultaneity	: Physical comfort, rhetoric and music, logic and analogy

Cognitive Hierarchy   *Cognitive Hierarchy*

These analogies represent rather than exhaust the relentless and omnipresent process of binding through which an image of Aetna's fires in book 2 becomes one with the medium of prose in book 5, through which Philosophy's smile in book 4 becomes one with the whole of book 1, through which the disparate multiplicity of a temporal work achieves the simplicity and simultaneity of divine consciousness. It achieves that simultaneity by affirming not the identity of all things, but the participation of all things in a single unity. In the transition from the multiple cognitive perspectives to the analogical binding made possible by those perspectives, in the transition from the hierarchy to the sphere made possible by that hierarchy, the beneficent intent of that hierarchy begins to emerge. As that which begins by revealing the distinctions among all things goes on to reveal the unity of all things, the ordered ranking of the hierarchical gives way to the absolute uniformity and sameness of the spherical. The final end of the cognitive hierarchy is not exclusion but *inclusion*: its ultimate purpose is not to divide and differentiate Creation into diminishing degrees of divinity, but to assure that no part of Creation will be lost from the immediacy of the divine present.

This chapter has shown four manifestations of the cognitive hierarchy in the *Consolation*. The cognitive hierarchy is described in the climactic three prose sections of the final book; it is present in the technical elements, persona, verse, prose, and book divisions; it is again present in the structural progression from the realm of sense in book 1 to the realm of Insight in book 5; and it is once more present in the analogical binding of the work. There is, finally, a fifth manifestation of the hierarchy, a manifestation visible in the first four. Just as man — or evil or knowledge or cosmic order — can be seen through the four cognitive faculties, so the hierarchy itself can be seen through those four faculties. The technical elements represent the sensitive manifestation of the hierarchy; this is a static and atemporal manifestation. The progression through books 1, 2, 4, and 5 represents the imaginative manifestation; just as the imagination mediates between sense and reason, so it is the mediating progression through the four books that leads us from the sensitive manifestation, the introduction of the technical elements in book 1, to the rational manifestation, the explicit analysis of the hierarchy at the end of book 5. That those final prose sections represent the rational manifestation is suggested by three factors: just as the rational is based on the sensitive and the imaginative, so it is only by going through the technical elements and the structural progression that one reaches the concluding prose sections; just as the rational faculty is intimately related to man's capacity for speech,[29] so it is only here that the hierarchy is explicitly articulated; and just as the object of reason is the form of the universal, so the language of the passage is that of abstract universals — for example, when describing the object of the imagination it provides not a specific image but the universal form of specific images apprehensible in the term *immaterial particular*.

Finally, the analogical binding of the work represents the hierarchy as it manifests itself to Insight. Just as Insight combines all aspects of knowledge simultaneously, so the analogical binding combines the other manifestations of the hierarchy simultaneously. While, then, the hierarchy of

cognitive hierarchies contains as its highest term the analogical binding, it is itself contained in that analogical binding. It, too, is part of an
analogy —

The techni- cal elements	:	Progression from book 1 to book 5	::	The four structural manifestations of cogni- tive hierarchy	::	Climactic three prose sections	:	Analogical binding

Cognitive Hierarchy in Structure of *Consolation*	Cognitive Hierarchy in Structure of *Consolation*	Cognitive Hierarchy in Structure of *Consolation*

— an analogy in which, once more, all terms are interchangeable. Just as
the quintessential fifth element is above yet simultaneously present in
earth, water, air, and fire, so the fifth manifestation of the hierarchy, the
hierarchy of hierarchies, contains yet is contained in the other four. It
becomes a part of the analogical binding that generates the final shape of
the *Consolation*, the well-rounded sphere, the sphere that enables one to
see, as though with the eye of Insight, the whole of the work in a single
glance.

Boethius's achievement of God-likeness reveals itself in three dimensions of the work. First, just as God is the coincidence of form and substance, so the *Consolation* achieves a coincidence of form and substance:
the idea of the work presented in the closing prose sections is everywhere
visible in its structure. Second, just as the final unity of the *Consolation* is
achieved through analogical binding, so Boethius's goal is itself an onto-
logical analogy: he does not want to become God; he wants to become
God-like (3. pr.10–12). Finally, the shape generated by this analogical
binding is, according to the Platonic writings to which Boethius explicitly
alludes, a sphere everywhere equidistant from its center, the shape that
Philosophy designates as the form of the Divine substance, "in body like a
sphere well-rounded on all sides" (3. pr.12.106).

It is regrettable that through the ages so much has been lost from a
work whose single purpose was to assure that nothing should be lost. That
Fortune's wheel rather than the well-rounded sphere should be the image
most often associated with the *Consolation* is symptomatic of our neglect of
the work's structure, its aesthetic integrity, its moral beauty. While the
foregoing description of the *Consolation* is perhaps imprecise and certainly
incomplete, its underlying assumption is correct. It is inconceivable that
Boethius, exhilarated by the form residing in mathematics, in astronomy,
in music, in human thought, would in that work he knew to be his final
work abandon his love of structure. It is inconceivable that the aesthetic
rigor he considered a corollary to metaphysical conviction would be diminished by his recognition of his approaching execution. It could be only

intensified: he had learned from his beloved Cicero and his more beloved Socrates that "Philosophy is learning how to die." The *Consolation of Philosophy* is an act of learning how to die, an act in which man's death is displaced by his potential divinity. While the outcome of the act is moral and metaphysical, the act itself is essentially aesthetic, for it is in the final and perfect shape of the work, the well-rounded sphere, that the nature of divine consciousness is apprehended. In creating that shape, Boethius intended the work to be, like Plato's perfect cosmos, "able of itself because of its excellence to company with itself and needing none other beside, sufficing unto itself as acquaintance and friend" (*Timaeus* 34). Boethius, Boήθεια, his name so close to the Greek word for helper, created a work meant to be — even in the most extreme crises of isolation — a consolation, acquaintance, and friend.

Notes

1. While the playful element in the *Consolation* must be recognized, the words of Boethius in *Quomodo Substantia* should be remembered: "[I] would rather bury my speculations in my own memory than share them with any of those pert and frivolous persons who will not tolerate an argument unless it is made amusing. "*Quomodo Substantia* is found in H. F. Stewart and E. K. Rand, trans. and eds., *Boethius: The Theological Tractates and The Consolation of Philosophy* (Cambridge, Mass., 1962), p. 32. All further references to the *Tractates* and the *Consolation* will be given in the text and will refer to these Latin texts. English translations of the *Consolation* come usually from this Loeb edition (Stewart's revision of "I.T."'s 1609 translation) but sometimes are from *Boethius: The Consolation of Philosophy*, trans. and ed. V. E. Watts (Harmondsworth, England, 1969) and occasionally are collated from these and other translations. References to Boethius's *De Institutione Musica* are to *Patrologia Latina*, vol. 63.

2. Pierre Courcelle, "Le personage de Philosophie dans la littérature latine." *Journal des Savants* (Paris, 1970), pp. 209–52; Joachim Gruber, "Die Erscheinung der Philosophie in der *Consolatio Philosophiae* des Boethius," *Rheinisches Museum für Philologie* 112 (1969): 166–86; Rand, *Founders of the Middle Ages* (Cambridge, Mass., 1929), pp. 160f.; V. Schmidt-Kohl, *Die neuplatonische Seelelehre in der Consolatio philosophiae des Boethuis, Beiträge zur klassiche Philologie*, 16 (Meisenheim am Glan, 1965); E. T. Silk, "Boethius' *Consolatio Philosophiae* as a Sequel to Augustine's *Dialogues* and *Soliloquia*," *Harvard Theological Review* 32 (1939): 19–39. My thanks to William C. Hale for several bibliographic references on the classical antecedents of Lady Philosophy.

3. *The Basic Works of Aristotle*, ed. Richard McKeon (New York, 1941), p. 595.

4. Boethius's emphasis on music's mediating power is reflected in the definition of music adopted by the later Middle Ages: "*Musica est de numero relato ad sonos*" (definition cited in Oliver Strunk, *Source Readings in Music History* [New York, 1950], p. 88 n.). Perhaps, too, it was in part Boethius's emphasis on this function that led his student Aquinas to designate sound as the vehicle of revelation.

5. One of these final meters, that in the third book, has often troubled readers

for what Rand calls its "somewhat perverted application of the story of Orpheus and Eurydice that no lover . . . would approve" (Rand, *Founders of the Middle Ages*, p. 172). The importance of music's function as a vehicle to a higher sphere should make intelligible, if not wholly acceptable Boethius's treatment of the myth: the Orpheus story provided the author with excellent material for a cautionary tale since, in attempting to rescue Eurydice from the lower world, Orpheus addresses his music to the lower sphere.

6. Alfred North Whitehead, *Modes of Thought* (New York, 1968), pp. 50, 174.

7. The verb *ratiocinari* as used by Boethius refers both to the power of reasoning and to the power of discoursing (e.g., 5.pr.5.21–24, 36–39; 4.pr.2.25,26). As one progresses through the *Consolation*, the distinction between mental and verbal acts becomes increasingly small: a truth arrived at by reasoning is repeatedly designated as an act of spoken assertion (e.g., 3.pr.2.10–13; 3.pr.12.42–43; 4.pr.2.19,20; 5.pr.3.69). This identification between reason and discourse is not necessarily evidence of an identification between reason and prose, since "discourse" in antiquity referred both to prose and to poetry (see E. R. Curtius, *European Literature and the Latin Middle Ages*, trans. W. R. Trask [New York, 1953], p. 147). However, Boethius seems to use "discourse" only in referring to the content of the prose sections. Perhaps he thought of his alternations between prose and meters as alternations between speaking and singing.

8. See, for instance, the *Shorter Oxford English Dictionary*.

9. On the medieval attitude toward the triangle, see Russell Peck's essay, "Number as Cosmic Language," in Caroline D. Eckhardt, *Essays in Numerical Criticism of Medieval Literature* (Lewisburg, Pa., 1980).

10. Other readers have also considered the third book, and in particular 3.m.9, in some ways a pinnacle. See, for example, Friedrich Klingner, *De Boethii Consolatione Philosophiae*, Philologische Untersuchungen 27 (Berlin, 1921), p. 66.

11. Watts, trans. and ed., *Boethius: The Consolation of Philosophy*, p. 98n.16.

12. That Philosophy's mode of argument in the second book is rhetorical and that rhetoric is intimately related to the imagination are suggested by two additional factors. First, in classical times rhetoric was closely associated with the law courts. Significantly, in book 2 Fortune is put on trial. Second, like the imagination, rhetoric in book 2 is used to examine immaterial particulars, the false forms of happiness, the multiple forms of mortal and material pleasure. The difference between book 2 and book 3, sections 1–9 (which again examines the false forms) is like the difference in the *Phaedrus* between the opening speech of Lysias and Socrates's first speech: while both speeches examine the "false forms" of love, Lysias's speech is a subrational approach to the subject, Socrates's a rational approach.

13. In the fifth book of Euclid's *Elements* (a work translated by Boethius) ratio and proportion are made applicable to incommensurates.

14. Significantly, the imagery of the *Consolation* progresses from the vegetable and nonsentient in book 1 to diminutive animals (worms, flies, mice) in book 2 to higher-order animals (wolves, tiger, swine) in book 4. In book 5 no specific animals other than man are mentioned.

15. To illustrate his concept of necessity, Boethius in prose 3 uses the image of "man sitting." In prose 6 Philosophy, when talking about necessity, changes the example from "man sitting" to "man walking," a change consonant with her insistence on man's capacity for free will.

16. The decreasing emphasis on biography can be seen by examining the references to other philosophers as well as to Boethius. When famous men (e.g., Socrates) are introduced in the early books, it is their biography, the course of events of their personal life, that is the subject. In the higher books it will instead be their ideas that are called forth.

17. This hierarchy of cosmic order is, for example, suggested by the fact that having just discussed the relation between fate and Providence in 4.pr.6, Philosophy at the opening of 4.pr.7 begins, "'Perceives thou now what followeth of all that we have hitherto said?' 'What?' quoth I. 'That,' quoth she, 'all manner of fortune is good.'"

18. Except for bk. 5, pr.2, which explicitly examines the nature of chance.

19. Philosophy will revise this definition of chance in book 5, prose 1.

20. In examining the cognitive progress from book 1 to book 5, section 2 of this essay focuses on the prose sections and on the changing imagery in the verse. It is possible that a study of the changing meters in the verse would also reveal this progression.

21. The function of verse as a memory aid was frequently emphasized during the Middle Ages, as it was again during the Renaissance (e.g., Sidney, *Apologie for Poetrie*).

22. The concepts of atemporality and eternity (time seen by sense and time seen by Insight) should not be confused. As Lewis S. Ford points out ("Boethius and Whitehead on Time and Eternity," *International Philosophical Quarterly* 8:38–67). Boethius made a very clear and exciting distinction between the two, which Aquinas obliterated, making the two indistinguishable. Whitehead has recovered the distinction for us.

23. *Timaeus*, in R. G. Bury, ed., *Plato* (Cambridge, Mass., 1942), pp. 59f. This passage in the *Timaeus* was also important to Hegel (G. W. F. Hegel, *The Difference Between Fichte's and Shelling's System of Philosophy*, trans. H. S. Harris and W. Cerf [Albany, N.Y.: 1977], p. 158).

24. The importance of unified numbers is suggested by Boethius's definition of goodness as unity, evil as division.

25. Boethius's interest in including a predetermined number of prose and verse sections in each book is suggested by the fact that the length of any given prose section does not usually seem to be dictated by the subject matter or by the structure of the argument: that is, he does not end a particular prose section when he has exhausted a topic or worked through an approach. The apparent arbitrariness of some of his divisions is a clue to the crucial importance of the numbers themselves.

In selecting the number of prose and verse sections for each book (13, 16, 14, 11), he could have chosen several alternative groups of numbers and still have successfully created the *first* set of numerical analogies shown here. However, the range of numbers from which he could have selected is much smaller than it at first appears; in finding numbers of prose and verse sections that he could then play off against the book numbers and against the internal number divisions of book 3, he was considerably more restricted.

26. While this discussion shows that the relation between book 3 and the other four books is a structural parallel to the relation in the *Timaeus* between the world-body and the world-soul, it ignores the further possibility that book 3's own

internal division parallels Plato's description of the world-soul. Plato's soul was composed of three terms, one material, one immaterial, and one a combination of the other two. One might find, for example, corresponding divisions in book 3: sections 1 through 8 might represent the material; 10 through 12 the immaterial, and section 9, which contains the conclusion for 1 through 8 and the first premise of 10 through 12, the intermediate third term.

Other aspects of the *Consolation*'s numerology have not been dealt with here. For example, it is entirely possible that the number of lines in each poem was significant to its author: it is probably no more accidental that 3.m.9 has twenty-eight lines, the triple ternary plus one, than that Dante's *Divine Comedy* has 100 cantos, ninety-nine plus one.

27. Significantly, in the *Republic* (6. 508d–511d) Plato talks about four modes of cognition and their analogical relationship.

28. Here I have appended to the terms specific book numbers (4, 5) even though any book number would be valid. The particular book numbers are specified in order to suggest the analogical binding uniting apparently disparate elements of apparently separate books.

29. See n. 7 above.

Acknowledgments

I am grateful to Oxford University Press for bringing together these essays about "resisting representation" that would otherwise exist only in scattered locations, as I am also grateful to those scattered locations — the journals *Representations*, *Word and Image*, *James Joyce Quarterly*, *Wisconsin Monographs*, and the book *Numerical Criticism of Medieval Literature* — for permission to republish them. The reproduction of the paintings in the second chapter has been made possible by the permission of the Museum of Fine Arts in Boston, the National Museum of Wales, the National Gallery in London, and the Musée du Louvre in Paris. A year of support by the Institute for Advanced Study in Berlin let me complete, among other writings, the introduction to this book.

To Eva Scarry, Philip Fisher, Stephen Greenblatt, and D. A. Miller, my abiding thanks: their steady concern for this book was decisive. I am grateful to Eva Scarry for our hours and days of shared reading aloud (like the characters in Beckett's "Enough," we moved side by side over pages rather than meadows) and to D. A. Miller for solving every unsolvable dilemma that turned up with clarity and ease.

Individual chapters are bound up in my mind with many people, some of whom I wish to thank here: Chapter 1, Mark Crispin Miller, Joe Scarry; Chapter 2, Todd Kelly, David DeLaura, Frances Ferguson, Walter Michaels; Chapter 3, J. D. O'Hara, David Gates, Ann Beattie; Chapter 4, Marc Wanner, Roger Wilkenfeld, Joseph Wittreich, Alison Byerly; Chapter 5, Charles Owen, Jack Davis, David Anderson. In preparing the book for publication I was helped by my research assistant David Gammons, as well as by many people at Oxford, especially Elizabeth Maguire, Ellen Fuchs, Elda Rotor, and Rosemary Wellner (for whose copyediting, now as in the past, I am grateful). Finally, for his steady insight about the making of books, my thanks to Bill Sisler.

Index

Accident, 66

Acts, embodied: brevity of, 53; combining and separating, 97, 98; dance, 72, 73; flirtation, 61, 72–73; perpetual vs. discrete, 65, 67, 68–70; reading, 54, 55; visiting, 67; walking, 53, 54, 76, 78; yawning, 54. *See also* Entry and Exit, Play, Work

Acts, mental. *See* Mental acts

Advertised object: Advil, 16, 41; American Express, 14; Anacin, 17, 41, 42 fig. 20; APF, 17, 41, 43 fig. 21; Aspercreme, 30 fig. 8; Bayer aspirin, 16, 26; blue jeans, 18; Bufferin, 16, 17, 18 fig. 3, 27, 43; Cheer, 19; Clinoril, 26; Darvocet-N 100, 30–31, 32 fig. 10, 33, 34; Empirin Compound c̄ Codeine, 26; Encaprin, 28, 31 fig. 9, 41; Excedrin, 16; Geocillin, 34, 45; Hart Schaffner and Marx, 15 fig. 2; Indocin, 26; Michelin all-season tires, 14 fig. 1, 16, 19; Morton Salt, 44; Mylanta-II, 33, 34; Nubain, 44–47, 46 fig. 23; Nuprin, 20, 26; Percodan, 26; Samaritan Nervine, 44, 45 fig. 22; sleeping pill, 39; soap, 15; Sunkist oranges, 11*n*.11.; Tampax, 17; Teldrin, 20, 21 fig. 4, 26, 27, 41, 42; Tide, 17, 44; Tolectin, 33, 34; Total, 19; True, 19; Tylenol, 16, 20, 21, 22 fig. 5, 26, 27, 29 fig. 7, 41, 43; Vicodin, 33 fig. 11, 34; Vistaril-i.m. (Calm), 23–26, 45

Advertising, 10; emotional symmetry in, 38; four categories of claims in, 13, 14, 16; object acts as locus of scepticism in, 40; picturing the competition in, 41; political, 40; product disappears in, 40; product identification in, 27, 41–47; product information in, 45; professional medical audience for, 22, 40; public audience for, 22, 40, 47; public service, 40;

restrained quality for pain remedies, 13, 14, 16, 17, 19, 20, 44; unrestrained in medical, 22, 23–26, 30, 33, 40, 45, 46. *See also* Advertised object

Aesthetic structure: as corollary to metaphysical conviction, 176; reflects conception of cognition in Beckett, 93–96; reflects conception of cognition in Boethius, 144, 146 (*See also* Sphere); reflects conception of cognition in Thackeray, 103, 105, 111–13, 117–18, 131, 137; unity and diversity, 157

Allen, Walter, 138*n*.7

Allergy, relief for, 20, 21

Amar, Akhil, 11*n*.7

Amendments. *See* Constitution

Analogy: as binding power, 167–76; and God-likeness, 176; and Hegel, 179*n*.23; of ideas about cognition, 171–76; as mode of argument, 159–60, 174; numerical, 169–71; in Plato, 168, 180*n*.27; as vehicle to insight, 159, 167

Animals, 187*n*.14; and cognition, 161–62

Aquinas, 177*n*.4

Arendt, Hannah, 15, 16, 88*n*.31

Argument: modes in Boethius, 158–61, 162, 178*n*.12

Aristotle: *De Anima*, 150; *Rhetoric*, 152

Artifice. *See* Creation, Work

Aspirin or nonaspirin substitutes, 13, 16–22, 25, 26, 27, 28–29, 33, 34, 37, 38, 39, 40, 41–44; giant, 42; and modest enablement, 17; as philosopher's stone, 19; prevents heart attacks, 16; stays stable in ads, 17; surface lacks sensuous detail, 42, 43; and willow bark, 44. *See also* Advertised object, Pain remedies

Assertion: as verbal form, 160–61

Astronomy, 176

Asturias, Miguel, 83*n*.2